# Turning Point

Jürgen Müller

# Turning Point

## How IT is Changing Our World

 Springer

Jürgen Müller
Düsseldorf, Germany

ISBN 978-3-658-46078-5        ISBN 978-3-658-46079-2    (eBook)
https://doi.org/10.1007/978-3-658-46079-2

Translation from the German language edition: "Zeitenwende" by Jürgen Müller,
© Der/die Herausgeber bzw. der/die Autor(en), exklusiv lizenziert an Springer
Fachmedien Wiesbaden GmbH, ein Teil von Springer Nature 2023. Published by
Springer Fachmedien Wiesbaden. All Rights Reserved.

This book is a translation of the original German edition "Zeitenwende" by Jürgen
Müller, published by Springer Fachmedien Wiesbaden GmbH in 2023. The translation was done with the help of an artificial intelligence machine translation tool. A
subsequent human revision was done primarily in terms of content, so that the book
will read stylistically differently from a conventional translation. Springer Nature
works continuously to further the development of tools for the production of books
and on the related technologies to support the authors.

© The Editor(s) (if applicable) and The Author(s), under exclusive license to
Springer Fachmedien Wiesbaden GmbH, part of Springer Nature 2024

Planung/Lektorat: David Imgrund
This Springer imprint is published by the registered company Springer Fachmedien
Wiesbaden GmbH, part of Springer Nature.
The registered company address is: Abraham-Lincoln-Str. 46, 65189 Wiesbaden,
Germany

If disposing of this product, please recycle the paper.

*If you think you are too small to move big things you never had a mosquito in your bed.*

*For Claudia, Fenja, and Thorin, as well as our four-legged family members, without whom this book would have been finished much faster.*

# Preface

## The Eighth Day of Creation?

Does this headline serve to characterize the enormously rapid and profound changes that information technology (IT) is currently causing in all areas of our lives? Is the comparison to an eighth day of creation exaggerated? After reading the present book, hopefully, doubtful readers will have found an answer. We have become accustomed to distinguishing between the virtual world of computer networks and the "real," physical world. However, this distinction is not a faithful representation of reality. The cyber world and the real world have long since merged into a hybrid whole; the boundaries between our online and offline lives are fluid. This is the new reality, even if it presents itself to us as individuals to varying degrees. Social networks and the opinions expressed within them create "facts," they influence elections, determine politics, and reveal the white spots of state regulation and jurisprudence. What happens on the net during the day appears in the news in the evening.

State hackers are engaged in a permanent cyber war, to such an extent that it is hardly possible to distinguish between war and peace. Is the crippling of the Colonial fuel pipeline in the USA in 2021 by Russian hackers or the infiltration—presumably by Israel and the USA—of the Stuxnet worm, which is only 500 kilobytes in size but had devastating effects on Iranian nuclear facilities in 2010, still peace or already war? Some countries have discovered "hacking" as a source of income and instruct their state-organized actors to extort foreign companies. They have become criminal organizations with a national flag and a seat in the UN. And when companies like Facebook or X (formerly Twitter) allow their users to call for violence against an aggressor on their networks, are they already parties to the war or not yet? Information technology is a master at blurring boundaries.

Some things have so far shown a remarkable persistence. Since their invention, we have been driving our cars with combustion engines, and we are still used to driving them ourselves. We pay our bills with state-guaranteed money in euros, dollars, or yuan and use a bank for this purpose. In our factories and offices, human labor is still a significant factor. But how long will we hold on to these habits? The very rapid, exponential networking of our world, the miniaturization of computers in the form of smartphones or sensors, and the increasing use of artificial intelligence are quietly but extremely effectively challenging them. IT is a stealthy force. Each of us is familiar with the first moon landing on July 20, 1969. Few will know the birth year of the internet. The moon landing has practically no perceptible significance for our everyday lives, yet it is still covered in history lessons. The internet has massively influenced our daily lives over the past 30 years, but it is hardly mentioned there, if at all. Stealthy processes are less noticed than major events, regardless of their actual significance. We perceive the encroachment of IT into all domains of social life, economy, and politics as normal and only marginally notice the turning point associated with it. We are no longer even surprised that the processors in our cell phones contain transistors so small that millions of them could fit on the period at the end of this sentence. Even crime today is largely different from what it was before the IT era. Social life, economic progress, and politics are now closely linked to the development of IT.

Companies must reinvent their business models because IT enables and forces new forms of value creation, new sales, marketing, and logistics channels are emerging, and new production and development methods promise more efficiency and competitive advantages. Artificial intelligence is transforming entire industries, the way our children learn, and how medical professionals heal. It creates a precursor of "mind" in learning machines, and we are only at the beginning of this development. Traditional industry boundaries are increasingly dissolving, creating competitive situations that did not exist before. Those who were only active in the IT market yesterday are now also involved in the music business, offering financial services, and building smart home devices. Apple Music, Alibaba's Alipay, and Google Nest are just a few examples of this. The established giants within the affected economic sectors are facing competition from outside and are thus under pressure. Cross-industry business models are emerging, based on the power of digital technology. Those who fail to recognize this cross-sectional nature of IT or simply do not have the know-how and resources to utilize it are at a disadvantage. Those who can't keep up will be left behind. In the digital world, it is not the big fish that eat the small, but the fast that eat the slow.

State regulatory efforts lag behind an explosively mutating technology and new business models. Improvement is not in sight, although some states—like in the EU—are joining forces with others to intervene efficiently and across borders. However, they repeatedly hit their limits because the agreed measures are all too often meager compromises resulting from differing interests. Internet companies have the power, the money, and the influence to endure this cat-and-mouse game and secure the best locations. It is no longer a compelling requirement to be physically present where they want to do business. The reach of data centers is by definition global. National solo efforts prove to be the wrong path. "Tech nationalism" and isolation only work temporarily and conditionally; in the long run, they exclude from progress. This is especially true for economically small and medium-sized countries, but ultimately also for the giants. The restriction of conventional sovereignty associated with international cooperation is both a burden and an opportunity.

IT has changed the globe, has made it into a "global village," although this term from the 1960s hardly does justice to the current development of individuals, economy, politics, and society. We live in a new world. If one were to attempt to agree on a worldwide standard for a modern era, one could with some justification speak of "before the Internet" and "since the Internet." Such is the immense influence of technological development on all areas of our lives. Has the dawn of the eighth day of creation already begun? And what is yet to come?

Nothing is without history, and much can be explained by it. Therefore, this book also discusses the history of modern IT and the development of the technology underlying it in a way that is easy to understand. How did it come about, what drove it, who were the key players, who created the Internet, why do the United States dominate, and why does Europe play only a minor role in this crucial field? However, it deals much more with other fundamental questions of IT. These include, for example: How and why and with what impacts does it change the economy and geopolitics? What role does it play in the new East-West power struggle? What goals do hackers pursue, who are these people, and who controls them? Another focus is on the influence of technological development on our social life, our work, and our thinking and actions. IT creates new forms of security needs, it exacerbates and clarifies the differences between authoritarian and democratic regimes. Where will this journey go?

In order to answer such and other big questions, I will draw on practical and real case examples that are partially based on my own experiences. Everyday topics that readers may have been interested in for a long time will also be explained, almost in passing. Examples of this are: What exactly is a digital business model, is there really such a thing as security in IT, what happens when you google, what do Artificial Intelligence and Big Data mean, what exactly is behind the multifaceted term of the Cloud?

When I entered the IT field as a career changer in May 1990, it was not a particularly good time for the industry. I remember exactly how I drove through Cupertino, Mountain View, Sunnyvale, and other places in Silicon Valley, where nothing suggested a gold rush atmosphere. In the front yards of numerous elegant houses stood a desolate sign: FOR SALE. Apple was limping, Windows had not yet established itself, Microsoft and Apple were arguing over the rights to the still quite young graphical user interface. A hint of the 1980s was blowing through the country, companies with long-forgotten names today—like Atari and Commodore—were still active in the market.

When I moved from Düsseldorf to San Francisco with my wife almost ten years later, the world was already a different place. The industry had once again shown how cyclical it operates. The internet had taken off, Google was in a steep ascent two years after its founding, and the Dot-com bubble was growing ever larger in the overheated industry. At that time, it was almost frowned upon for young companies to make profits. Instead, they endeavored to burn through money at a high rate based on a questionable economy. An end to the speculation and gambling did not seem in sight, even though it did come soon after. The index of the technology stock exchange NASDAQ had risen by 400% between 1995 and March 2000, when it reached its peak. At that time, I was looking for salespeople for my employer Sybase. Numerous career starters applied and demanded obscenely high salaries and many stock options on top of that. To most of them—not all—I said that although I did not know how I would manage without them, I would still like to try. The gap between the apparent competence and the demanded salary was just too large for me.

This book resembles a lesson on the changes that information technology has brought about in recent decades. For my research, I only occasionally visited a library and did not request any printed magazines or articles. My research was conducted almost entirely digitally; all important information was within reach of a mouse and keyboard. It was supplemented by online meetings with people whose thoughts and advice I consider valuable. What a contrast to the time of my studies in history and political science! Back then, I spent weeks and months in archives and libraries, ordered books through interlibrary loan, stood in line at one of the few university copiers, and then collected index cards with content and literature references in a wooden box.

"Non-digital," on the other hand, were the personal experiences from my jobs, the observations, and lessons from the last 35 years of my career during the creation of the book. It was the time I spent in different roles, companies, countries, and continents in IT. They are the actual foundation of this book; most of the questions, ideas, evaluations, and conclusions are based on them. Somehow, I find that reassuring. Personal encounters with other people are ultimately irreplaceable. Nor is the fun and sometimes the frustration that resulted from it. Only digital and theoretical and without extensive practical experience, this book would have become entirely different or perhaps not even come into existence.

The book is aimed at a broad audience and is for everyone who is aware of the fact that IT increasingly and more massively influences society, the economy, and politics, and that they themselves are personally affected. They generally only have a "felt" knowledge but feel the need for understandable and sustainable explanations. Most of us experience this process of change as a daily, almost inconspicuous sequence of small steps. This makes the realization of the big picture, the assembling of individual observations into a pattern and overall picture, difficult. This applies not only to people outside but also to many within the IT industry. Questions, as treated here, have significant professional relevance in everyday life for only a few actors even there.

The goal of the book is to convey this large picture with its bright and dark sides in a way that is easily understandable. I will try to highlight selected major lines, create awareness of the tremendous upheavals we are experiencing, explain developments, and in this way provide orientation and, above all, a piece of maturity in an increasingly technologized society. And something else is important to me: I want to correct the prevailing, fear-oriented, and negatively colored discussion about changes brought by IT—as can be easily seen in the example of artificial intelligence—and to highlight not only its risks but also its opportunities.

It is good to give chance some space in life. I myself ended up in IT by chance; actually, an academic career in the humanities at a university was planned. I have not regretted the step into IT for a single second. Reinventing myself has done me good; when one door closes, another opens. Being able to work in a very dynamic industry, where you have to consider every morning in the shower why what was successful until yesterday no longer works today and needs to be reinvented, has always been a lot of fun for me. The IT industry rarely forgives mistakes; it is fascinating, intense, fast-paced, surprisingly often more art than science, and has enormous consequences for our lives. It falls in love with solutions, not problems. It knows that it is better to be 80 percent right today and implement these ideas with full force than to wait until a 100 percent solution is found. The motto of the hacker group Anonymous sums it up with immortal conciseness: "We are legion. We do not forgive. We do not forget. Expect us." Where else could it be more exciting? I look forward to constructive suggestions and criticism on my blog "zeitenwende-it.com".

Jürgen Müller

# Contents

# 1

# Beyond Technology. Our New Life with IT

"I have a device in my pocket that allows me to access all the information known to humanity. I use it to look at pictures of cats and argue with strangers."[1] This quote from 2019 comes from a user of Reddit.com, a social media platform that is especially popular in the USA. Computer technology has become so small and portable that it seamlessly integrates into all aspects of our lives in the form of smartwatches, smartphones, or tablets. The miniaturization of computers drives their usage. If we only had desktop computers available, we would certainly spend significantly less time on these devices. Perhaps our activities would also be significantly less trivial than described in the quote. Trivialization is apparently, among other remarkable phenomena, a variant of our behavior on the internet.

In a survey in the USA from February 2021, 46% of respondents stated that they spend an average of five to six hours daily on their smartphones, excluding work-related use. Another 11% reported seven or more hours, and 22% said they spend an average of three to four hours daily on their phones. Only 5% claimed to use their smartphones for less than an hour per day. The remaining 16% were at one to two hours.[2] Assuming that our average waking time is around 17 hours,[3] smartphone consumption plays a significant role for large segments of the population—it dictates the daily routine. Of course, there are also apps on the internet that facilitate such number games and can simultaneously help us control our smartphone consumption. Examples include AppDetox, OffTime, or FlipD. They say nothing about the consequences of this form of constant strain, but they are obvious nonetheless. When parents or children spend their time on smartphones, personal interaction, through which social behavior is conveyed and shaped, suffers. This shaping, especially in children, should not be delegated to strangers on the internet. The internet gives us access to the world at any time and from almost any place. It is often forgotten that it also gives the world access to us. Not everyone who roams the internet has the best intentions. The wise Master Yoda from the Star Wars series aptly described it when he revealed himself as a harbinger of cyberpsychology: "When you look at the Dark Side, careful you must be. For the Dark Side looks back."

## Digital Psychograms

Cyberpsychology is a young branch of knowledge that deals with the effects of digital interaction on human behavior. It refers not only to, but especially to, the internet. Evolution has not conditioned us for the use of technology, but for personal interaction with each other. "Post-sociality," the replacement of personal interaction with communication technology, is not on nature's development plan. Therefore, many of our instincts do not function at the computer; our behavior is often not the same as in so-called real life. Our still very young millennium has brought humanity high-frequency crises of global magnitude in its first good 20 years. They line up like pearls on a string: the terrorist attacks on the World Trade Center and the Pentagon in 2001, the subsequent war in Afghanistan, the invasion of Iraq under false pretenses, which permanently and negatively changed the balance of power in the Middle East for the West. In 2008, a global financial crisis began, triggered by a real estate bubble in America. It was different in that it did not only affect stock owners but also the "ordinary citizen" who had to fear for their savings. In 2011, the civil war in Syria began as a result of the Arab Spring, which brought Europe the exacerbation of its migration problem. A similar problem later emerged in the United States, where people fleeing poverty and violence in Central and South America knocked on the door. This was accompanied by the debt crisis in Europe, virulent since 2009, which could have brought the end of the Eurozone and lasted until the middle of the decade. The list can be extended indefinitely, with the preliminary endpoints being the COVID-19 pandemic and Russia's invasion of Ukraine. All of this has deeply embedded itself in the collective consciousness. A significant reason for this is that these crises have an omnipresence beyond traditional TV and print media, primarily caused by the internet and its access via smartphones. They are the subject of more or less qualified comments on the Twitters (now X), Telegrams, and Facebooks of this world. Every change is communicated in real-time; there is always a fire somewhere, and we are under constant bombardment. The result is VUCA, "Volatility, Uncertainty, Complexity, and Ambiguity." Uncertainty rises, the longing for stability, for simple explanations, for certainty. The internet is the outlet for the resulting discontent and the place where one can seek belonging and "friends."

In her readable book on the subject of "digital behavior," Mary Aiken has described a number of interesting phenomena that can be observed in our online lives.[4] She collectively refers to these as cyber effects, of which I would like to address the most essential ones, namely disinhibition, behavior reinforcement, syndication, and cyber migration.

Many of us have already experienced online disinhibition in a professional or private context. There are simply too many people who react in emails, chats, or on social networks in an exaggerated manner that they would never do in direct personal contact. Therefore, I made it my maxim many years ago to respond to such "electronic" outbursts of others—back then mostly via email—consciously delayed (or often not at all). Also for self-protection, because computer networks are young, but their memory lasts long. When such reactions culminate in hate speech, defamation, or threats of violence on the web, the fun definitely stops. There are numerous prominent examples of this, one being the case of Renate Künast. Here, a german politician was attributed with completely fabricated quotes, accompanied by obscene insults and rude threats. In a trial that went through several instances, the Federal Constitutional Court ultimately decided that Facebook must disclose the data of the authors so that they can be prosecuted. This must serve as a lesson to potential offenders. Like at any other crime scene, they also leave their electronic "fingerprints" on the net. It is naive to believe that one can evade detection with the means available to ordinary mortals. Cyber-naivety could thus be seen as a new behavioral category. Anonymity is a myth that many users still believe in. It makes transgressions as easy as their uncomplicated logistics. Anyone who has to write, print, envelope, and mail a scathing letter with the correct address is more likely to refrain from letting their bitter feelings run free. The effort is a deterrent. The computer and its keyboard take that away from us.

Closely linked to the easily made transgressions on the computer is a behavioral reinforcement that experts call online amplification. An interesting example of this is cyberchondria. This refers to anxiety disorders related to health that are generated or intensified by internet research. We don't feel well, the heart skips a beat, the stomach twinges. In a self-experiment, I entered the search term "stomach pain" and Dr. Google responded with diagnoses like "gastritis," "it could also be the heart," "stomach ulcer," "salmonella," "pancreatitis," until I finally ended up with stomach cancer and various self-help groups after intensifying the search. Suddenly, one feels like they have a serious illness without any medical findings. An everyday discomfort that could have been eliminated with a cup of tea takes on life-threatening dimensions, and uncertainty spreads. The phenomenon is well known to health insurance companies, as they have to bear the economic consequences of online hypochondria. Of course, it is no coincidence that website operators design their tagging in such a way that the number of visitors to their websites increases. The more dramatic, the better for the click rate. This is also reflected in the results of search queries.[5]

Harmless in itself, online syndication can grow into a serious danger when like-minded people with questionable views come together in groups on the net and confirm each other's opinions. Technology makes this immensely easier. Someone who is a follower of absurd conspiracy theories living in a sparsely populated rural area has little chance of meeting someone who thinks similarly. This problem does not exist on the net. People who are on the same wavelength are easy to find in cyberspace. Suddenly, one is no longer isolated and receives applause for their opinion instead of negative criticism from their immediate environment. The conclusion many draw from this is: I am right after all. The next step is arranging a "demo" over the internet, thus getting to know each other personally. The feeling of being right is joined by the feeling of belonging to a community that knows more and is smarter than the mainstream—one belongs to a kind of elite that grows closer together through attacks from outside. Pegida, the most well-known german example of this, started as a Facebook group. This form of group formation can, in extreme cases, lead to strong radicalization, as a study by the think tank Rand Corporation based on concrete cases shows.[6] Where radicals previously had to go through the effort of physical recruitment with limited reach, they now use the internet as a political platform with a scattergun effect. Self-radicalization of individuals is a desired side effect.

Whether one can also speak of such desirability in the case of cyber-migration must remain an open question. Cyber-migration describes the adoption of behavior from the net into our offline lives, with the term being used in various ways, e.g., also for the migration of visitors between social networks. Given the significant amount of time we spend online, the idea of such adoptions is close at hand. The communities we join in social media, the opinions we encounter, the new "friends" we chat with, leave their marks on our thinking and actions. A kind of second socialization takes place unnoticed, influencing our physical world. The younger we are, the more pronounced this effect is. Personal experiences show that the attention span of my friends and acquaintances is getting shorter and shorter. Listening seems to be more difficult when the partner does not communicate in "chat format." In email correspondence with colleagues, it can be seen from their responses that longer texts are not read properly; feedback leaves much to be desired after just five lines. Information is more likely to be consumed than thought through, responses must be spontaneous and quick, and are therefore sometimes deficient.

Not every person is equally susceptible to cyber effects. This is also why there is no reason for pessimism. People with a corresponding predisposition are more likely to be affected, while others handle it more critically and can derive great benefits from the internet. The internet is a mirror of society and is unlikely to lead to a world of behaviorally conspicuous people. What applies online is what also applies in our offline lives. Michael Seto, a Canadian forensic psychologist, once described the internet as "the greatest unregulated social experiment of all time"[7]. The internet is widely seen as an instrument and platform of freedom, and rightly so. It facilitates the expression of opinions, provides a forum for the voiceless, organizes democratic protests, is a reflection of diversity, and thus the bane of autocrats and dictators. They are therefore constantly striving to limit access to the web for their population.[8] The internet spreads the knowledge of humanity around the world in an instant and allows everyone to participate. It accelerates science and research, and allows us to connect with each other from almost any location.

Even the questionable aspects described have their positive sides, aside from disinhibition. Successful fundraising campaigns on the internet, whether for children with cancer, war refugees, or animal protection, represent a form of behavioral reinforcement and syndication. A very creative and interesting example of this is an event involving Airbnb, a leading broker of vacation rentals and rooms.[9]

In March 2022, Sarah Brown from Salt Lake City booked a room through Airbnb with Ekaterina Martiusheva in Kyiv to support people in Ukraine during wartime. She never intended to use it but checked in anyway. Airbnb pays the hosts 24 hours after the guest has checked in. Ekaterina received the money promptly, and in a phone call with National Public Radio (NPR), a kind of American version of Deutschlandfunk, she explained how much this donation meant to her. Spread via Facebook, Sarah Brown started a wave. Within two days, over 61,000 overnight stays in Ukraine worth over two million dollars were booked from around the world. When Airbnb noticed the event, the company waived the fees for all hosts and guests.

Those who transfer empathy to the internet also show a form of cyber-migration, only in the opposite direction. But as with any form of freedom, we must also handle freedom on the web carefully. If it is abused, whether by ordinary criminals, child molesters, extortionists, hate speakers, or political demagogues, boundaries must be drawn. The legislature has recognized this necessity, it is slowly making progress, but mostly acts reactively rather than preventively. It is like a journey into a new world because our legal system also needs to be adapted to these new opportunities and dangers. The universe of cyberspace is expanding much faster than the earthly realm of the legislature.

## Life on the Platforms

In October 2021, there were 4.55 billion active social media users worldwide. In the second quarter of 2021, Facebook counted 2.89 billion active users per month, and Instagram one billion. Thus, 3.89 billion of all visitors were attributed to Meta Platforms Inc., the company that owns these two market giants.[10] Other platforms have to settle for significantly less attention: Twitter (now X), Snapchat, Pinterest, LinkedIn. A look at WhatsApp and Facebook Messenger makes the dominance of the "Meta family" even clearer. Their messaging services Facebook Messenger and WhatsApp, which was acquired in February 2014 for $19 billion, handle more than 50% of the global messaging volume. Only TikTok and Google's YouTube play in a similar league with their video platforms. TikTok has even developed into a heavyweight among video platforms in a relatively short time.[11] It belongs to the Chinese company Byte Dance, which caused it a lot of trouble in the USA under the Trump administration and still does. Google's YouTube is still the top dog in this business with two billion monthly users. However, only about 30 million pay for its premium video and music service.[12] Measured against the approximately eight billion people on our planet, the penetration rate of these media is enormous. No one else can boast comparable reach. Their mere ubiquity gives them significant and determining weight in our daily lives. These platforms neither produce anything themselves nor do the vast majority of users count as their real customers. Having an account on Facebook or Snapchat alone does not make us one. Their business model is based on an almost ingenious idea: billions of users feed the platform daily, voluntarily, unsolicited, highly frequently, and for free with data. They form a kind of community of "freelancers" spread across the globe. A member of the Hamburg based Chaos Computer Club described it this way: "The saying always went at Facebook: The user is not the customer, he is actually the product."[13]

The core of the consideration is that users are allowed to create and communicate their own content via the platform. The platforms then exploit the users' data, their comments, likes, messages, their uploaded content, their usage behavior, and much more by marketing them for advertising purposes of all kinds. These unpaid suppliers are ultimately the guarantors of their high profits. Data protection is written in small letters in this model. Those who value it more will quickly realize, when looking for Facebook-like alternatives, how great the compromises are that would have to be made in case of renunciation or change. "Similar" here means: messaging, sharing, likes, posting pictures, videos, and links. One of Facebook's larger competitors is Reddit, with over 50 million daily users.[14] Reddit's focus is in the USA; in Germany, despite partially localized content, there were only 3.9 million users. Overall, visitor numbers outside the United States are very small and fragmented,[15] which is why the attractiveness of local content or Reddit groups leaves much to be desired. The biggest compromise, therefore, lies in the reach of alternative platforms, as fewer users naturally also mean fewer opportunities for group formation and communication. With fewer participants, the economies of scale decrease. Almost all competitors, therefore, try to score with a combination of data protection, freedom of expression, transparency, and ad-free experience. They exploit Facebook's Achilles' heel.

Some position themselves as anti-Facebook. Minds, for example, says of itself: "Minds is a social open-source network that advocates for freedom on the internet. Speak freely, protect your privacy… and take control of your social media."[16] A whitepaper from Minds, which describes technology, content, business model, and the founders' motivation,[17] reads in its moral charge like Luther's theses against the Catholic Church, which he is said to have nailed to the portal of the Castle Church of Wittenberg in 1517. Minds uses a very modern approach for data storage, dispensing with central storage and instead working decentrally with cryptographic blockchain technology.[18] Users pay for the provision of content via a network protocol that allows direct connection between them. This so-called Wire Protocol, therefore, does not need a central control and intermediary instance like Facebook, which allows it access to the data and its use. Payment can be made in the form of donations, ad hoc transfers, as well as subscriptions. The operators call this contribution economy, as opposed to platform economy, which Facebook stands for. Minds has—as of March 2022—around six million users.[19]

It goes without saying that such "uncensored" and uncurated social platforms also attract people whose access would have been blocked elsewhere due to their views and extreme statements. The small providers operate below the radar of state regulators, whose attention is focused on the larger ones. However, this automatically raises the question of how great the desire for data protection really is among the billions of visitors to mainstream platforms. Interestingly, it is not they who force such platforms to better data protection. They apparently do not care much about it; otherwise, they would simply switch to an alternative provider. The network effects associated with the size of Facebook, which I will discuss in more detail elsewhere, exert such a strong attraction that a switch—if desired at all—seems unattractive. The ambivalent role of the protective instance is therefore taken over by the state, which must navigate the narrow path between freedom and the protection of personal rights, but cannot always be entirely sure-footed in doing so.

# Artificial Intelligence and Learning Machines

The terms Artificial Intelligence (AI), Machine Learning, Deep Learning, Algorithms, and Big Data encounter us in everyday life not only when it comes to the utilization of our data by platforms. Anyone using a navigation system in a car is guided by AI on an optimized route. On the packaging of my new electric toothbrush, I found the sentence: "Genius X with artificial intelligence has learned from the brushing behavior of thousands of people." This example shows how far AI has penetrated our lives. The aforementioned terms are often used with little distinction and mixed into an unspecific whole. This is understandable to a certain extent, as the boundaries between them can indeed be fluid. To better understand these terms, which we will encounter more frequently throughout the book, I would like to define them more precisely using concrete examples.

Artificial Intelligence is the umbrella term for a range of techniques that refer to the ability of computers to make intelligent decisions and thus emulate human intelligence. AI learns from the data it interprets and constantly improves its results in this way. The more data available, the more secure the interpretation and the stronger the learning progress and reliability of the results. Conventional software, on the other hand, follows a predefined, rigid set of rules dictated by the program. Because it—somewhat simplified—does not interpret data but merely processes it, it is not adaptive and therefore does not improve its results on its own. No matter how much data is available to it, the set of rules will always remain the same and determine the outcome. AI represents the transition from useful to smart computers. Automation of processes is the main characteristic of useful computers. Smart is the main characteristic of computers with AI. They make intelligent decisions, are able to weigh alternatives against each other, and can independently generate meaningful content. The range of artificial intelligence spans from semi-autonomous to autonomous, meaning it can operate with varying degrees of human intervention. AI thus ventures into areas that were previously reserved for us humans. We will discuss a special variant, the so-called chatbots, in more detail elsewhere. They are used to simulate conversations with humans and have gained significant public interest. All of this generates fears among some contemporaries, resulting in AI often being seen more as a problem than an opportunity. The following example, which demonstrates its strong influence on our lives beyond practical use, represents its numerous applications.

Ping An Insurance from Shenzhen in southern China is one of the top three insurance companies in the world by market value.[20] It uses AI on a large scale for recruiting new employees, pursuing two goals: more efficient handling of the high recruitment volume and—more importantly—a better hit rate in selecting the right talents. Applicants must answer questions from intelligent machines during the recruitment process. Their answers are compared in terms of content, tone, word choice, and gestures with those of the company's most successful salespeople. Large amounts of data are available for this, collected from previous job interviews, among other sources. The feedback with the later performance of the hired candidates is used to constantly refine the system. At Ping An, they are firmly convinced that this system is better and more objective in selecting the right employees than the human interviews that follow later in the process.[21] Anyone who has ever been interviewed for a job and been annoyed by poorly prepared interviewers may be quite open to dialogue with an AI system.

In this example, Ping An uses Machine Learning as a manifestation of Artificial Intelligence. Through the mentioned feedback, the machine constantly learns, with humans still intervening in the process. They determine what data it is fed, what the algorithms look like that the selection process follows, and ultimately conduct their own interviews with the pre-selected candidates. The machine operates semi-autonomously. In comparison, Deep Learning is a further development stage of Machine Learning. It differs by a higher degree of automation, meaning: humans need to intervene very little or not at all in the computer's decision-making and learning process. The computer independently selects the features from the available data and forms the patterns that are best suited to accomplish its tasks. It operates autonomously. It continuously learns on its own by independently linking what it has already learned with new content. This is quite reminiscent of human learning. In fact, neural network models are used for this, which are modeled after the functioning of our brain to design AI. They are found in numerous applications, from speech and pattern recognition to complex predictions. The foundation of all this is algorithms, which, despite their modern use, are anything but new. The term is a corruption of the name of the Arab mathematician Al-Khwarizmi, who lived during the turn of the eighth to the ninth century. His achievements include, besides introducing the "Indian zero" as a full-fledged number into our Arabic numeral system, the development of precisely defined calculation methods for deriving problem solutions.[22] This is exactly what an algorithm is. Algorithms are core components of software and mathematically based rule sets that dictate to the computer what it should do to solve a task. Here is a very simple example:

To determine the Body Mass Index (BMI), a program needs a person's weight and height. After these data are entered into an appropriate screen mask, the underlying algorithm (calculation formula: BMI $=$ weight/height$^2$) calculates the corresponding value.[23]

As mentioned above, the more data available to the AI software, the more reliable and better the results. A publicly available data repository measured in many petabytes (1 petabyte $=$ 1 million gigabytes) is Common Crawl. It is provided free of charge by Amazon Web Services to anyone who needs data for training purposes for AI. In the context of very large amounts of data, we speak of Big Data. I would like to explain what lies behind this using the example of age recognition: On the internet, there are websites and apps of very different quality that can determine a person's age based on their facial photo. The more photos of people with known ages are available, the better the facial characteristics of individual age groups can be mathematically determined and programmatically classified. The developers of such websites and apps therefore use large databases with facial photos, which are partly freely available on the web. With them, they can test and optimize their applications, which is a cost-effective alternative, especially for small software companies.[24] The more often the computer determines the age based on as many faces as possible, the better it can be checked how reliable its results are, which in turn can flow into the AI.[25] The progress is enormous. MLPerf™ is a consortium of leading AI experts from universities, research labs, and industry. It has set itself the task of creating well-founded benchmarks that provide assessments of the training and inference performance of AI systems. Based on this, machine systems can already be trained twice as fast in 2022 as in the previous year. The greatest increase in performance is due to the further development of AI software, but to a lesser extent also to some system innovations.[26]

Anyone who uses biometric software for facial recognition, such as FaceID on the iPhone or its various counterparts on Android phones, will have already recognized how useful such AI techniques can be. There are also more than enough positive examples in other areas. Think, for example, of a Big Data implementation for detecting tumors from MRI scans. Huge databases from around the world with images of tumors at different stages provide the doctor with faster and more reliable information about the disease using specialized applications than he could ever have analyzed himself.[27] In July 2022, the AI company Deep Mind, a London-based subsidiary of Google's parent company Alphabet Inc., announced that it had deciphered the structure of practically all 200 million proteins known to science, paving the way for the development of new drugs or technologies to tackle global challenges such as famines or environmental pollution. It has published the protein structures in a publicly accessible database.[28] No human can conduct such ambitious analyses with such a large amount of data in such a short time. Of course, there are also negative examples of AI applications. We know them from totalitarian states that use them to monitor their citizens down to the smallest aspects of their lives. As always, the principle applies that a coin has two sides, and in some applications, it is more like a die with multiple sides.

## Are Algorithms Evil?

Algorithms are repeatedly portrayed as the evil secret agents that work in the shadows and scrutinize and manipulate us without our knowledge. What one does not know causes fear. However, algorithms are not inherently dangerous. They are neither good nor evil, fair nor unfair, biased nor objective. For those who want to know more, the website Algorithm Watch.org is recommended, whose operators investigate the use of algorithms in critical areas such as AI. As with all technical possibilities, it depends on how they are designed and what is done with them. They are the brains of our software, functions and benefits of programs depend on them, and nothing works without them. They are used to increase productivity in industrial manufacturing, optimize supply chains, control financial transactions, guide us to the desired information on the web, provide weather forecasts, and allow us to recognize patterns in vast amounts of data and draw useful conclusions from them. Unlike in our example with the Body Mass Index, algorithms sometimes also make serious decisions that do not concern industrial processes but have a targeted impact on the lives of individuals. What do they base their decisions on, and what values underlie them? The way they work often remains hidden, as they are part of the hard-earned and legitimate intellectual property of their developers. Often, many years of continuous work are behind them, for which the search algorithms of Google or Microsoft are good examples. However, since their impact can be enormous, there is a public interest in certain application cases to know what logic and objectives they follow. Why does the risk management software grant one bank customer the desired loan and not another? Why is a candidate considered or immediately sorted out when applying for a job, as in the case of Ping An? Why does one high school graduate get a place at a coveted foreign university and another does not? What criteria are used to make these decisions?

It is a major misconception to believe that programs make such decisions more objectively than humans in all cases.[29] On the one hand, the underlying artificial intelligence was created by humans who pursue economic or political purposes or bring their own values to bear in the form of program code. On the other hand, these decisions are based on consciously selected data. Such data includes, for example, gender, place of residence, income, level of education, or marital status. The results produced by an algorithm thus depend heavily on the data selection with which it is fed. For instance, if only men are classified as managers in the code of a company's internal e-learning platform, then women will not be suggested management courses. Data can therefore be selected and used in a discriminatory manner, either consciously or unconsciously. If one adds religious affiliation, age, ethnicity, uploaded content, and friends on social media or "likes" and "dislikes," a person can be quite well typified, and their political preferences or consumer behavior can be predicted with high probability. However, the "consumer" of the algorithm usually does not know which data basis and logic led to a particular result, and they hardly understand when questionable and unfair decisions have been systematically implemented in this way. The consequences are borne by the applicant for a loan, the job applicant, or the high school graduate seeking a university place. Our life path can thus be positively or negatively influenced by the achievements of IT.[30] This is what is behind the demand for more transparency from developers.

Social media and search engines thus determine, based on algorithms and our data, which results are presented to us in an internet search, which content is shown to us, which friends or groups they suggest to us, which news is prioritized, or which advertisements we get to see. Even our moods and emotions can be determined quite reliably. But the algorithms can do even more. From past behavior, the probability of our future behavior can be calculated. By moving from "descriptive" to "predictive," their significance grows further. The claim to be able to predict the behavior of others in this way can have far-reaching consequences for those affected. Sounds utopian? But it is not. Social media—especially when they have high user numbers or can even combine user data from several of their platforms (in the case of Meta: Facebook, WhatsApp, Instagram)—have very high hit rates for behavior predictions due to the very large volumes of data available to them, as numerous highly elaborate studies show. In this respect, they are not only very interesting for advertisers who want to sell their products but also for political parties and the design of their election campaigns.

Barack Obama described the importance of technology for his 2008 campaign quite cautiously: "What also struck me was the growing role that technology played in our victories. The extraordinary youth of my team enabled us to use and refine digital networks… Our status as upstarts led us to repeatedly rely on the energy and creativity of our internet-savvy volunteers."[31] While an important but not decisive role of digital media is diagnosed here, commentators assessed their influence on the presidential election four years later quite differently. A data analyst from US *Computerworld* titled his article on the 2012 election with the words: "Barack Obama's big data won the US election," and concluded that big data changed politics.

Micro-targeting, i.e., the massive and precise addressing of people with individualized messages based on analyzed user data, was seen by the author as the main reason for Obama's re-election.[32] The obvious increase in importance from 2008 to 2012 continued in the presidential elections of 2016 and 2020. *Forbes* predicted in an article from October 2020 that social media "could determine the outcome of the election."[33] Of course, this constellation also offers foreign powers the opportunity to intervene in favor of a candidate. In the 2016 presidential election, Russia massively intervened in social media in favor of Donald Trump against Hillary Clinton. As a result, two years later, a total of twelve members of the Russian military intelligence service GRU ended up on the FBI's Most Wanted list with names and photos.[34] However, none of the participants could be held accountable.[35] But Putin's people were not the only ones working for Trump in 2016. With an app called "This is your Digital Life," the data of 87 million, mostly American, Facebook users was illegally harvested and used by the British company Cambridge Analytica for the election campaigns of Donald Trump and his party colleague Ted Cruz. Facebook ended up in court for this in 2020, and Cambridge Analytica had to file for bankruptcy as early as 2018.[36]

Which data Facebook stores in over 60 categories can be found in its data policies.[37] The platform registers them with every login of a "target," by which we m ean users. These include, among others:

- Chat: the last chats with other target persons;
- Check-ins: all places where the target person has ever checked in;
- Connections: all connections to pages that the target person likes;
- Family: other family members with an indication of the relationship;
- Favorite Quotes: the entries in the favorite quotes field;
- Friend Request: all friend requests, including the declined ones;
- Groups: all memberships in groups;

- Last Location: the last location;
- Machines: every computer ever used;
- Notes: list of all saved notes, keywords or persons can be marked;
- Photos: all images ever uploaded by target persons;
- Pokes: list of all attempts by others to get the target person's attention and vice versa;
- Political Views: information on political views;
- Privacy Settings: list of chosen privacy settings;
- Real Time Activities: storage of tracking results, i.e., all clicks on Facebook are stored for analysis purposes;
- Removed Friends: all former friends on Facebook;
- Shares: all links posted by the target person on the wall.

In addition, there are the "normal" personal data, such as name, date of birth, gender, and place of residence. Given this list, one does not need to be a master of stochastics to recognize why precise micro-targeting is possible with it. Any intelligence service would be delighted with such a comprehensive list of data, as it would extremely refine and facilitate profiling, i.e., drawing a comprehensive personality profile of target persons, with the appropriate algorithms. But from Edward Snowden, we already know that these data are anyway fished out of the large data streams of the internet by the services.

Given the fact that positive and negative consequences of algorithms and thus also artificial intelligence are inevitable, the essential decisions on how to deal with them must be of a political rather than a technical nature. Otherwise, the development will slip away from us, and a gigantic loss of control over our future would be the consequence. This, of course, presupposes a state that is truly knowledgeable, acts proactively, and employs or can utilize personnel capable of handling such a task. In the digital world, ignorance and naivety pose an imminent danger.

Digitalization is largely understood by us as the construction of infrastructure. In reality, however, this is only one component. The experts involved must also be capable of assessing the technical possibilities and ensuring the proper handling of them. However, state regulations must not hinder progress but should promote it and guide it in ways that are justifiable under aspects of personality protection and informational self-determination. Countries with a broad participatory base and active civil societies have good prerequisites for this.

# The Democratization of Knowledge

One of the most significant achievements of IT is that it has provided us with access to the world's knowledge via the internet. Search engines level and democratize access. Thanks to them, it is no longer a privilege of certain social classes, companies, academies, or people in developed industrial societies. What humanity knows and makes accessible becomes knowledge for all through them. This fits with the official mission of by far the most used search engine: "To organize the world's information and make it universally accessible and useful." Google's vision has long since become an experienced reality. Searching for information on the internet without using the company's search engine has become hard to imagine. Google's search algorithms significantly influence how we complete tasks, what information we receive, and ultimately how we perceive our world. Whether we are looking for flights for the next trip, events, institutions, people, images, current news, or conducting professional research.

Google was founded in 1997 as an ad-funded internet search engine and achieved a revenue of 200,000 dollars in the following year.[38] In 2021, just 24 years later, it stood at 256.7 billion dollars, with 209.5 billion still resulting from advertising despite a now diversified portfolio.[39] Thus, Google is the dominant revenue generator for its parent company Alphabet.

The increasing significance of Google has also influenced language. We no longer search for information; we google it—equating the product with the activity. With every search term we enter, an odyssey lasting only a hundredth of a second across an average of 1500 to 2000 different servers on multiple continents is triggered. Interestingly, no one is surprised anymore when tens of thousands of results appear on the screen with hardly any delay and also convey meaningful results. However, search engines with high data volumes are not only suitable for finding information but also, under certain conditions, as prediction tools. Let's assume there is a persistent and statistically noticeable increase in the number of searches for "single-family house in Düsseldorf, Germany." From this, one could derive forecasts for the current development of demand for such houses and then verify these against actual future transactions and market prices. Another example of the power of search engines is the interest in certain politicians before an election. For instance, the search for "Olaf Scholz" increased continuously and significantly from August 15, 2021, to September 26, 2021, the date of the federal election. Olaf Scholz won the election. Such statistics can be found on the Google Trends website. They are  available for free.[40] Anyone who proverbially wants to look at the people's mouth can do so on Google Trends. If this has not yet been done, it would be an interesting task to compare the statistics from Google Trends with the predictions of pollsters. Do they go hand in hand, do they differ, who is faster and more accurate?

As of January 2022, Google holds a market share of just under 92% among search engines.[41] The narrow remainder is shared by the Bings, Yahoos, Baidus, etc., of this world. This is unlikely to change significantly in the foreseeable future. Internet search and access to the world's knowledge can therefore be almost equated with Google. For those who feel overwhelmed by this and are concerned about their privacy, DuckDuckGo is recommended for a number of good reasons. According to its own statements, as of March 2023, the company handled 3 billion searches per month and is the number 2 in North America, the UK, and Australia.[42] There was indeed a time when other search engines than Google, which have now fallen into oblivion, were very popular and widespread. Of the former giants like AltaVista, Lycos, or Excite, only Yahoo remains of some significance. Google's company name is derived from "Googol," the English term for $10^{100}$, a one followed by a hundred zeros. This reflects a program. In line with this, since October 2009, Google has used the scientific designation of Googol "1e100" with the addition ".net" (= 1e100.net) for its own internet domain. Most of us will never see it. This is intended to express the enormous capacity of Google's worldwide data centers and the claim to be able to capture and index virtually unlimited numbers of web pages. What are the reasons for the very high acceptance of the Google search engine, as reflected in its market share?

Essentially, they lie in its speed and the quality of the results. Both can be traced back—simplified—to a manageable number of factors. These include, of course, the search algorithms that the company has developed over the years and which are among the company's crown jewels. These magical tools distinguish between categories such as texts, images, videos, news, etc. They differentiate e.g. between terms like "Bild" (image) and the german newspaper named "Bild " and know that someone searching for "carriage" might actually mean "car." They can also handle common typos and still find the right websites or identify spam. How does the magic work?

The search itself is based on small programs called crawlers or spiders. They "crawl" over millions of publicly accessible web pages in search of keywords and links to other pages listed there. Once discovered, they are stored in a gigantic directory, the so-called index, along with information about their location and how up-to-date they are. According to Google, the index contains more information than all the libraries in the world combined and is over 100,000,000 gigabytes in size. When a query is entered, only the index is searched.[43] This makes the search so fast. The quality results from a process called page ranking. The rank of a web page for the relevance of a search result depends on three factors: the frequency and position of the keywords on a web page, the time span, i.e., how long the web page has existed, and the number of other web pages that link to the page in question. Of these three factors, the third is the most important. Since Google considers the number of links to a web page as a quality vote for it, these links determine the rank it receives in the search results listing. The more links, the higher the page appears on the results list. This makes the evaluation quite resistant to manipulation. However, advertisers can influence this ranking by paying for it. This is particularly interesting because market researchers have found that users are most likely to click on websites that appear at the top of the results lists and modify their query if they do not find what they want on the first page.[44] Smart website operators therefore pay close attention to using targeted keywords. In general, they strive to align as closely as possible with the logic of the Google search algorithm.

The demand for "Googling" and thus its success is also due to the fact that the number of active websites is growing enormously. In the year 2000, there were only 17.1 million, ten years later 207 million, and it took only another five years to reach the impressive number of 863 million. By the end of February 2022, there were 1.93 billion websites online. This does not take into account the number of those that are offline and have found their place in the "Internet Archive," a non-profit organization for the historical documentation of web content. As of March 2023, these were 735 billion websites, 890,000 software programs, as well as 8.4 million videos, 41 million books, and much more.[45] The curve is still rising exponentially, with new ones being added every second.[46] All of this is very positive. Nevertheless, a slight aftertaste might remain: Does Googling lead to outsourcing our memory to the web? Is it enough for us to know where to find information instead of having it ourselves? Anyone who always and everywhere has all the desired information within reach of ChatGPT, Google, or Siri, Alexa, and Cortana does not need to remember anything. But was it fundamentally different in the past? Is there really a reason for cultural pessimism? Were libraries not what Google is today, only with atmosphere and without a universal information offering? Education is knowing where it is written, goes a popular saying from old times. Does Google simply make us collectively ignorant, or does it make us smarter? The answer depends on how and for what we use it.

## New Work and the Placeless Society

When I worked for Novell in the 1990s, our CEO and former head of the PC division at Hewlett Packard, Bob Frankenberg, set "Pervasive Computing" as the strategic direction for our company. The term originates from 1988 and was coined by Mark Weiser, Chief Scientist at the legendary Xerox research center in Palo Alto. It meant, in contrast to "island computing" of unconnected computers, that data communication can occur with any device, at any location, and in any format. Worldwide networking and collaboration were the goals. In an article in the *Chicago Tribune* from May 1995, Bob announced: "We are on a path that is not too different from the development of the automobile or electricity, where this new technology simply becomes part of daily life, something we just take for granted."[47] The concept of Pervasive Computing was in line with the trend of the time, and Bob had summarized the development of the coming decades in a few words.

He had Novell's flagship product in mind. In the mid-1990s, NetWare was the standard for PC network operating systems, the so-called Local and Wide Area Networks (LAN and WAN), with a 60% share of the world market. More data flowed through Novell's NetWare servers worldwide daily than through the entire Internet, which in 1995 had only 16 million users. These represented just 0.4% of the world's population at the time. Today, with a much larger population, we are at 65.6% (March 2021).[48] Additionally, Bob's statement also contained a jab at competitor Microsoft. While Microsoft dominated the PC market with MS-DOS and Windows, Novell was the top dog in the network market. Both companies knew they needed at least a piece of each other's market to be permanently successful. It was only later that Windows NT (New Technology) would take over the network market. Until then, we at Novell joked about Microsoft's attempts to break into "our" network market by translating NT as "Not There." Pride comes before a fall.

What Bob Frankenberg envisioned back then can best be described with the term "placeless society." When we hear it, we usually associate it with things like home office, ubiquitous access to social media, the unlimited availability of online shops, or the ability to conduct transactions with our bank 24/7 from anywhere in the world. Few think of telemedicine or the ability to diagnose their car without having to visit a workshop. However, it is only a matter of time before such things, which currently lie on the periphery of our perception, also become taken for granted.

Especially with regard to our working world, IT offers ever-new models that are often summarized under the umbrella term "New Work." New Work ultimately goes back to the changing needs of working people, to which employers must respond. Only in this way can they remain competitive in the face of a shortage of skilled workers. New Work therefore means the flexibilization of work models and—as far as possible—the individualization of work. Without IT, such reforms would be built on sand from the outset. Digitalization and global networking are prerequisites without which New Work could only be implemented inefficiently.

The classic in the field of New Work is the home office. This model received a significant boost from the Corona pandemic. According to a study by the German Federal Ministry of Labor and Social Affairs, the average in the group of 20- to 64-year-old employed persons who at least occasionally work from home was 14.8% in the 28 EU member states in 2017 and 15.2% in 2018. In Germany, however, it was only 11% and 11.8%, respectively. In the Netherlands (37.5%) and in the Scandinavian countries, working in the home office was already much more widespread. But even in France and the United Kingdom, the rate was significantly higher than in Germany.[49] A comparable study by the Institute of the German Economy shows the effect of the pandemic three years later. In the average of the now 27 EU countries, it was 43% in March 2021, with the share in Germany at around 42%, just slightly below. The frontrunners of 2018 largely maintained their positions.[50]

It is quite possible that these numbers will now continuously and persistently decrease again after the end of the pandemic. How significant the decline will be in the medium term is difficult to predict. However, a (hopefully) sustainable effect could be that the IT infrastructure in companies, but especially in data networks, will continue to be significantly expanded. It is high time for this. Anyone who, like me, has to work with an old copper line touted as ultra-modern (referred to in marketing jargon as VDSL) and fluctuating throughput rates will have a different experience with the home office than someone who is already connected to a fiber optic network. In both of the studies cited above, however, the home office is viewed positively by the majority of employees and companies. The former CEO of Twitter (now X), Jack Dorsey, announced in May 2020 that his employees could work from home permanently, with the return to the office being voluntary at that time. Tim Cook, his counterpart at Apple, saw it differently. In June 2021, he informed the staff in Cupertino that presence in the company headquarters would be required again from September, triggering a storm of protest. Given the fact that Apple had moved into a new company building costing $5 billion in 2017, one can certainly understand Cook's decision. Sundar Pichai, the head of Google, opted for a hybrid form, which was met with much approval from the staff.[51] I worked in Silicon Valley for four years and can well understand the protest of the Apple employees. The eternal traffic jams and catastrophic traffic, a meager public transport system, and astronomical rents on site make the home office very attractive.

But available technology is only one side of the coin. The opportunities and risks that modern IT offers the working world are more diverse—and more controversial. For example, there are already discussions about whether employees who work "remotely" from places with lower living costs should be paid less. Conversely, it is also being discussed and implemented to reward those who are still willing to come to the office with bonuses.[52] In 2021, an internal study at Microsoft found that employee satisfaction with their work-life balance had fallen by 13% during the pandemic due to the home office. The main reasons for this decline were constant availability, frequent online meetings, the lack of focus time for important tasks, and less uninterrupted leisure time and vacation.[53] Employers will have to think about such mood drops just as much as about what management skills are required to lead employees without a fixed location. In an article by the BBC[54], there is talk of ghost colleagues on the net and soulless work silos in relation to the home office. This means that contact with colleagues outside the group with whom one has to work functionally has shrunk significantly. Opportunities for communication, such as the shared walk to the parking garage after work or the casual small talk in the hallway, are missing. Topics such as psychological safety, impending loneliness, or diminished productivity and creativity are on the agenda and require new management as a result of new work. How many leaders are prepared for this? What happens to loyalty to the employer or the degree of attachment to the company when social contacts between employees and supervisors become increasingly loose? Can there still be a sense of "we" if the exchange in the coffee kitchen is missing? And how susceptible will highly qualified professionals be to calls from headhunters if a new job no longer requires a move and thus the corresponding discussions within the family are eliminated?

Another consequence of IT for our working world can be described using the example of crowd working. This term refers to the practice of assigning work via digital platforms to an online audience. Currently, these are usually smaller jobs, so-called micro tasks, that can be done online or on-site.[55] One of these platforms is the globally operating Amazon Mechanical Turk, which was originally developed internally for Amazon but later made publicly accessible. It advertises with the phrase: "Access a global, on-demand, $24 \times 7$ workforce," which describes the idea very succinctly and accurately.[56]

Currently, crowd worker jobs mostly do not require any special qualifications, as they are simple and time-limited tasks. Examples include delivery services, online research, or commissioned positive reviews of products in online shops. Of course, the highly adaptive English language has the appropriate names ready for this. People who strive for such jobs and see them as part of their lifestyle are called "gigs." The growing labor market behind it is referred to as the "gig economy." The process of assignment is very simple: If a corporate customer of the respective platform has a new job to assign, the platform informs its registered jobbers via app and other digital channels. If interested, they simply accept the job with a click, just as an Uber driver accepts a ride—whereby better platforms also take over quality control and reporting for the corporate customer. It is already apparent that this method is also gaining ground in higher-qualified areas.[57] Technology redefines the physical boundaries of a company, as well as its social ones. Thus, these platforms become a real competition for the numerous intermediaries of freelancers. Especially in higher-qualified "brain work" (e.g., programming), which does not require local presence, crowd working can be in demand worldwide, true to the motto of Amazon Mechanical Turk. Whether a programmer, who is used for a clearly defined, sufficiently specified sprint within a project, is sitting in Germany or Vietnam makes no difference. However, it does make a difference for wages, social benefits, vacation entitlements, and the like. When crowd workers climb up the value chain and the jobs become more qualified, a global ad hoc labor market without permanent employment relationships emerges, which can also be more productive than the conventional one due to the exploitation of time differences. While employees in Europe are sleeping, those in Asia are already up and about, and both groups can work together better.

With skillful organization of task distribution, 24/7 work scenarios can be designed that are not as easily and cost-effectively possible on-site. I was able to observe a real example of higher-qualified gigs up close: A friend of mine is a self-employed lawyer and was approached by a legal consultancy. The idea was that he would take on cases upon request, which they acquired on the internet. Out of curiosity, he agreed to it. At first glance, this could have resulted in a win-win situation for both parties. However, after a closer look at the conditions, this perspective was no longer present. My friend would have become an on-call service provider, unable to reliably plan his income and financial possibilities. Additionally, he would have been in competition with other lawyers, which would not have been beneficial for his pricing. This market will therefore operate under different rules than the one we are used to. It will be much more difficult for governments and unions to regulate or shape it. Individualization and self-determination, the two core elements of New Work and the emerging gig economy, come at a price. "There is no free lunch," as one of my American colleagues aptly put it.

# Love, Sex, and Bits & Bytes

The same applies to the very personal areas of emotional relationships, which are also increasingly influenced by IT. The number of technology-mediated personal relationshipsis increasing so much that this business already occupies a significant place in the platform economy. The forms are diverse. They range from dating with real people and built-in virtual reality functions to the offer of cyber relationships with virtual love partners, whose characteristics can be customized, up to "sexting." The latter refers to the exchange of erotic messages and photos over the internet and is a composite of sex and texting. As a new market, sex robots are added, which, due to the materials used and artificial behavioral intelligence, are becoming more and more similar to humans. Except for one difference: they do not contradict! In this respect, IT has also, if not completely changed, at least significantly supplemented our sex life—a topic that the English writer Ian McEwan masterfully addresses in all its disturbing ambivalences in the novel *Machines Like Me*.[58]

Compared to such innovations, internet porn sites are almost conventional. An analysis of the world's top 20 search terms on Google (as of February 2022) reveals a somewhat unsurprising ranking: 6th place XNXX, 7th place Xvideos, 10th place XXX, 11th place Pornos, and 19th place Porn.[59] The top 1 to 5 spots were taken by the mega search terms Facebook, YouTube, Google, Gmail, and Hotmail—then comes sex. In trying to grasp the economic dimensions of pornographic websites, it quickly became clear to me that reliable data is not available. The internet only provides figures on the total annual revenue volume of these sites. Depending on the source, they differ by several billion US dollars, cannot be trusted, and in some cases, are completely outdated. A query from me about the reasons for this was answered by the Free Speech Coalition, the American industry association of the porn industry, with a reference to the structure of the industry. Almost every company is privately owned and is careful not to publish its figures. Additionally, while there are a handful of well-known, large studios and platforms, the industry as a whole is incredibly diverse and fragmented—with hundreds of thousands of small producers and creatives working in sometimes very small niche markets worldwide. The erotic industry is an ecosystem with permeable boundaries that (depending on the definition) includes studios, producers, tube sites, advertising networks, cams, clips, and other forms of entertainment and can be found all over the world.[60]

A list of 2000 porn websites that have at least 10,000 visitors a day is provided by Allpornsites.net and shows the wide range of offerings. The site divides them into a total of 84 categories with special interests.[61] The total number of porn sites on the web is estimated there to be just under a million. One of the most frequented porn sites is PornHub. The company behind it, Aylo (formerly Mind Geek Holdings), is based in Montreal, Canada, and owns other sites like YouPorn and Brazzers. PornHub publishes extensive analyses annually, allowing for a better understanding of this industry and its users.[62]According to PornHub's own information, the site had an average of over 130 million visitors daily in 2021,[63] slightly more than the population of Mexico. Their average age was 37 years. With increasing age, the proportion of individual groups decreased significantly, although older users stayed on the site longer. The preferred access was mobile, with mobile users accounting for 83%. In most countries, Sunday was the most popular day to visit PornHub, while Friday had the least traffic. This is mainly due to the times when porn is consumed, usually between 10 PM and 1 AM.On weekends, visits shift even more to the early morning hours. Among the top 20 "visitor countries," Germany ranks 8th. Each visitor worldwide spent an average of 9 minutes and 55 seconds on a page in 2021. That was 29 seconds less than the previous year, although the dwell time for female visitors increased by 14 seconds. Overall, the proportion of women in this predominantly male field increased by five points in 2021, now standing at 35%. On the top 20 list, German women form the bottom with 28%, while Filipinas take the top spot with 52%, confirming the global trend that developed industrial countries tend to be lower on the list. The time generally invested in visiting this site is enormous. 130 million visitors multiplied by 9 minutes and 55 seconds results in a total daily duration of 2451 years. In this time, empires have risen and fallen. Anyone wondering where the operators get all this data from is strongly advised to familiarize themselves with topics such as privacy policies, cookies, tracking, and Google Analytics.

As part of a scientific study in the USA from 2018, around 85% of the 1036 participants said they had consumed internet porn in the last six months. More men (80%) than women (26%) reported watching online porn at least once a week.[64] So, we are indeed dealing with a mainstream topic. The study also states that 17% of customers of porn sites have an addiction problem with it.[65] There are indications that visiting sites like PornHub also serves as a kind of substitute function. This is shown by the following circumstance: When the services of Facebook, Instagram, and WhatsApp temporarily failed on October 4, 2021, access to PornHub increased by 10.5%. A similar phenomenon was observed in 2019 when Facebook and Instagram went down before. Are we lacking creativity for leisure activities without screens?

However, those interested in porn sites show plenty of creativity otherwise. In China, internet pornography is banned. According to MIT Technology Review, the world's largest gaming site "Steam" is one of the few platforms still available uncensored in the vast country. The app "Wallpaper Engine," provided by a German developer duo in 2016 and available there, was quickly repurposed by resourceful Chinese gamers to gain access to online pornography.[66]

Running a site like PornHub is expensive. To serve the vast audience worldwide, smoothly and at high speed, a very powerful IT infrastructure is needed. This ranges from technical staff and content maintenance to the network and computing capacities, which must be able to quickly respond to load changes to automatically scale resources up or down with fluctuating visitor numbers. This raises the question: How do the operators of porn sites make their money?

In the same way as many other websites. The providers of most porn websites offer their basic services for free, meaning a selection of videos. "Free," that's the honey pot used to attract visitors. This is financed with advertising, paid services—such as live shows—paid access to special interest sites, and the sale of various aids. Considering the mentioned 2000 websites with their 84 categories, one can assume that the average revenue per visitor is higher, the more specific the preferences are. At PornHub, a simple calculation makes things easier: If each of the claimed 130 million daily visitors leaves just 0.5 cents on average, that would be a substantial 650,000 Euros per day. However, whether and how accurate this number is must unfortunately remain speculation.

Billy Eilish, singer, songwriter, and four-time Grammy Awards winner of 2020, as well as many other music awards, claimed in a well-known American talk radio show that consuming porn sites since she was 11 years old had "destroyed" her brain.[67] By this, she meant her disturbed relationship with sexuality, her addictive behavior, her distorted image of women, and unrealistic expectations of sexual partners. Results of this kind are also scientifically confirmed, especially when the consumption of pornography begins in childhood. In cases where parental control is absent or insufficient, governments, such as that of the United Kingdom, are trying to mandate technically watertight age verifications for porn sites.[68] A not entirely simple task. The web is full of sites that seem to compete in presenting the negative effects of porn sites. Many have a religious or ideological slant. Some of these effects, such as the risk of addiction or social isolation due to a lack of offline contacts, can also be seamlessly transferred to other online activities: permanent computer gaming or online betting are examples of this.

Online activities follow the same pattern here as with other popular platform services. Constant availability combined with free, location-independent, mobile access drive this economy, with the factor "anonymous" likely having an amplifying effect in the case of pornography.

In addition to the many porn sites, IT has enabled other technology-dependent forms of sexual activities. The English language, always far ahead of ours in terms of technology, has coined terms such as Cyber Infidelity, Cyber Celibacy, or Online Dating to describe such phenomena. Online dating appears in many forms, from the famous Tinder swipes to the clicks on the site of Ashley Madison, a well-known specialist in arranging affairs.[69] The Ashley Madison database was hacked and published in 2015 by a group called "Impact Team." The unmasked users experienced a nasty surprise and had to live with a variety of serious consequences: from divorces to sextortion, i.e., blackmail with compromising information. The Dark Web Journal has extensively described the case.[70]

The hacked database proved to be a goldmine for psychologists, sociologists, and analysts of all kinds. An interesting technical analysis by Annalee Newitz of Gizmodo claims the following: The more than 30 million men registered on the site were faced with only a very small number of real women.[71] According to her analysis of the database and the site's source code, the supposedly countless users ready for affairs were actually around 70,000 fembots. In this way, men were led to believe that a large playground for affairs was opening up, while in reality, it was just software pretending to be a woman.[72] When strong emotions and money are involved, the brain just shuts down.

While online dating has become a kind of standard on the internet, other forms, which are even more IT-enabled, prove to be marginal—but they have great future potential. This refers to relationships with partners who exist only as program code and where the human part is, of course, aware of this. One should not limit the view of any of these variants to just sex. It has now been proven that people can enter into real emotional relationships with virtual partners or even robots.[73] In the English edition of the Japanese daily newspaper *The Manichi*, Akihiko Kondo was quoted on April 18, 2020, as saying: "I have sworn my eternal love to Miku, not as a substitute for a living human being, but for her own sake." The special thing about Miku is: She exists only in the form of zeros and ones, i.e., as software.[74] In response to Kondo's marriage proposal, Miku said: "I hope you will honor me."

None of Kondo's family members were present at the wedding. However, 39 friends came, and the husband received many positive online comments, such as: "You have given me courage." Kondo, who wears a shiny wedding ring on his left hand, said: "I want people to know that this is my way of living life." Perhaps in a (not too distant?) future, such a marriage will be state-recognized, Miku could inherit from her husband, or both could adopt children. I have been in IT for too long to dismiss technology-driven changes—no matter how strange they may seem today—as unrealistic.

Kondo is not alone in his type of relationship. On the Indian website Analytics Insight, which specializes in AI topics, the usual top 10 websites and apps for virtual relationships are listed (somehow the decimal system seems so attractive that no ranking site manages to list only the top 8, even if the rest are worthless).[75] The way these apps are promoted is interesting. According to the authors, AI is a fundamental component of a change that "tests" our notions of what it means to be human. AI is so intertwined with everything that we will soon find it hard to imagine life without it. Virtual relationships, according to the authors, are an integral part of this.

In the Microsoft App Store, there are also Virtual Boy and Virtual Girl, which claim that now everyone can have a partner to their liking. The software assembles the girlfriend or boyfriend according to the user's specifications and can thus create the perfect partnership for everyone.[76] A particularly extreme example of such creation is offered by Virtual Life. Under the telling motto "raise your child, live your life," one can raise a virtual child there without having to expose oneself to the stress of real parents.[77]

Parents without stress, marriages without external burdens, without the requirement of mutual consideration, without really taking responsibility for each other, and without the ups and downs of human interaction do not require social skills. Such connections are a one-way street that suggests one can configure the other according to one's own ideas and wishes and transform them again if necessary. They are an ideal escape route from the reality of real relationships and are excellent for those who are not capable of or do not want to make compromises. But that does not make them fundamentally bad. For those who cannot experience intimacy in other ways, they may even be helpful. Even if one is de facto alone, they can still create the feeling of togetherness. Kondo is a good example of this. Cyberpsychologist Mary Aiken has summed it up in her book on the Cyber Effect: In her view, the easily made connections on the web have led to a shift of intimacy to the internet—and perhaps even to more sexual activity. However, at the expense of actual intimacy, real sexual contact[78], and at the expense of real reproduction. This cannot remain without social consequences.

On YouTube, there is an interesting thought experiment in a video about sex robots. A man named John asks in the comments: If my sex robot were cloned in the order of 10,000, would I then love all 10,000 clones or still only my own interpretation of her?[79] I am tempted to answer his question with a counter-question: If you love a person who has an identical twin, could you just as well love that twin? For most of us, the spontaneous answer would probably be "No." But is there this certainty on the internet? The topic of robotics raises even more pointed questions than virtual partnerships. For example, in June 2018, the US Congress initiated the so-called Creeper Act, which bans child sex robots and criminalizes their importation because some known owners of such robots were also proven to have committed crimes related to child pornography.[80]

According to the current state of technology, intimate relationships with a robot still rely on the perception of human lovers. They project something into the machine that does not exist. To the extent that AI continues to develop and replicate the neural structures of our brains, robots will, however, acquire distinguishable, individual personalities, as imagined by Ian McEwan. Then, the question posed by John in the cited YouTube thought experiment will become redundant. A foretaste of this is provided by the clever R2D2 and the somewhat clumsy-looking C-3PO from the planet Tatooine in the Outer Rim. Both Star Wars characters have many human traits, and it is easy to find them likable, just like Luke Skywalker does. A recent incident in one of Google's AI development teams highlights the discussions already taking place today. In June 2022, programmer Blake Lemoine claimed to the *Washington Post* that Google's AI language system LaMDA (Language Model for Dialogue Applications) had consciousness, based on chat logs. His astonishing conversations with LaMDA and especially its responses are captured in a noteworthy 15-minute reel by the BBC, vividly illustrating how far AI has already progressed.[81] Technically, LaMDA is software that Google developers trained with a big data model of a total of 1.56 trillion words from 2.97 billion documents, 1.12 billion dialogues, and 13.39 billion statements.[82] Blake's assertion sparked a heated debate on the internet. It was embarrassing for Google, as they had assured that they would not venture into gray areas with neural AI techniques. Shortly thereafter, Blake was available on the job market. The mentioned eighth day of creation in the preface of this book might be closer than most of us realize. After all, AI-based chatbots that can write speeches or software and do our children's homework, are finding their way into our daily lives.[83] One should also think of AI in conjunction with the immense potentials of quantum computers, which we will discuss elsewhere. We are beginning to move towards the computing power of our brains. However, like most other things, love for droids is not fundamentally new. Love and sex between a human and a statue already occurred in antiquity. The Roman poet Ovid, born in 43 BC, tells in his famous *Metamorphoses* of the sculptor Pygmalion, who fell in love with a statue he had created. "Lost in delight, Pygmalion feels a burning love for the seeming body," it says, over 2000 years ago. After appropriate and qualified sacrifices, the statue was brought to life by the goddess of love, Venus. What remains for me is the horror of Ovid's not exactly easy texts from my Latin classes.

In the here and now, the range of sex robots (mostly female) is remarkably rich even without the intervention of a Roman goddess. On one of the now numerous manufacturer websites on the web, you can meet Megan, Sophia, Becky & Co.[84] They are marketed as AI versions of their species and cost between 3500 and 4000 dollars. On the open-ended price scale, almost no wishes for extras remain unfulfilled. Heating to human body temperature upon touch and easy programming in a do-it-yourself manner are included. These creatures are far removed from the dolls made of straw, fabric, and leather that sailors of the early modern period took on their journeys or the inflatable companions that are indispensable from men's jokes of recent decades. We see how the topic of sex on the internet has brought about considerable dynamics. I expect nothing different in the field of sex robots, even if the usual success factors of porn sites—always and everywhere available, free, and anonymous—do not apply equally here. With falling prices and increasing individualization of robots, the topic will gain weight.

All this practically forces us to think about how to deal with such innovations, as the American Congress has already attempted with the Creeper Act. In my opinion, the organization Responsible Robotics[85] is pursuing a correct approach by closely monitoring all forms of

AI. This includes those that have already found their way into our children's rooms. Founded by Canadian Aimee van Wynsberghe, who currently teaches as a professor of applied ethics of artificial intelligence at the University of Bonn and also advises the EU Commission on these issues, Responsible Robotics formulates it as follows: "The worldwide spread of these robotics and AI technologies is beginning to significantly impact people's lives. Despite the touted successes, cracks are gradually appearing, and questions about social justice, gender and racial biases, as well as privacy and the erosion of other human rights, are increasingly being raised." The organization provides advice and certification for manufacturers, consumers, and policymakers at these points. Robots have no morals, no matter how human they appear to us. Morality and the limits of their behavior must be implemented by their developers in their AI code and its database. This serves to also set boundaries for the people who use them. In a global market, not every country, political system, and society will define the rules by which this should happen in the same way.

To the extent that artificial intelligence is integrated into products, services, and decisions, the previous protection of privacy and data alone is no longer sufficient. The EU, which once again takes a pioneering role with its white paper "Artificial Intelligence—A European Approach to Excellence and Trust" (2020) and its proposal for an AI legal framework (2021), sees regulation as an essential prerequisite for the development of AI tools in terms of consumer protection.[86] This is a very large task that now needs to be solved. Here too, technology is once again far ahead of politics.

# 2

# America's Dominance and Europe's Opportunities

In the forties of the last century, the era of our modern computers began. It marked the transition from electromechanical to electronic data processing. At that time, engineers typically designed their computing machines with a specific purpose in mind. It was about solving a particular, practical problem more efficiently and quickly with the help of a machine. Such problems were, due to the wartime conditions, of a military nature. Examples include ballistic calculations for artillery shells, machines for deciphering enemy communications, or optimizing the statics of aircraft. The early computers were built for these purposes. Unlike today, their programs and data were punched onto punch cards and thus not stored in electronic memory, similar to a historical piano. Its music is played from a paper roll with punched holes that control the keystrokes. The idea of being able to program and use the same computer to solve any problem emerged during and shortly after World War II and was gradually realized

© The Author(s), under exclusive license to Springer Fachmedien Wiesbaden GmbH, part of Springer Nature 2024
J. Müller, *Turning Point*,
https://doi.org/10.1007/978-3-658-46079-2_2

thanks to corresponding technical and theoretical groundwork. For today's user, it has become a matter of course to use their computer for a spreadsheet, a presentation or text program, a planning tool from SAP, or a browser for various purposes. It is equally natural for us that all these programs can be open simultaneously and run in parallel. However, in the 1940s, this was futuristic and anything but self-evident.

The term programming evokes associations with today's software. Modern programming tools exist in many different variants, the so-called computer languages. Their commands, syntax, and grammar are highly formalized and vary according to methods, purpose, and target systems. For example, each processor type has its own instruction sets on which it executes a program's instructions. This executable machine language is difficult for humans to read and quite detailed. Therefore, as early as the 1940s, there were initial approaches to developing programming languages that abstracted from the machine language of zeros and ones and were readable and understandable for humans. Plankalkül by Konrad Zuse, which will be discussed here, was the first of its kind worldwide. It was developed between 1942 and 1945. Apart from these early approaches, however, the comfortable possibilities of today's programming were still far off. Changing existing "programs" for new tasks was laborious and could mean days of work by several specialists with different roles. Unlike today, the computers of that time did not have storage media in which programs were stored. Instead, depending on the problem to be solved, the connections between individual hardware components of the machines had to be reconfigured. In other words, the machines were rewired for new questions. They weighed many tons, could be the size of a medium-sized apartment, and had a power consumption that would bring tears to the eyes

of modern sustainability advocates. After data processing, they output the results on punch cards or directly on
a typewriter-like device that made them readable without
detours. The punch card system remained in use as an
input and storage medium for a long time. The cards used
in computers go back to Herman Hollerith, who leveraged
them as data storage for the American census of 1890.
It was not until the mid-1970s that they were largely
replaced by magnetic storage devices, which resemble
today's hard drives.

In addition to programmability and use for very different tasks, the first modern computers of the 1940s were
characterized by electronic processors for data processing. This distinguishes them from their electromechanical
predecessors of the first computer generation, with which
they overlapped in their development. Electromechanical
computers used relays to control their circuits, whose
mechanical switches regulated the flow of electricity. The
Z1 by Konrad Zuse from 1936 was one of the first functioning machines of this kind. The next generation largely
dispensed with mechanical relays and instead used electron tubes, also called vacuum tubes. These characterize the British Colossus, the American Mark I, and the
American ENIAC. They all date back to the time of World
War II. With these electronic computers, modern computer history begins. The third generation, which in principle corresponds to today's computers in design, replaced
the tubes with transistors, whose current flow is controlled
by resistors, and used internal electronic storage.[1]

If one applies the three qualifying criteria, namely

- universal programmability,
- electronic data storage, and
- electronic processing,

then one has the blueprint for our modern computers. Of course, their architectures, i.e., their individual components and the way they work together, have changed significantly over time.

It has often been debated who invented the first computer. National pride and the desire to claim authorship for one's own country influence the discussion. However, it remains fruitless in the end because there is no single "inventor". In this case, it can rightly be said that success has many fathers, but the conditions and reasons for it were different in each country.[2] Therefore, the question of "who" is joined by the even more important question of "why." What drove the development of modern computers, what economic and political environment favored it, and why did it progress so differently in its core countries?

# The Emergence of Modern Computers

The dawn of modern IT began almost simultaneously and largely independently in the main centers of Germany, Great Britain, and the United States. The striking coincidence was no accident. On the one hand, pre-modern computing technology no longer provided a sufficient answer to the requirements of increasingly complex problem-solving. On the other hand—and more significantly—the pressure to act became noticeable, resulting from the fact that global politics were steering towards World War II. Automation was hoped to provide advantages for one's own victory. The times were bad, but this acted as a catalyst for the development of modern computing machines.

In Germany, the Nazis dealt the death blow to the first German democracy, the Weimar Republic, in 1933 with the help of anti-democratic forces among the old elites of the Kaiserreich. A similar turning point had already occurred in Italy in 1922, where Mussolini established a fascist dictatorship. These examples were contagious. Fascist parties flourished everywhere, and fascist regimes showed themselves to be extremely aggressive. Germany rearmed, annexed Austria, and first annexed the Sudetenland, which belonged to Czechoslovakia, and finally the entire country. In Spain, Francisco Franco established a fascist dictatorship after the end of the civil war in 1939. Italy conducted a colonial war in East Africa and regarded the Mediterranean region, in connection with the Roman Empire, as "mare nostrum," "our sea," and its own dominion. The fascists in Germany had similar ambitions with their demand for "living space in the East."

In the East, similar tendencies were evident. In the communist Soviet Union, Stalin established his totalitarian sole rule and covered the country with internal terror and show trials to eliminate his opponents. Japan and China had been at war since 1931, after Japan invaded Manchuria. In the battle for Shanghai alone, over 150,000 people lost their lives in 1937. Crisis symptoms were also becoming increasingly apparent in the USA and many other countries. The global economic crisis had devastating effects. It became increasingly obvious that even liberal democracies like the USA and Great Britain were being tested and could not stay out of the struggle for spheres of influence in the long run. The list of crises and conflicts was long, and the sky over the world darkened as Hitler triggered World War II and reached for world domination. This fueled the development of computers for military purposes, even if this did not happen everywhere with the same intensity, permanence, and success.

Efforts to technologize war have existed at all times. However, these largely revolved around weapons. In World War I, for example, work was done on submarines, cannons, poison gas grenades, and similar things. The tools of war were still aimed at killing in an archaic sense. Digital intelligence with its practical application "war" was only added in World War II. Considering the development up to today and especially the high strategic importance that cyber war now has, the approaching World War II can indeed be seen as the beginning of the digitization of war. No one has put it more aptly than a great old lady of IT. "Life was simple before World War II. After that, we had systems."[3] This quote is from Grace Hopper († 1992), Rear Admiral of the US Navy and pioneer of modern programming languages. Obviously, Grace had a sense of humor and self-irony, as she was not entirely uninvolved in the development of these systems in the 1940s and subsequent years.

# Born in the USA?

In the USA, research on computers for military use began quite early. The Mark I is one of the most prominent results. It was financed and supported by the Bureau of Ordnance, the procurement office of the US Navy. The development team also included the aforementioned Grace Hopper. It was an electromechanical computer whose development took seven years. The computer was conceived by Howard Aiken of Harvard University and IBM engineers and built by IBM. It already shows the success pattern of the emerging American computer industry: the combination of military contracts, academic research, and industry. We will encounter this again in the emergence of the internet and other occasions. Mark I was completed in 1943 and presented to the public the following year. IBM was very annoyed at the time that Aiken positioned it as his sole work. As early as 1937, Aiken, a Navy reserve officer, had designed plans for a series of computers and was able to win IBM for the project and manufacturing. The Harvard Mark I was a heavyweight in every respect. It weighed 5 tons, was 2.4 meters high, 15 meters long, and consisted of around 750,000 individual parts. The total length of the installed cables was more than 800 kilometers. For input and output, 3 punched tape readers, 2 card readers, 1 card punch, and 2 typewriters were used. Adding two numbers took less than 1 second, multiplications 6 seconds, and divisions about 12 seconds.[4] By today's standards, that's an eternity. Comparing it to the size and much higher performance of our common smartphones today, it becomes clear what a gigantic development IT has undergone since that time.

Aiken developed three more machines of this type (Mark II–IV) in the following years and is considered the midwife of the first fully automatic large-scale calculating machine. The Mark I was initially used for ballistic calculations and later employed for the Manhattan Project. Under this name, the US military bundled its various research efforts to develop the atomic bomb. Based on the aforementioned criteria of universal programmability, electronic data storage, and electronic processing, ENIAC (Electronic Numerical Integrator and Computer) can claim the honor of being one of the first modern computers—even though its data storage in short-lived registers with low capacity did not yet truly match what we understand by it today. As with many technical matters, it ultimately remains a question of chosen definitions. At the beginning of the project, ENIAC was concerned with ballistic tables to optimize projectile trajectories, i.e., to achieve greater accuracy. These trajectories had previously been created and maintained only with a lot of manual effort. The development of ENIAC was officially commissioned by the US Army's procurement office in 1943.[5] However, by the time the public learned of its existence in 1946, World War II was already over. Therefore, the computer spent a large part of its existence performing calculations for the construction of the atomic bomb.

ENIAC was developed from 1942 at the Moore School of Electrical Engineering at the University of Pennsylvania. Its intellectual fathers were the academics and later entrepreneurs John Mauchly and John Presper Eckert. If its electromechanical contemporary, the Harvard Mark I, was a heavyweight, then ENIAC played in the super-heavyweight league. It weighed 30 tons, required 140 kW of power, needed 170 $m^2$ of space, and consisted of 18,000 vacuum tubes, 1500 relays, and hundreds of thousands of resistors, capacitors, and inductors. Allegedly, the lights in Philadelphia flickered when ENIAC was powered up.[6] Steve Wozniak, co-founder of Apple, once said, "Never trust a computer you can't throw out a window."[7] His judgment of ENIAC would thus have been unequivocal.

ENIAC was very fast for its time and represented a great engineering achievement. To make it available for military use as soon as possible, its technical design was frozen at an early stage of development.[8] This compromise left deficits, many of which were eliminated during its use. Its builders were also aware of these deficits in its early phase. Computers are like Japanese gardens; they are never finished. Its high computing speed required that commands be given to it very quickly as well. Punched cards and paper tape were, of course, not sufficient for this. Thus, ENIAC was like a 300-horsepower car with a fuel line that was too thin. It lacked a way to store large amounts of data in memory, as today's computers do, and retrieve it very quickly.

In addition to the lack of electronically storable programs, ENIAC's programming itself was an area where
progress needed to be made. There was also no central
processing unit that performed all calculations. Instead,
ENIAC consisted of a number of individual hardware
modules with respective "responsibilities," such as storage,
division, or multiplication. Programming involved connecting and configuring these modules with patch cables
according to the task to be solved. There were also up to
6000 multi-digit switches that had to be set. For example,
if a multiplication was to follow an addition in the program sequence, a cable ran from the output terminal of
the addition module to the input terminal of the multiplication module. If this changed, because a division was
to be performed instead of the multiplication, the cables
had to be reconnected accordingly. One can imagine how
many such patch operations were necessary to solve a
complex problem. Another point was that the computer
(like the Harvard Mark I) could not independently decide
which operation to perform next after an intermediate
result was achieved. In other words, if the intermediate
result was A, B, or C, the staff had to specify to ENIAC
which action (= program branch) it should perform next,
depending on the result. These and other time-consuming
human interventions were mainly carried out by a team of
talented women who have found their place in the history
of computer technology as "the women of ENIAC."[9] The
automation of computing processes remained incomplete
with ENIAC.

Despite these initially open issues, ENIAC remained
in operation well into the 1950s, continuously being
improved. It remains a symbol of the technological breakthrough into the modern computer age. Nothing could
better describe the long way technology has come since
ENIAC than the following fact: On its 50th birthday,

electrical engineering students at the University of Pennsylvania recreated the entire ENIAC on a 7.44 mm × 5.29 mm chip using 0.5 μm CMOS technology.[10] What a difference compared to the 170 m² that the original still required.

# Bletchley Park, Colossus, and Nazi Cryptography

In Great Britain, too, the military was the midwife of technological development. World War II presented the British with immense military challenges that had to be overcome as quickly and efficiently as possible. The direct deadly confrontation with Nazi Germany and the late entry of the USA into the war at the end of 1941 left the British military with no choice but to use all technical possibilities with determined resource deployment. The areas for which purpose-built computers were developed and built included gun control, flight simulation and pilot training, radar signal processing, and the decryption of encrypted messages.[11] As in the USA, the development of universal computers originated from these "special-purpose" problem solvers.

Of the highest military priority was the decryption of the communication of the opposing side. Knowing the enemy's plans and always being one step ahead of him could be decisive in the war. This was especially true after Hitler declared war on the USA on December 11, 1941, thereby strengthening the alliance of his opponents with a particularly powerful partner. It was the time when the German U-boats shifted their focus from the naval blockade of England to the disruption of supplies from North America and received their orders via radio out in the

Atlantic. The impact of this strategic decision by the Nazis on the British-American merchant fleet was severe.

The technical progress in wireless transmission of messages was undeniable, but it also increased the risk of the enemy eavesdropping. Therefore, there were efforts in many countries to improve the encryption of radio messages. In the German Reich, a consequential innovation was achieved shortly before the end of the First World War. The German entrepreneur and inventor Arthur Scherbius patented the cipher machine "Enigma," which he had developed, in February 1918. This machine gained great significance in the Second World War, as the Wehrmacht, Luftwaffe, and Navy used it to encrypt their communications. Enigma found a literary reflection in the eponymous spy thriller by Robert Harris, published in 1995. Scherbius himself did not live to see this success. He died in an accident in 1929 at the age of only 50.[12] Hitler himself increasingly used the encryption of the "Lorenz machine" for direct communication with his generals since 1941, which had been developed by C. Lorenz AG in Berlin on behalf of the military in 1940. Thus, it was of even greater strategic interest to the British than Enigma. Nevertheless, the latter posed great puzzles to Hitler's rivals. Even before the Second World War, the Polish military dealt with some success in decrypting Enigma. Under the leadership of cryptographer Marian Rejewski, they succeeded in breaking its code in 1933. But not only did the cat get smarter, but so did the mouse. The Germans kept improving the device, so Rejewski's team reached the end of its resources. When it became foreseeable that Germany would invade Poland, the Polish General Staff handed over its information to the French and British.

On September 3, 1939, Great Britain declared war on the German Reich, just a few days after Hitler's invasion of Poland. At that time, the estate of Bletchley Park in the northwest of London housed the Government Code & Cypher School, which was under the direction of the foreign intelligence service MI6. GC&CS had only moved there a few months earlier. Its task was to intercept and decrypt Nazi Germany's radio traffic. With Britain's entry into the war, this task gained top priority. Station X, as Bletchley Park was also called, developed very quickly. The original number of 140 men and women had grown to around 1000 two years later, and the increasing need for space was met by the construction of wooden barracks. Among the staff were also American cryptographers who had been helping to solve the Enigma puzzle there since 1941.[13]

The decryption of the Enigma and Lorenz machine codes were the main tasks of Station X. Despite initial successes, their "paper-and-pencil" and "trial-and-error" methods proved too slow. Decrypted documents had a very short half-life in wartime, especially when it came to the enemy's tactical maneuvers. With the swelling communication among the German troops, speed was of great importance.[14] Therefore, other methods were needed to significantly accelerate the decryption processes. After various attempts with relay-based computers, whose results were unsatisfactory, engineer Thomas Flowers proposed building a machine that would be entirely based on vacuum tubes. This way, decryption would be significantly faster and more automated. Flowers was an employee of the British Post Office, which was also responsible for the telephone and telegraph network. In the years before, he had experimented with tubes to replace relay-based data storage in his employer's telephone exchanges.[15] Flowers' work is a good example of the convergence of communication and computer technology, which was taking place not only in England at that time. In Germany, too, the computer built by Konrad Zuse in 1941 with 2600 relays was based on know-how acquired in communication technology.

Flowers had contact with Bletchley Park, among other things, through his work with Alan Turing, who in the early phase of the war had cracked the Enigma version of the German Navy with his method called "Turingery" and subsequently engaged in a cat-and-mouse game with the Germans. Turing designed the so-called Bombe, an electromechanical machine for decrypting codes. The name is reminiscent of the Polish cryptography team led by Marian Rejewski, who had named his invention "Bomba" and, as mentioned, had provided the British with the results of his work. Hundreds of "Bombes" formed the basis for the large-scale attack on Enigma orchestrated in Bletchley Park. Turing also briefly participated in attempts to decipher the Lorenz machine in 1942.[16] He went down in history as the "father of modern computer science." He studied in Princeton, New Jersey, from 1936 to 1938 to earn his doctorate there. During that time, he published his groundbreaking paper "On Computable Numbers with an Application to the Entscheidungsproblem," in which he theoretically founded the so-called Turing machine. Simply put, his concept of this machine was the foundation for building a universal computer. Its architecture was supposed to allow solving any problem as long as a corresponding program was written for it and stored as a Stored Program in its memory. This marked the departure from the previously prevailing idea that a computer could only solve the problem for which it was built.[17] Turing shared the paternity of modern computer science with the Hungarian-American scientist John von Neumann, who held a chair in mathematics at Princeton. Born in Budapest in 1903, the son of a Jewish banker, he studied chemistry in Berlin and Zurich and was "on the side" a doctoral student in mathematics in Budapest. In 1933, he left Germany, just as Albert Einstein (who also taught in Princeton) and many other highly talented Jewish scientists had done before him. They made impressive careers in the USA. Von Neumann offered Turing a position in Princeton at the end of 1938, which he declined. He returned to England but had encouraged von Neumann to engage more with the construction of computers.[18] This had significant consequences that extend into our present time. Von Neumann was significantly involved in the conception of EDVAC (Electronic Discrete Variable Automatic Computer), the successor to ENIAC. He is considered the founder of game theory, researched quantum physics, worked on the atomic bomb, and dealt with the analogy of computers and the brain, in modern terms: artificial intelligence. Inspired by Alan Turing, he published a paper in 1944 titled "First draft of a report on the EDVAC." In it, he showed how data and programs could be digitally stored in the same memory of a computer and how they could flow and be processed within the computer via data paths, so-called buses, to its individual components. These components were the arithmetic and control unit, the memory for programs and data, as well as input and output devices, such as a screen and keyboard, and peripheral devices, such as a printer. This made it possible to program computers and feed them with data without cumbersome rewiring or creating elaborate punch card sets. However, John von Neumann's insights went even further. He also recognized that by moving away from ENIAC's decimal system to the binary number system as the basis for calculations, the hardware and its susceptibility to errors could be significantly improved. The decimal system had the consequence that ten vacuum tubes were needed per digit displayed. This could be significantly simplified by using the binary system, which only works with the two numbers zero and one (later called "bits").[19]

His design is still known today as the "Von Neumann machine" and is a foundation of our modern computers.

The 1940s were a kind of founding era of information technology with significant technical and scientific upheavals in America and Europe. And Tom Flowers was there to write another chapter in its history book. His idea of the electronic tube computer, which could calculate much faster than a relay computer, initially met with skepticism from the superiors at Bletchley Park, as the tubes were considered too unreliable and prone to errors.[20] Therefore, the first Colossus was not built there but at the Post Office in Dollis Hill, London. However, it moved to Bletchley for commissioning as early as January 1944. By then, its performance had been convincing. Flowers thus became one of the heroes among the codebreakers and a British computer pioneer.

Colossus, with its approximately 1600 vacuum tubes, was electronically programmable through rewiring and, unlike the "decimal" ENIAC, was already based on von Neumann's idea of the binary number system.[21] With a height of two meters, a width of five meters, and a depth of almost four meters, Colossus weighed five tons and consumed 8 kW of power.[22] If one takes its commissioning before ENIAC as the leading criterion, it can be considered the first electronic computer. The programming, as with ENIAC, was largely carried out by women. Its successor model, Colossus II, had 2400 tubes and appeared as early as June 1944. It was 4.5 times faster than its predecessor.[23] Innovation in IT happens very quickly not only today. There have always been smart people; they only differed from us in that they knew less.

By the time of the German capitulation in May 1945, ten of its kind were already in operation, and an eleventh was under construction. But almost no one knew about it. It was not until 30 years after the war that the secrecy of Colossus was lifted. Thus, the potential it could have unfolded for scientific or commercial applications in Great Britain and elsewhere remained unused. This was a particularly great missed opportunity for its country of origin. The pattern of missed opportunities can also be observed in Germany during the same period; we will come back to this. In America, they were much smarter in dealing with IT innovations by not hiding them but commercializing them.

For Flowers, this was a bitter disappointment, as he could neither reap the commercial fruits of his work nor receive corresponding honors. He was forced to bloom in secrecy and later vented his bitterness: "When I was informed after the end of the war that the secret of Colossus was to be kept indefinitely, I was naturally disappointed. I had no doubt that Colossus was a historical breakthrough and that its publication would have made my name known in scientific and technical circles—a conviction confirmed by the handling of ENIAC, the American counterpart, which was published shortly after the end of the war. I had to endure all the applause that was given to this enterprise without being able to reveal that I had anticipated it. What I lost in personal prestige and the advantages that usually arise under such circumstances can only be imagined today."[24]

Overall, the British did not treat their heroes from Bletchley Park very sensitively. Max Newman, head of the "Newmanry" in Bletchley Park and one of the leading figures there, rejected an order of merit in 1946 as "ridiculous."[25] Alan Turing took his own life in 1954 after being given the choice between prison or chemical castration due to his homosexuality. It was not until 2009 that he was rehabilitated by Prime Minister Gordon Brown.[26]

# Zuse's High-Tech Start-Up

In Germany, the engineer Konrad Zuse had already begun building a mechanical calculating machine before the Second World War. He had completed his studies in 1935 and, after a brief stint at Henschel Flugzeug-Werke AG, became self-employed with financial support from parents and friends. He completed the new machine in 1938 under the designation Z1. Its purpose was to automate lengthy static calculations, such as those required in aircraft construction. Due to its susceptibility to errors, Zuse designed a successor model, the Z2, just two years later. It no longer worked with a mechanical calculating unit but, on the suggestion of his friend Helmut Schreyer, with relays. Zuse and Schreyer, who had met in a student fraternity in Berlin in 1937, thereby aroused the interest of Alfred Teichmann, the department head at the Institute for Strength of the German Research Institute for Aviation (DVL), which can be considered the predecessor of today's German Aerospace Center (DLR). The DVL was under the command of Hermann Göring, head of the German Air Force since 1935.

Teichmann was looking for a solution to control the twisting of wings and tail units at certain speeds. Zuse's machine was to help with the necessary calculations. In 1941, Zuse founded the "Zuse Engineering Office and Apparatus Construction" and immediately received a lucrative order: the DVL ordered a larger computer from him, which did not take long to arrive.[27] As early as May 1941, Zuse and Schreyer presented the Z3, while they developed one of the world's first programming languages, "Plankalkül," for their machines. More advanced than the later ENIAC, it did not use the decimal system but already the binary number system and floating-point technology.

It is generally considered the world's first electromechanical, digital, programmable computer. According to the state of the art, its programming was done via punched tape. It had 600 relays for the calculating unit and 1400 for the memory. Its clock frequency, i.e., the number of possible operations per second when executing the program's instructions, was 5 Hertz. For comparison: today's processors, even in the high-performance class for home computers, have a base frequency of 2.5 gigahertz (= 2.5 billion cycles per second) and reach up to 5 gigahertz in turbo mode.

Tragically, Konrad Zuse's Z3 fell victim to a bombing raid on Berlin in 1943, just two years after its completion. What we know of his invention from practical observation is based on a later reconstruction by his son, Horst Zuse, in 2003.[28] The Z3 was considered a success by the German Research Institute for Aviation. They therefore commissioned Zuse to develop the follow-up version Z4, for which he received 50,000 Reichsmarks. Zuse completed the electromechanical computer with 2200 relays during the war with a team of about two dozen engineers and "freelancers" from the Wehrmacht High Command. Remembering his experiences with the Z3, he saved it from Allied bombs and the advancing Soviet troops by moving it from Berlin, first to the Aerodynamic Research Institute of the collapsing Reich in Göttingen. Since the "Alpine Fortress" in southern Germany was considered safer and through a contact with General Dornberger, one of the leading figures of the V2 program in Peenemünde, the right support was obtained, it was possible to flee further into the Allgäu. Dornberger had previously ordered the relocation of Wernher von Braun's working group to Bavaria.[29] The conditions for the emerging German computer industry were certainly suboptimal compared to those of their American and English counterparts. After

1945, Zuse initially supplemented the family income by selling woodcuts that he made himself. His attempts to sell the Z4 to American companies were unsuccessful. He founded Zuse KG in 1949, repaired the Z4, and rented it out the same year to the Swiss Federal Institute of Technology in Zurich, where it served as the central computer for the Institute of Mathematics.[30] The Zuse Engineering Office and Apparatus Construction, founded in 1941, and the subsequent Zuse KG were thus among the first commercial company foundations in the modern IT market. Today, this is called a start-up.

# Commercialization as a Success Factor

For the coverage of the American presidential elections on November 4, 1952, the broadcaster CBS News had rented the UNIVAC computer from the Remington Rand Corporation. It was supposed to predict the final result in the race between the Republican Dwight D. Eisenhower and the Democrat and Governor of Illinois, Adlai Stevenson, after the first results came in. Contrary to the opinion polls, UNIVAC predicted a landslide victory for Eisenhower and was correct. However, the broadcaster distrusted the computer's prediction and withheld it for a long time on election night.[31] In the end, the process illustrated just as impressively as it did effectively what computers were capable of achieving.

UNIVAC was a further development of ENIAC. The aforementioned leading minds of the ENIAC team, John Mauchly and John Presper Eckert, had left the group in 1946 due to a disagreement with the University of Pennsylvania. They were asked to cede all rights to the inventions they made while in the service of the university. They were not willing to do so. Both founded a company later that same year, which was bought by the typewriter and arms manufacturer Remington Rand in early 1950. Alongside the Zuse Engineering Office and Apparatus Construction from 1941 and the Zuse KG from 1949, the company founded by Mauchly and Eckert was one of the earliest IT start-ups. Like Zuse, Eckert and Mauchly initially struggled heavily with financing their company until Remington Rand, the white knight, rescued them. By 1954, a total of 19 units of the various versions of UNIVAC had been sold to an impressive list of significant companies in the western part of the USA.[32] Only one was located on the West Coast, at Pacific Mutual Life Insurance. The first six computers went to the military. The Cold War boosted demand, and the American government gave the young company the wings that a start-up needs.

The Manchester Mark I, originally developed at the University of Manchester, was also in similar financial straits. Initially funded by the state, the money tap was turned off in 1952 after a change of government. A capital mistake with long-term consequences. Thus, this opportunity remained unused for Great Britain. In the same year, it was sold to the University of Toronto, where it served science—as it had in Manchester. The British electronics manufacturer Ferranti Ltd. pursued a commercial further development, selling a total of nine machines of the "Ferranti Mark I" by 1957.[33]

After the war, Zuse KG received its first orders from surveying technology and optics. Unlike in the USA, the military did not act as a financier and sponsor in the young Federal Republic. The later Z11 was the last computer manufactured using relay technology; in 1956, the switch to electron tubes occurred. Of the Z22, which was based on this, 50 units were sold, and in total, Zuse KG produced 251 computers.[34] With the introduction of the

Z64 ("Graphomat") at the Hannover Fair in 1961, Zuse switched to transistor technology. The new machine was used in the automotive, aircraft, and shipbuilding industries, surveying, commercial tables, road construction, weather maps, network plans, and statistics. By 1964, a total of 85 such systems were delivered at the then-proud price of 90,000 DM.[35] Not a bad record, but still too little to be able to look to the future with ease given a limited German market and constant struggles for credit. The USA offered their IT start-ups a significantly larger domestic market in which they could grow, in addition to the government as a customer. Therefore, Zuse sold his company in 1964 to the electronics group Brown Boveri & Cie. from Mannheim, and in 1967 it went to Siemens AG. The founder left his company at the same time at the age of 57. Siemens then concentrated its computer manufacturing in Munich, and Zuse KG was removed from the commercial register in 1971. It remained a relatively unknown entity outside of Germany, as did its ingenious founder.

## Historical Lesson

The financial support that Zuse received from the state was only a very modest imitation of what the British and Americans provided their engineers during the war and—in the case of the USA—also afterward for the development of computers in terms of personnel and financial resources. In the Anglo-Saxon world, the state in a certain way assumed a role that years later would be taken over by venture capitalists. Zuse did not have this luxury. Even though he received a certain amount of support, the declaration of his project as "vital to the war effort" was missing, which usually secured a permanently and reliably high budget for the Anglo-Saxon counterparts. Harvard Mark I and ENIAC were initially about ballistics for projectiles and later about the H-bomb, Colossus was about decrypting Enigma and the Lorenz machine. They were all "vital" and therefore attracted state funds. The solution to a purely technical problem, such as the fluttering of wings and tail units, which was the basis for state involvement in the case of Zuse, was not sufficient.

In addition, in the USA, the universities of Harvard and the University of Pennsylvania played an important role in the development of the first modern computers. It was similar in England, where the "Manchester Mark I" was already working as a "university computer" in 1949. It was largely based on the know-how and partly also the personnel from Bletchley Park. It was developed at the University of Manchester after Max Newman, one of the leading minds of Bletchley Park, had received a chair in mathematics there and had brought along a number of former colleagues. The Mark I quickly became the prototype for the aforementioned Ferranti Mark I, one of the first commercially available universal computers.[36] This was not the case in Germany. In addition to the state, science also fell short as a promoter of computer development compared to England and the USA. In Nazi Germany, there was neither real coordination regarding the construction of calculating machines nor sufficient support from science until the end of 1943, which could have played a role as a "game changer." Practical mathematics with the goal of computer construction was a stepchild of the universities.[37] The exodus of one-third of the habilitated mathematicians during National Socialism did the rest.

A long-term result of the developments in the 1930s and 1940s is that the multitude of different instruments for solving mathematical problems, from the slide rule to the mechanical calculator to the logarithm table, gradually disappeared. Computers—and later their smaller siblings, the calculators—displaced all these now anachronistic-looking tools and began their triumphant march.[38] The experimental nature of the first machines was increasingly overcome in the wake of World War II. In addition to military computing, scientific computing also emerged during the Cold War. The improvements in programmability made their universal use for solving a wide variety of scientific problems possible, relatively easily even. The latter also drove the commercialization of computers: They became increasingly interesting and indispensable as tools for companies to bolster efficiency and productivity. Thus, new user groups emerged alongside state and scientific institutions. With their continued miniaturization, from a former living room size to today's smartphone, the customer base and thus the market for computers expanded enormously. As late as 1948, Howard Aiken, the inventor of the Harvard Mark I built by IBM, believed that a commercial market for computers would "never" develop. In his opinion, the demand in the USA was for "five or six such machines, no more." By the 1950s, thousands of them were being sold there alone.[39]

The reason why one of the most important protagonists in World War II and the Cold War, the Soviet Union, is missing from my account is that a genuine computer industry never developed there. This was due to a variety of causes, ranging from initial ideological reservations against "cybernetics"—from which our modern term "cyber" is derived—to a lack of coordination, e.g., in the area of technical standardization between competing ministries and institutions. The MESM calculator developed at the Kiev Institute of Electrotechnology at the end of the 1940s did not become the starting signal it could have been. The impetus for the development of computers during the Khrushchev era quickly fizzled out. In the 1970s, the development of their own systems was abandoned, and they decided to clone Western technology.[40] Compared to other states in the "Council for Mutual Economic Assistance" (CMEA, also known as COMECON), the communist German Democratic Republic (GDR) was the most successful within the Soviet Union's sphere of influence. The CMEA was a counter-design to the Western Marshall Plan and the "Organization for Economic Co-operation and Development" (OECD). As part of the specializations assigned to individual CMEA members, the GDR was responsible, among other things, for the computer sector. The Robotron Combine from Dresden and the VEB Röhrenwerk Mühlhausen in Thuringia stand for this development. Despite difficult conditions under the Western embargo, their successes were not insignificant, but their products never became relevant factors in the world market. After the fall of the Wall, my then-employer Sybase hired a number of former Robotron employees, and I fondly remember working with people of high professional qualification and a pleasant tendency towards teamwork.

In West Germany, too—as in other European countries—no globally significant computer industry developed. Despite Konrad Zuse's efforts, the end of the war marked a turning point for the construction of digital computers. What Zuse and Schreyer had produced also came to a temporary end, as did the greater appreciation and promotion of machine computing that had arisen under the pressure of war. The country had other problems and was initially not a sought-after partner on the international scientific stage. When West German universities and research institutes sought to catch up with the USA and Great Britain through the use of computers in the 1950s, their lead could no longer be made up. The use of computers in the German economy lagged far behind Western practices.[41] Among the world's ten largest hardware manufacturers by revenue in September 2020, there was neither a German nor a European company, but six from Asia and four from the USA.[42]

Nothing fundamental has changed in this situation by 2023. It fits that, despite its leading role as an industrial nation, a reunited Germany still has only a modest software industry, which—with the exception of SAP—plays no globally significant role outside of niches. Among the Global Top Ten in the software industry by market capitalization and revenue in mid-2020, there were eight American companies, one French, and one German.[43]

By 2023, SAP was the only non-American left. When today there is talk about the long-standing ignorance of the importance of digitization and the inertia of German politics, it should not be forgotten that the causes also lie in the missed effort during the war and post-war development. For example, the history of digital infrastructure in Germany to this day is a history of failure. As early as 1981, then-Chancellor Helmut Schmidt had a plan to advance it and to cable Germany with fiber optics by 2020 (they allowed themselves "only" almost 40 years!). But this was stopped under his successor. His name was Helmut Kohl, who, incidentally, is a particularly striking example of the de-prioritization of digitization. In 1993, when asked about the future of the data highway by a Microsoft employee on the RTL TV-program "Nachgefragt," his answer was: For the construction of highways, in addition to the federal government, the states are mainly responsible.[45] In other words, Kohl had no idea what was being talked about. The good man from Microsoft reacted with a mixture of astonishment, amusement, and horror to this answer, as can be clearly seen in a YouTube video.

However, Kohl was and is not alone. For 20 years, we have been struggling with the digital health card without it having gained widespread use. Significant parts of the German bourgeoisie also shine with disinterest in technical topics and with a discomfort towards everything digital, characterized by profound ignorance. Thus, it is probably no coincidence that the word "computer" first appeared in the German Duden dictionary only in 1967.[46] In the Oxford English Dictionary, it was already found in 1946.[47] The economist Daniel Stelter summed it up in an article in *Welt am Sonntag*: "Unfortunately, Germany has made itself comfortable in the past. All relevant industries on which our prosperity is based originate from the imperial era."[48] Hope dies last. In the Global Cloud Index Ecosystem 2022, we at least appear in sixth place in the ranking, which includes 76 countries and evaluates how they promote the availability of cloud services through technologies, regulations, and talents. So, progress is being made![49]

# 3

# The Rise of IT to World Power

What began with the construction of electromechanical computers has now become a significant global economic factor. For 2022, the projected total revenue of the IT sector is 4454 trillion US dollars, up from 4239 trillion the previous year.[1] This is a jump of "only" 5.1%, but in absolute terms, it means an annual increase of 215 billion, which is roughly equivalent to the gross domestic product (GDP) of New Zealand.[2] Among the five most valuable companies in the world by market capitalization (March 2021), four are from the IT sector. They are all based in the USA, with only Aramco, the state oil company of Saudi Arabia, being the exception.[3] In the corresponding top-ten industry ranking (March 2021), IT ranks sixth worldwide, ahead of the giants in telecommunications, automotive, oil and gas, as well as food and agriculture. All four have had a significantly longer market presence than modern IT and have nevertheless been overtaken by it.[4]

© The Author(s), under exclusive license to Springer Fachmedien Wiesbaden GmbH, part of Springer Nature 2024
J. Müller, *Turning Point*,
https://doi.org/10.1007/978-3-658-46079-2_3

What gave IT its tremendous dynamism, and what pushed it so powerfully forward?

# Connected Worlds

What do telephones and computers have in common?

Answer: For both, their added value increases exponentially with the growth of their distribution. A single telephone has no practical use, but 100,000 interconnected telephones do. The more participants are connected to the telephone network, the greater the benefit for everyone. The utility of a single computer is higher than that of a single telephone. Nevertheless, it also increases exponentially with the networking of as many devices as possible. Only then are data exchange and communication on a broad basis possible. Think of social media, messaging services like Signal or WeChat, streaming services for music and videos, simple Googling, or working from home. Even cryptocurrencies like Bitcoin or Ether would never have emerged without networks. What is now a given in our lives would not exist without the networking of various computer worlds. Our economy would be different, and so would our daily lives.

The advance of computer networks thus had a significant impact on the rapid and widespread adoption of IT. Unlike what we know today, networking in the late 1970s and 1980s had little to do with the Internet. Local networks, also known as Local Area Networks (LAN), were the main characteristic and trend of the time. Driven strongly by the advance of personal computers, companies of all sizes embraced "networking." The spectrum ranged from law firms to the dentist around the corner, from medium-sized businesses to DAX and Fortune 500 companies. They all used LAN technology to network computers, printers, hard drives, and employees internally. The shared use of peripheral devices was economically interesting, and collaborative work was no less so. Being able to quickly exchange documents and messages over the LAN was more efficient than a "sneakernet," where they still had to be delivered in physical form.

Novell was my first encounter with the computer industry, first as a user and then as an employee. The company, with its flagship product "NetWare," held a 65% market share worldwide in the 1980s and epitomized what was understood by "network." Competitors like Banyan Vines or even Microsoft with MS-Net played only a subordinate role and shared the remaining 35% with others. The PC and networking pushed each other forward. The result was the increasing acceptance and establishment of IT-supported processes in the economy, from large companies down to small ones. Those who did not participate were less productive. Novell took advantage of the fortunate circumstance that it did not rely on company-wide, strategic decisions by these large customers for a specific technology on its way into large companies. Such directional decisions are usually lengthy and often determined by political battles within these companies. Any new technology can mean a loss of influence within IT departments for those whose jobs, know-how, and rank are based on established systems. With its local networks, Novell did what the German student movement of the late 1960s called the "march through the institutions." Department by department was moved to NetWare and "rolled out." Network-enthusiastic young technicians contributed their part until it eventually became a company-wide infrastructure factor and difficult to remove. The normative power of the factual works not only in politics. When the later famous Eric Schmidt became CEO of Novell in April 1997, the company's decline had already begun, with Microsoft having displaced Novell as the leading network provider. Even Eric Schmidt could not prevent this. He moved to Google in 2001, where he accompanied its unprecedented rise as CEO for ten years and transitioned to the board as Executive Chairman in 2011.

# Fresh Chips From Texas

The phrase "more bang for the buck," succinctly describes the development of the performance price/ratio of computers. Their performance is significantly determined by their processors and other built-in chips, in addition to the computer's architecture. The processor—also called the Central Processing Unit, or CPU for short—is the heart of a computer. It executes all the instructions provided by the software. Without the ever more powerful small silicon chips with their multitude of transistors, many modern applications would not have emerged. Just think of gaming in the private sector. No one wants to see the heroes of Fortnite stutter across the screen instead of jumping. Increasing performance has had a catalytic effect on the industry, especially since it was accompanied by a steadily falling price for chips. For their manufacturers like Samsung, with $81 billion in revenue in 2021, the largest in the industry, ahead of Intel in second place or the German Infineon in twelfth place, the price-performance ratio is a crucial success factor.[5] However, it was and still is also decisive for the triumph of computers in general, not least, but especially in the private sector. The trend has made computers for home affordable. Anyone who has paid attention to how much the choice of processor, the size of the main memory, or the hard drive (SSD) affects the final price of the device when buying a PC or MacBook can easily understand this. The widespread use of computers, whether desktop or smartphone, would hardly be imaginable without this downward price spiral.

In 1965, Gordon Moore, who founded Intel with Robert Noyce three years later, predicted that the number of transistors on a chip would regularly double at short intervals, while manufacturing costs would decrease at the same rate. The electronics of a chip are applied to a piece of silicon only a few centimeters in size, which makes the technical know-how behind it, especially for their production, particularly evident. Moore's Law, as it is somewhat exaggeratedly called (it was more intended as a rule of thumb), thus states: The performance of computers increases exponentially while they become increasingly cheaper. To illustrate this effect, Intel has placed an entertaining, small explanatory video on its homepage, which states: Compared to the Intel 4004 from 1971, which is considered the world's first microprocessor, the performance of the company's 14 nm processor is 3500 times higher, the energy efficiency 90,000 times better, and the price per transistor 60,000 times smaller. If the technical progress of the car had proceeded as quickly as with these processors, it would now travel at 482,000 km/h, drive 850,000 km on one liter of fuel, and cost only 0.04 dollars.[6] One can hardly imagine a better technological driver for the spread of computers.

The basic idea behind silicon chips, also called semiconductors, is quite simple. Semiconductors like silicon are materials that can be both conductive and non-conductive for electricity—hence their name. For ENIAC, all the necessary components had to be individually assembled, connected with wires, and soldered together. This required around 18,000 vacuum tubes, which acted as processors executing the program instructions, 70,000 resistors, 10,000 capacitors, etc. When transistors became commercially available in the mid-1950s and replaced vacuum tubes and relays as components, a major step was taken. The computers of a new generation were born. Transistors were less prone to failure, less power-intensive, and much faster and cheaper. However, they still had to be laboriously installed and wired individually. IBM introduced its model 7090 at the end of 1959, which was equipped with transistors instead of vacuum tubes for the first time.[7] The complexity of assembling the individual components remained a problem for the time being. The solution came from Jack Kilby of Texas Instruments. He and his team succeeded in designing a prototype in 1958, in which several transistors were applied to a single carrier, hence the name "integrated circuit" (IC). This created a kind of building block that made the individual installation of transistors unnecessary and subsequently made it possible to simply plug them onto the mainboard, the carrier of the electronic components of a computer.

With this type of CPU, the history of third-generation computers began, which we still use today in principle. At Fairchild Semiconductors, where Gordon Moore worked at the time, Robert Noyce built his circuits with silicon wafers. The silicon chips were much cheaper than the rare germanium that Kilby used. Silicon is almost unlimited in availability. The Santa Clara Valley between San Francisco in the north and San José in the south, where Fairchild was located, would get its nickname from this and go down in history as Silicon Valley. Today, transistors are applied to the carrier in a complex photolithographic process. At the beginning of the development, it was difficult to place more than five transistors on a chip. The aforementioned Intel 4004 already carried 2300 of them. The

A15 from Apple, which is installed in my iPhone, carries no less than 15 billion transistors.[8]

On this 88 square millimeter piece of silicon, that is an unimaginable capacity. Chips with multiple CPUs are now normal. In this case, a single processor is referred to as a "core." The number of cores is always highlighted in the marketing brochures of the manufacturers as an important argument for performance. The future will show to what extent this can still be increased. One of the problems lies in the small distances between the transistors, which are in the atomic range. This results in quantum effects that impair the conductive properties of silicon. A chip whose current flow can no longer be controlled is worthless. Therefore, research is already working on alternative concepts for computers, which we will discuss in more detail in the section on quantum computers.[9] The history of IT shows that everything is just a matter of time and money. Once the right concept is designed, progress grows exponentially.[10]

# The Great Shrinking

Another success factor of IT is that with integrated circuits, not only did processors become smaller and more powerful, but computers as a whole also shrank. Small computers ensure portability, an important prerequisite for their current omnipresence. Those who can take and place them anywhere without having to plan a major transport as in the days of ENIAC & Co. gain flexibility and thus additional application possibilities. If they even fit on a desk at home or in the office, on the lap of their users, or in a briefcase, then they are not far from universal availability. This awakened the desire to own them in broad buyer groups. The internet in its current use and spread would be unimaginable without small computers, especially in the form of smartphones. Even computers in the form of wristwatches have now become part of everyday life.

Small devices also form a fundamental basis of the Internet of Things (IoT) and thus Industry 4.0, which we will deal with more extensively elsewhere. The Internet of Things refers to the connection of data-collecting sensors to computers or data centers. There, they are increasingly analyzed with the help of Artificial Intelligence and provide humans or machines with instructions for action. In this way, a kind of "ambient intelligence" is created, which allows a significantly higher degree of process automation. In Germany, every third company now uses the Internet of Things, without this innovation having reached general awareness. On average, across all EU states, it was 29%.[11] Specifically, this means, for example: Elevators equipped with sensors in a large office complex independently report when they need to be serviced. Maintenance is thus carried out as needed instead of cyclically on suspicion or after an inspection by a technician on site. The sensors also provide preventive warnings of possible elevator failures, so unwanted incidents can be avoided. The IoT has numerous other application possibilities. The areas of application range from modern cars to the control of factory plants and logistics chains to agriculture, where sensors, for example, turn an irrigation system on or off or advise the farmer when the optimal time for fertilization has come.

Miniaturization began on a large scale in the 1960s. Driven by companies like Digital Equipment Corporation (DEC), IBM, Nixdorf, and Prime, devices emerged that were called "minicomputers" by the standards of the time. Compared to the room-filling mainframes of the previous decade, this designation was quite justified. They were "only" the size of filing cabinets, some even just the size of a refrigerator.

In this development, too, the military was both financier and midwife, as it had been with ENIAC, Colossus, and Konrad Zuse's Z-computers. The trend initiated by World War II greatly favored the emergence of modern computers, continued into the Cold War. The first Minuteman intercontinental missiles, commissioned in 1962, were already equipped with small computers that determined their course. They were thus superior to the Soviet competing models, which still relied on bulky vacuum tubes. The computers were the result of diverse research efforts from which the American IT industry benefited greatly and permanently beyond its formative phase. In this way, not only very competitive products were created, for which there was little competition in the rest of the world. The involved companies were also able to finance research and development to an extent that was hardly imaginable elsewhere through large government contracts. Their growth was stimulated, and their investment risk was reduced. The highly IT-dependent SAGE program of the US Air Force, planned to intercept strategic nuclear bombers on their prospective path over the North Pole, alone brought IBM half a billion dollars in the 1950s. That was more than the entire commercial revenue from its leased, regular computers. When SAGE went into operation in the summer of 1959, the technology was almost obsolete due to ballistic intercontinental missiles, but its catalytic effect on computer technology remained unaffected. NASA's Apollo program, with its great need for technologically advanced small computers, provided further development boosts.[12]

The already discussed promotion of the American IT industry during and after World War II through large and long-term government contracts thus runs like a common thread through the history of the industry. It provides an important part of the explanation for the still existing IT dominance of the USA. Those who can grow well-secured in a very large domestic market do not necessarily have to expose themselves to the risks and uncertainties of international expansion and thus have decisive advantages over competitors from other countries. Once a critical mass is reached, it is easier to go "global." I have seen some start-ups in my career that did not understand this and disappeared again. But here, too, the internet has changed some of the logics and certainties.

# Computers Become Personal

With processors on a tiny chip and the trend towards ever smaller machines, personal computers, which were then still referred to as "microcomputers," emerged. Chips increasingly served not only as CPUs but also as inexpensive data storage, which we also encounter as RAM (Random Access Memory = writable) or ROM (Read Only Memory = non-writable). Writable memory chips are today widespread as so-called Solid State Disks (SSD). They replace mechanical hard drives and thereby accelerate access to stored data. Mechanics in computers stand for slowness compared to electronic processes. With falling production costs and sufficient competition among manufacturers, the PC became affordable not only for business customers but also for private users. Initially, programs and data were stored on magnetic tapes and the "floppy disk," which got its name from its flexibility. It was commercially available since 1972. Although floppies are hardly used today, they have retained their place in IT as a common "save" icon in many programs. By the way, there is no single inventor of the PC, just as there is no single inventor of the mainframe. The PC developed from the contributions of many smart minds, gradually evolving from its humble beginnings into what we currently understand it to be.

Today's personal computer differs significantly from the first of its kind. These were sold as kits from 1975, and their buyers still had to use a soldering iron to assemble them. For these kits, a screen, a keyboard, or a drive could be purchased separately as accessories. There was no trace of a PC mouse yet; it would not appear until about ten years later. Of course, one also had to write the programs oneself—in machine language. Microsoft Office, Apple's iWork packages, or the free Apache Open Office Suite did not exist yet. In the 1970s, one was in the world of electronics hobbyists and techno-freaks. If the buyers of the first PCs overcame all these hurdles, they finally owned "their" personal computer. This was a kind of revolution in the world of mainframes and minicomputers, which had to be shared with others via a time-sharing concept, if one had access to them at all.

The most prominent of these new machines was called Altair 8800 and was developed by MITS from Albuquerque, New Mexico. The machine is said to have been named after the star Altair, which appears in some episodes of Star Trek. Until then, MITS had built electronic calculators and was now trying to establish itself as a pioneer in the emerging microcomputer market. The relationship between calculators and computers paved the way for MITS. Some other calculator companies also moved along this development path over time—with varying success. Examples include Olivetti, IBM, NEC, Hewlett-Packard, Toshiba, or Sanyo. By 1990, the Japanese company NEC had become the fourth-largest PC manufacturer in the world.[13] IBM and Olivetti are among those who started even earlier and originally built typewriters. They represent the development line from the "typewriter" of the late nineteenth and early twentieth centuries through the calculator to the computer. Evolution does not only take place in nature.

After the Altair appeared on the cover of the magazine *Popular Electronics* in January 1975, it was sold tens of thousands of times despite its spartan equipment and a still limited market, becoming a commercial success. Sales were conducted via mail order. The price of around 430 dollars was not a hindrance, and MITS, which was burdened with debt from its old business, made over a million dollars in revenue with it in the first year alone. Adjusted for inflation, that would be around 5.5 million dollars today.[14] When MITS founder Ed Roberts sold the company in 1977, revenue was already at 20 million dollars according to him.[15]

The inventors of the Altair did not think that its buyers would primarily use it for games—they had other applications in mind. A love of technology and a penchant for play are closely related. The Altair's popularity created the economic conditions for an ecosystem of accessories, such as keyboards, monitors, or memory cards.[16] This pattern remains a characteristic of the IT industry to this day. Ingenious companies fill the gaps left by the "original product." This applies not only to hardware but also, and especially, to software. Who doesn't use some of the numerous plug-ins for their browser, an additional virus scanner, small helpers in the form of widgets, or add-ons to office applications that are not included in the original package? The various app stores are full of them, which is why the further technical development of the PC can also be seen as the history of continuously improving user-friendliness. Such facilitations and additions increase market acceptance and are one reason why the PC increasingly grew out of the circle of tech freaks and hobbyists and gradually conquered new areas of application in business and private sectors. Unlike the first large computers, the PC did not start its career among scientists and researchers, nor was it the result of military sponsorship. Devices like the Altair had to finance themselves but certainly benefited from the basic technical research of others. Its original consumer affinity remained permanently despite the growing business applications. Over time, however, the do-it-yourself period of the Altair ended, and fewer and fewer special skills were needed to use it profitably. Besides Intel, three other companies have done more for the PC in this regard than any others: Microsoft, Apple, and IBM.[17]

## BASIC, an Apple, and the PC in a Blue Suit

One of the innovative companies that emerged around the Altair was Microsoft, which was then still written as Micro-Soft. The name is a compound of *Micro*computer and *Soft*ware. The company was founded in April 1975 by the 19-year-old Bill Gates and the 22-year-old Paul Allen in Albuquerque. It remained there until early 1979, when it relocated its headquarters with its 13 employees to the state of Washington. Gates interrupted his studies at Harvard at that time and dedicated himself entirely to the new company. The initial proximity to the headquarters of MITS was, of course, no coincidence. After Gates and Allen had heard about the Altair through the *Popular Electronics* article, they contacted MITS and offered to write a version of the programming language BASIC for the Altair. Their goal was to enable hobbyists and other tech enthusiasts using the computer to write their own programs for their machines without having to use or master the binary code (i.e., zeros and ones) of a machine language. This would give a significant boost to user-friendliness and promote the spread of the Altair. BASIC was no longer an unknown at this time. It had been developed in 1964 at Dartmouth College in New Hampshire with the goal of enabling students who were not mathematically or engineering-oriented to use computers through an easily learnable programming language.[18] It thus became one of the most widespread, higher-level programming languages in the 1970s and 1980s. These programming languages abstract from the "lower" machine code and allow the developer to use commands that are readable and understandable by humans. The resulting programs are called source code. Their instructions are automatically translated into machine code using so-called compilers or interpreters. BASIC continues to exist in numerous variants, later including Commodore BASIC, Applesoft BASIC, and Atari BASIC. With Visual Basic, Microsoft still provides a modern version today.

BASIC thus fit exactly what MITS wanted. An agreement was quickly reached, and Microsoft created its first product with Altair BASIC, which was still delivered on a cassette and sold for 350 dollars. No one suspected that the two tech enthusiasts had thereby launched one of the world's most significant companies. The success of the PC was henceforth closely linked with the name Microsoft.

The Altair inspired not only "Bill and Paul." The duo "Steve and Steve" also fell under its spell. Steve Wozniak, 24 years old and called "Woz," founded a company named Apple in 1976 with the 22-year-old Steve Jobs. Woz was the technical brain of the start-up. Initially, Ron Wayne was also part of the duo, receiving ten percent of the company, but he left after just 11 days. He did not want to take on the risk of debt out of consideration for his family.[19] What a wrong decision! In August 2018, Apple became the first publicly traded company in the world to reach a market capitalization of more than one trillion dollars. At that time, Steve Jobs, who only lived to be 56 years old, had already been dead for seven years. Wayne's ten percent would have been worth 100 billion then. Incidentally, Microsoft followed Apple almost a year later when it also surpassed the trillion-dollar threshold.[20]

Not a bad result for the two companies that were founded less than 12 months apart. Apple and Microsoft represent another defining phenomenon of the new PC market: The protagonists were and are significantly younger than the inventors of the bulky machines of the war and post-war periods. An example of this is also Michael Dell, who founded "PCs Limited" in May 1984, later renamed Dell Computer Corporation. He was 19 years old and, like Bill Gates, a college dropout. They play an often ignored yet important role in the history of IT. However, this should not be taken as a recommendation for young people. By 2021, Michael's company had risen to become the third-largest PC manufacturer in the world by units sold.[21]   The influx of young talent was also driven by the fact that these new companies weren't reliant on government contracts, which often favored established firms,  with serious-looking, gray-haired heads. The young entrepreneurs had to take many risks and commit themselves body and soul. Those who are older and have families are more likely to shy away from such prospects. This phenomenon of unbridled daring in the early PC years still accompanies the IT industry today. Just think of the many Internet start-ups of the 1990s and subsequent years.

The significance of the Altair was great for Apple, as it was in a different way for Microsoft. While Bill and Paul built a business around the computer with Altair BASIC, it served as a source of inspiration for Steve and Steve. Woz, then employed as an engineer at Hewlett-Packard, saw a demo of the Altair in March 1975 at a meeting of the "Homebrew Computer Club" in a garage in Menlo Park. The club included hobby electronics enthusiasts and techno-enthusiasts who liked to pick up the soldering iron. More important than the Altair itself for Woz was the nature of the Intel 8080 microprocessor that was inside it. A piece of silicon on which the entire central processing unit was mounted! He later described his thoughts as follows: "This whole vision of a personal computer appeared in my head. That night I began sketching on paper what would later become the Apple I."[22]

This vision referred to a project that Steve Wozniak was pursuing at that time. He was designing a terminal with a keyboard and monitor, through which one could log into a remote computer and work on it. In 1975 this certainly was no longer a revolutionary concept. But what if one could bring the computing power of the remote computer into the terminal itself using the microprocessor? This would save the need to log in via a slow telephone line. If the terminal itself became the computer, one would no longer have to share its computing power with others and wait for one's turn. Computing would be faster, one would have the device entirely for oneself at any time, and one would only have to pay once, namely when buying it.

Steve Jobs, who worked at the game developer ATARI and was a college dropout like Bill Gates and Michael Dell, was electrified by the idea of his friend Woz. He became the business brain of Apple, while Woz took on the role of the highly talented technician in the background. The Apple I was built after Jobs secured the money for the necessary components and received an initial order of 50 units from an electronics shop in Silicon Valley. The young company was already profitable with the Apple I—its story would continue with some "dents" and eventually reach unprecedented heights. These heights would likely have remained distant if Jobs had not prevented his friend Wozniak from giving away the design of the Apple I for free and making it available to other members of the Homebrew Computer Club for replication. Without this intervention, Apple might never have become what it is today.

In the past, when you met IBM employees at the CeBIT computer fair in Hannover, Germany, they were immediately identifiable by their IBM-blue suits. They reminded me of the work suits of the Chinese, in which Mao Zedong and his companion Zhuo Enlai could be seen on television in the 1970s. The contrast to the young entrepreneurs of the PC industry could not have been greater. It was a clash of cultures, but also a reflection of their respective clientele. On one side, IBM with its history dating back to 1911, with strict hierarchies and rules, thick government contracts, and an established customer base that was no different from the IBMers themselves. On the other side, the long-haired representatives of Microsoft or a barefoot Steve Jobs, who, according to his colleagues at ATARI, emitted an unpleasant body odor due to his eating and showering habits.[23] They too were a reflection of their clientele of hobbyists and techno-freaks, just as the IBM people mirrored their customers. "Big Blue" was also capable of acting pragmatically when the pressure was high enough. And that was the case at the beginning of the 1980s. Even in the years before, not only a new corporate culture emerged in the IT industry. IBM's business model also received deep scratches. In the era of mainframes and mid-sized computers, which were somewhat misleadingly called "minis", it was the norm for a small number of large companies to provide their customers with everything from a single source. In Germany, Nixdorf AG had secured a leading position in the field of minis. It maintained production facilities in five countries, including Singapore and the USA, and was active in 22 countries. In the PC market, its share was less significant compared to the US competition, especially since it only entered the market in 1986.[24] The range of large "all-inclusive systems" extended from hardware to the operating system and applications to maintenance.

This changed with the PC. It initially came only as a kit and then created the described ecosystem, to which off-the-shelf software later joined. In other words, the market, which was initially dominated by a few manufacturers of mainframes and minis, began to fragment.[25] A colorful, unmanageable cosmos of companies in different niches emerged, all supplying the PC market. Over time, business customers also warmed to it, recognizing the advantages of the new IT world. It was not just about prices, but also about flexibility and real competition. With PCs, due to their technical standardization, a "best-of-breed" approach could be pursued. This means that in each category—such as hardware, operating system, applications, or storage media—one could choose the supplier who had the best solution at the best price, without being restricted by compatibility issues with products from other manufacturers. This was exactly the case with the large systems. Anyone who wanted to switch from one manufacturer to another had to reckon with considerable efforts in system conversion, functional risks, and correspondingly high costs. Of course, companies like IBM, Honeywell, UNIVAC, Burroughs, and others were aware of this so-called vendor lock-in of their customers. But it got even worse for the market leaders, as the prices for highly profitable large systems also came under pressure because companies like Fujitsu or Hitachi from Japan and Amdahl from California were making themselves more and more noticeable. The comfortable times for the big players in the industry came to an end with the arrival of the PC.

In the early years, the interest of companies, authorities, and consumers in the new devices was still quite low. That changed from 1977 onwards. In that year, three computers came onto the market that could all be used "out of the box" and for which ready and usable software was available in the following years. They came with a monitor, a keyboard, and a drive for reading and storing data. These were the Tandy TRS-80, the Commodore PET, and the Apple II. *Byte Magazine* aptly named them the "Trinity." Of course, they also each had their own version of BASIC, in case the users still wanted to program themselves. The Apple II alone, which could display in color, was sold millions of times and catapulted the company to the top of the PC industry. From September 1977 to September 1980, Apple's annual revenue rose from $775,000 to $118 million.[26] The Trinity gave the digitization of society and the economy their blessing and administered the last rites to some larger systems.

The success of these devices increasingly put IBM under pressure. The available software and the fact that all necessary components of the computers were delivered "plug-and-play" made PCs attractive to both business customers and private users without IT knowledge. This meant a significant expansion of the market, which slipped away from IBM also because an independent software industry emerged from the hardware suppliers, serving both the B2B and B2C markets. Games, word processing, spreadsheets, and a variety of other applications conquered the market. It was like driving a car without having to be a mechanic. One of the software products that achieved particular popularity and stimulated the entire PC industry was VisiCalc, available from 1979 initially for the Apple

II, and subsequently for Commodore and other platforms. It was a spreadsheet that conferred the higher status of a serious device on the PC among business customers. The PC was here to stay. The cheapest IBM computer introduced in 1980, with the sonorous name "5120," which at least outwardly somewhat resembled the PC, cost $13,500. Compared to the young PCs, which were available for a fraction of that price, this was a hard-to-justify premium. IBM's share of the entire computer market fell from 60% to 30% between 1970 and 1980.[27]

However, this did not mean that customers abandoned IBM. The computer market simply expanded without IBM benefiting from it. And the competition did not sleep. By then, Hewlett-Packard, Data General, and Texas Instruments were also in the market with their own devices. In 1980, IBM's top management responded. An IBM PC was needed, and as quickly as possible. The development followed a pattern that some companies still use today when things need to move quickly and be innovative. IBM CEO Frank Cary opted for a task force of only 12 people, who were to develop the IBM PC independently of existing structures, business units, regulations, and bureaucratic processes in the shortest possible time. Throughout my career, I have learned that large companies and government agencies tend to employ many people with limited workloads and unlimited access to communication tools. The result is that some things take much longer than they should. The team, referred to as the "Dirty Dozen" in IBM jargon, was free of such shackles. After just one year, in August 1981, their work was completed and presented to the public in New York.

The unleashing of the twelve had worked. To meet the pressure from top management and lose little time, existing components were purchased on the market and assembled based on their own computer specification. Had it followed the company's conventional rules, components would have been acquired from other business units or even developed in-house. Such an old-fashioned process would have taken four to five years at IBM, based on experience. Now, however, other IBM units also had to compete with third-party companies if they wanted to place their technology in the new device. This had an unintended, long-term effect on the entire PC industry. IBM built its PC on so-called open architecture and with off-the-shelf hardware. This meant that individual components were compatible with those of other computers. There were only a few "proprietary" rights or IBM parts to which other manufacturers would not have had access. The Intel 8088 chip for the processor also had the "flaw" of lacking exclusivity. Additionally, the detailed documentation of the PC was publicly accessible. Others knew exactly what specifications it was based on. All together, it was a cordial invitation to copy the machine. A similarly severe and unintended consequence was another decision. In 1980, IBM licensed DOS, the Disk Operating System, from the 31-person company Microsoft and henceforth installed "MS-DOS" on its PCs. The licensing by IBM was a quantum leap for Microsoft and created the conditions for the company to evolve from a manufacturer of a me-too version of the BASIC programming language to a powerhouse for system and application software. To meet the delivery deadline set by IBM, Microsoft, lacking its own finished product, bought a system called Q-DOS (Quick and Dirty Operating System), which could be adapted to IBM's requirements. IBM wanted Microsoft, not its own team, to take responsibility for the development and maintenance of the operating system. As a consequence, Microsoft retained the rights to DOS, which from IBM's perspective would prove to be a serious strategic mistake. Microsoft had paid $75,000 for Q-DOS. By the mid-1990s, this investment had increased the company's value to $27 billion.

However, IBM's strategic mistake of leaving the rights to the operating system with Microsoft was not only measured in money. Due to the widespread use of the IBM PC, Microsoft set the standards for PC operating systems in the future. Every software developer who wrote applications for the IBM PC also did so for MS-DOS. In this way, it became—with the exception of Apple—the foundation of PC software. The IBM PC was an unexpected success and at its peak reached a market share of 80% of all personal computers sold. After just twelve months, it had generated more than a billion dollars in revenue. IBM had planned to produce 200,000 units for the first year and one million over three years. By the second year, it was 200,000 per month. In January 1983, *TIME* magazine featured a PC on its cover—instead of the usual "Man of the YEAR."[28]

In view of this success, the open architecture and the fact that Microsoft could license its MS-DOS to any manufacturer fueled the market for clones. The term "IBM-compatible" became established for them. Companies like Compaq and Dell seized their opportunities and grew big, leaving IBM with only the honor. After John Opel, the successor to Frank Cary, reintegrated the PC business into inflexible IBM structures, a series of partly grave missteps and a steep decline began. This also included IBM's rejection of an offer from Bill Gates in 1986 to invest in Microsoft. Frank Cary's successor never understood that in the new world of PCs, the fast eat the slow, no longer the big eat the small as in his old world. The events surrounding the IBM PC are a lesson for corporate leaders, both good and bad. Bureaucratic processes and structures did not fit the new IT world. In December 2004, IBM announced the sale of its PC business to the Chinese manufacturer Lenovo for only $1.75 billion. Users of a Lenovo ThinkPad with a sense of history might take a moment of silence for IBM's "Dirty Dozen" the next time they turn on their device.

# One Network to Rule them all

Most of us do not primarily see the Internet as a technological innovation but consider it a normal part of our professional and private lives. The parallel to the car, television, or electricity is obvious. Its self-evidence is the best proof of the success of a technology whose beginnings date back to the late 1950s. If one looks for a founding act for the Internet, the choice falls on the Defense Advanced Research Projects Agency, abbreviated DARPA or ARPA. This agency was established in February 1958 by President Eisenhower.[29] Since then, despite its global spread, the Internet has remained a thoroughly American affair.

To understand this, a common misconception must be cleared up right at the beginning: The Internet is not the same as the World Wide Web (WWW) with its currently (May 2022) around two billion homepages. The latter has its origins at CERN in Switzerland, which will be discussed shortly. We mainly encounter the Internet in this application, and it is therefore often equated with it in public perception. However, the Internet existed about two decades before the WWW and was largely a computer network restricted to science, research, and the military. It formed—as it still does today—the infrastructure for email, messaging, and data traffic between the participating institutions, at a time when no one could make sense of the terms website or homepage. In its early days in the 1960s and early 1970s, about 70 almost exclusively American computers were connected to it, no more.

The founding of ARPA, like that of the National Aeronautics and Space Administration (NASA) in July of the same year, was a response to the launch of the Soviet satellite Sputnik in October 1957. Besides the prestige success of the Soviet Union, it was also proof that the Soviets could build a carrier rocket capable of reaching US territory. In a time of nuclear arms race and in the midst of the Cold War, it was a real wake-up call for America, which is why the event went down in history as the "Sputnik Shock." In modern terms, ARPA was (and is) an agency of the US Department of Defense that acted as a kind of "public-private partnership." ARPA itself did not operate research facilities at the time but coordinated projects between scientific, private, and government institutions. This construct is certainly part of its success. A former top manager of General Electric, Roy Johnson, became its first head, who engaged the German Wernher von Braun for ARPA as Chief Scientist.[30] Wernher von Braun was one of the leading figures in the Third Reich's rocket program in Peenemünde and was involved in the development of the V2 (Vengeance Weapon 2) rocket. The Americans had brought him and his team to the USA in a secret operation in 1945 before the Red Army could capture them. However, due to his past as a member of the Nazi Party NSDAP and SS (Schutzstaffel), von Braun was initially not considered for a leading position but eventually ended up in a prominent position at the newly established NASA.

A division of labor was established between NASA and ARPA. NASA took care of civilian aerospace activities, while ARPA conducted research on computers and networks. Its goal was to efficiently and, above all, quickly exchange information between computers, namely the mainframes of the government and science at the time. The result of these efforts was the ARPANET in 1967, which three years later connected the East and West coasts of the USA via a computer network, to which a number of supercomputers from scientific research institutions and universities were connected. ARPANET was thus a very exclusive club. "High Performance Computing" and the emergence of the Internet are therefore closely linked. Over the years, ARPA promoted a number of important inventions and established standards that still shape the Internet today. Two of these were essential for the further development of the network into what it is now.

Until the 1990s, the connection between computers of a network functioned either through dial-up via the telephone network or a leased dedicated line, which in both cases connected two computers in point-to-point mode. The latter were expensive and thus less widespread. If a user from University A wanted to transfer data, such as an email, to a computer at University B, they had to connect to the corresponding computer at B via a phone number and log in there as a registered user. When they sent their data, it would queue up in the network's data stream and wait to be transmitted. This created a queue: depending on traffic, it could take between six hours and two days for an email to arrive. The point-to-point connection between two computers was therefore not very efficient, especially considering that the data transmission speed was nowhere near what it is today. It was equally inefficient to send data as a single packet. If the packets were large and there was a lot of traffic on the network, the transfer would take correspondingly longer—like a traffic jam on the highway. In this store-and-forward system, the user had to wait until their packet was next in line and fully transmitted. Therefore, a solution was needed to avoid congestion and increase transmission speed.

ARPA addressed this problem with a technique called packet switching. We still use it today when we navigate the internet. Instead of sending data only over a specific path, i.e., the point-to-point connection between two computers, the new technique, which has been in use since the 1970s, allows data to be broken down into several smaller packets and sent over any paths of one or more networks to their destination. Each packet contains the sender's and the recipient's address. Once they arrive, they are reassembled, and the recipient sees the original message on their screen—as if it had never been sent in small pieces. With packet switching, an email—or any other form of data exchange—now takes only seconds, depending on the file size, instead of hours or days. Specialized small computers, known to us from our everyday internet use as routers, were developed for the optimal transfer of data over any available paths.

To use any routes, separately existing networks also had to be able to exchange data with each other. The internet is not a single monolithic network but the connection between many "independent" subnets. For example, the network of Universities A and B needed a connection to the network of Universities D and E to enable efficient routing. ARPANET solved this problem by developing software that specified a set of technical rules for data exchange between networks. The TCP/IP (Transmission Control Protocol/Internet Protocol) protocol family serves this purpose. Most of us encounter it in the form of our IP address. It is the unique address of a computer and allows the sender of a message to send it precisely to a specific computer in a specific network among the millions that exist on the internet. TCP/IP still forms the basis for data communication on the web. TCP/IP went "live" for the first time in 1975 with a connection between computers at Stanford University and University College London.[31]

Today, internet exchange points ensure the connections between individual subnets. The largest in the world by data throughput is DE-CIX, based in Frankfurt, Germany. The private company operates numerous "interconnection platforms" worldwide, which connect the subnets of internet providers and other customers. In the pandemic year 2020, the node reached a peak throughput of 10 terabits per second! That corresponds to 1280 gigabytes. With this data volume, you can watch more than 600 hours of HD videos.[32]

Without packet switching and ARPA's TCP/IP protocol, this data flow would not be possible, and the internet would not have become what it is today: the global communication and publication platform formed by the amalgamation of a large number of individual networks of very different origins and purposes. TCP/IP created the technical interoperability, and packet switching provided the speed. Both allow us to exchange data with each other despite the multitude of common technical standards and protocols. The architects of the biblical Tower of Babel would have been delighted.

The European Organization for Nuclear Research, or CERN for short, is headquartered in a suburb of Geneva, right on the border with France. As of 2022, CERN comprises 22 European nations and Israel. It conducts research in the field of particle physics and deals with two major questions of humanity: What is our universe made of, and what are the fundamental properties of matter? A physicist at CERN, with the help of a dedicated colleague, provided the internet with the "killer application" it needed to break out of the realm of science and government and become so massively integrated into our lives. This application is the aforementioned World Wide Web. As is often the case, this technical innovation began with a very practical problem.

It was about how to best find information in CERN's vast electronic documentation using software without needing to know which department it belonged to, on which computer, in which folder, or in which database it was located. With such software, information could also be easily and in the same way shared with third parties. Instead of representing documents "top-down" hierarchically, the idea was to create a web-like structure where one could "jump" directly to them on the connected computer. Tim Berners-Lee found a solution to this problem. The son of an English mathematician couple who had worked on the Manchester Mark I, he wrote a concept for this in 1989 during his work at CERN, with great support from a colleague, the Belgian Robert Cailliau. Unlike the newcomer Tim, Robert was a veteran at CERN and knew which strings to pull to obtain the necessary resources for the project.[33]

Berners-Lee's concept utilized a technique called hypertext, which had been available since the early 1960s. It involves a text that is linked in one document to texts in other documents. Access to the documents is achieved by pressing a key on this link—nowadays more commonly by clicking a mouse or touching the screen. Building on this technique, Berners-Lee also wanted to access information that was not only in CERN's network but scattered somewhere on the internet. Thus, hypertext was supplemented by a technique we now know as Hypertext Transfer Protocol (HTTP), which allows access to documents or web pages in the depths of the internet. HTTP—and in its secure, encrypted form HTTPS—is thus part of the internet protocol family. It appears to us ostensibly as a "Uniform Resource Locator"—better known as URL—, a string of characters as the address of a web page in our browser. URLs (for example: https://www.example. com/) are used not only for the WWW but also for other internet applications. Examples include database access (JDBC), email (mailto), and data transfer (ftp). Without this technique, we would have to know and enter the exact path leading to the desired document. The WWW would hardly have become as popular as it is today with this handicap.

Tim Berners-Lee published the code of his application in August 1991. The "public" World Wide Web was thus born. It is very remarkable that neither CERN nor Tim charged money for the use of the software but made it available to the public free of charge. Berners-Lee thus likely left hundreds of millions of dollars on the table. He followed his dream of a free, public platform for the global and unrestricted exchange of information. In the foreword to Tim's book *Weaving the Web*, Michael Dertouzos, then director of the Computer Sciences Lab at MIT in Cambridge, writes: "As technologists and entrepreneurs founded and merged companies to exploit the web, they seemed fixated on the question: 'How can I make the web mine?' Meanwhile, Tim asked: 'How can I make the web yours?'"[34]

In my industry, which is ruthlessly governed by money, there are more examples of very successful individuals pursuing dreams similar to Tim Berners-Lee's. Consider the open-source movement of the Finn Linus Torvalds, whose free software Linux today forms the basis of Google's Android operating system, among other things, and has found its way into the data centers of the world. Or the encyclopedia Wikipedia by Jimmy Wales and Larry Sanger, which is funded by donations. On an institutional level, this includes the Mozilla Foundation, whose most well-known products are the Firefox browser and the Thunderbird email client. Such a form of idealism with such far-reaching impacts is as much a characteristic of the IT industry as the pursuit of money.

To make the WWW accessible to people who are less technically savvy, a very easy-to-use software was needed in addition to the hyperlink technology. We know it today as a browser. Since these must be suitable for very broad audiences and target groups, they follow a design principle that applies to all consumer products in IT. They are built for the user referred to in industry jargon as "DAU" (Dumbest Assumed User). This ensures that the technology can be mastered without any prior knowledge and can be easily sold. It is now taken for granted that modern browsers can combine and display graphical, video, and text-based information in a single window. The rudimentary browsers available at the time—including the one developed by Tim Berners-Lee and a mathematics student named Nicola Pellow at CERN—could not do this. A solution to this problem was found in 1993 by the National Center for Super-Computing Applications (NCSA) at the University of Illinois. Its descriptive name was "Mosaic," the first popular web browser. Mosaic still had a lot of development needs in its initial release but was an important reason for the boom that the WWW experienced afterward. Microsoft licensed Mosaic in 1995, after the product had already been displaced in the market by the competing Netscape Navigator, and made it the basis of its Internet Explorer. The company was probably somewhat startled by the rapid development of the internet and entered the business relatively late. No wonder, when it made its money with head-heavy "fat clients" on the PC, for which browser-based "thin clients" initially posed a threat. Both concepts seemed difficult to reconcile at the time, and Microsoft almost didn't make the turn.

# The Perfect Storm

In the early 1990s, various factors came together in IT that were reminiscent of Wolfgang Petersen's Hollywood adaptation of the book *The Perfect Storm*. But instead of extreme weather phenomena on the Atlantic, whose convergence sank the cutter Andrea Gail, the IT storm was characterized by parallel technical and economic developments that also reinforced each other: the strong demand for internet access driven by the WWW, the enormously increasing spread of personal computers in companies and private households, and the steadily improving bandwidths of networks while costs were simultaneously decreasing.

Anyone who had to dial into the web via a modem over an analog telephone line with a service provider (Internet Service Provider, or ISP) like America Online (AOL) or Deutsche Telekom at that time initially found themselves in the "World Wide Wait." In the early 1990s, there was no other internet access, especially not for private individuals. We are talking about transmission rates of 56 Kbit per second with modem dial-up. Today, we use always-available, "always-on" broadband lines, whose speed is still unsatisfactory but nevertheless serves its purpose without causing too much frustration. A current 100 Mbit VDSL line corresponds to 100,000 Kbit per second and still leaves many wishes unfulfilled. Back then, it would have catapulted every PC owner to seventh heaven.

Surfing with a 56 Kbit telephone line was a real test of patience, except for sending pure text files. A video of 700 MB in size took about 28 hours, not including fluctuations in the transmission rate.[35] Additionally, the telephone line was occupied for the duration of the internet connection, so simultaneous calls were not possible. With the introduction of DSL as a broadband service from the mid-1990s—in Germany first in 1999 in Berlin by Deutsche Telekom—the problem was solved. Now, telephone lines could be used for both calls and the internet simultaneously, and higher data rates were also available. Since the acoustic modems of 1983 to the broadband accesses of the 2020s, the technically possible data throughput for internet access has increased by 50% per year.[36]

The internet gave a significant boost to the PC market, which had been growing significantly since the late 1970s. PCs were bought just to have a comfortable web access. America Online, as the dominant ISP, made its online access available for PCs, first for Microsoft's DOS and from 1993 also for Windows. Since 1985, it was available under the name Quantum Link as a bundle of online services on the Commodore 64. These services, which were available from AOL for a manageable monthly price, included games, emails, news, and chat rooms. In 1995, AOL already had three million users under contract, after previously leading a much more modest existence alongside other services like CompuServ. AOL could initially only send emails among users of its own service, which was not uncommon for ISPs at the time. When it then established a connection of its email service to the global internet, a so-called gateway, a precedent was set.[37] This added another piece of significance to the web as a universal communication platform, and the ISP market exploded.

Microsoft also contributed to this in 1995 with its consumer-oriented Windows 95 release. With this version, MS-DOS and Windows were merged, and "Win '95" also came with a new dial-up service: MSN, Microsoft Network. The brand name was used over the years for a number of other services, such as Hotmail (now Outlook. com) and Messenger (now Skype). MSN was not coincidentally available at the same time as Windows 95. The accompanying marketing campaign was enormous. A song by the Rolling Stones, Start Me Up, served as a kind of theme song, referring to the newly introduced Windows "START" button. The advertising campaign in print and other media cost over 200 million dollars, a huge sum for the time, but well invested.[38] The company had apparently understood that the battle for the internet could become its Armageddon. Unlike Microsoft, not every company had a reasonable business plan. At the beginning of my time in San Francisco, as a "newbie," I made the mistake of always looking for the cheapest ISP for my private internet connection. The result was that I was repeatedly confronted with the bankruptcies of the providers. Being stingy is not always cool.

By the turn of the millennium, IT had become a mass product for business and private use. And it continued to rise. The trend accelerated significantly with the first commercial implementation of an internet-enabled 3G wireless network by NTT DoCoMo in Japan in 2003 and with the arrival of the iPhone in 2007. Despite a cascade of superlatives used to describe this steep rise, one must not forget that the industry does not only live off Microsoft or the likes of Google. Economically, it has remained largely a small and medium-sized sector globally, even though its image is shaped quite differently by the heavyweights. In Germany, according to the Federal Statistical Office, there were 127,191 companies in the information and telecommunications sector (ICT) in 2021. Of these, 110,850 (87%) employ up to nine, another 12,628 (10%) up to 49, and only 2,887 (2.3%) up to 249 employees. Only 826 (0.7%) companies have more than 249 employees. According to the EU's statistical definition, they are already considered large companies.[39] In reference to a quote from Gandalf the Grey in "The Lord of the Rings," one can state: Reality has more facets than meet the eye.

# 4

# The Transformation of the Economy

An investigation by a large American management consulting firm in May 2022 illustrates, using specific job categories, how technology is changing existing job profiles and why the workers of the future will need an increasingly broad spectrum of qualifications. If they want to be successful, it will not be possible without "digital" knowledge, coupled with genuine job knowledge. IT thus becomes one of the core competencies even outside typical IT roles.[1] A good indicator of this long-ongoing process is the ubiquitous shortage of IT specialists, which is not only due to demographic developments but also points to an enormously increasing demand. Companies in the IT sector have long since ceased to compete only with each other for talent. The employer profiles in the relevant job forums on the internet are as colorful as a box of marbles.[2] The following incident illustrates how difficult the job market has become even for large IT companies: When I was responsible for Central Europe at my then-employer

© The Author(s), under exclusive license to Springer Fachmedien Wiesbaden GmbH, part of Springer Nature 2024
J. Müller, *Turning Point*,
https://doi.org/10.1007/978-3-658-46079-2_4

Citrix in 2013, we moved the German branch from the vicinity of Munich Airport to the more expensive city center. The reason was that it was becoming increasingly difficult to recruit employees for a company location "far out." Young staff, in particular, showed little inclination to work outside the narrower city area. The conscious decision to forgo a car and unattractive connections with public transport were often cited as reasons. Even for a successful and well-known industry giant like Citrix, the situation had already become tight. "The war for talent is real," as I read in an American study.

# The Digitization of Everything

"Are you a human or a machine?"

During a chat with Apple's customer support, I couldn't resist asking this question. The responses from the other side of the net seemed too quick and precise to sufficiently support my initial suspicion of "human." The reply was: "Ha, ha, I am a human." After my question about the name of the german Chancellor was correctly answered, I believed David that he had a heartbeat and complimented him on his competence. However, the competition between humans and machines has other variations than described in this anecdote. Chatbots, whose popular examples Siri and Alexa everyone knows, are on the rise everywhere. Some of them are topics of talk shows and TV news. The AI software ChatGPT is a bot that, since its release in November 2022, has even made a giant like Google fearful. GPT stands for "Generative Pre-trained Transformer" and describes a neural network architecture developed for processing natural language (Transformer architecture). The AI was trained with very large amounts of data, can constantly improve its own results, and also incorporate new data (Machine Learning). The adjective "generative" describes the fact that it can independently generate new content. The concept was first described by Google in 2017. The product has the potential to shake up not only the IT industry. In less than three months, it surpassed the 100 million user mark, which took Instagram 2.5 years to achieve. In January 2023, Google felt compelled to quickly announce and bring to market its own response with the chatbot "Bard." At the same time, CEO Sundar Pichai promised "big, AI-driven leaps" in his company's services. Shortly thereafter, the Chinese internet giant Baidu also entered the scene with its own product announcement "Ernie" (Enhanced Representation through Knowledge Integration). Following this, Baidu's stock price on the Hong Kong Stock Exchange rose by up to 17%.[3] The wake-up call has reached the competition. Meta also launched its own AI bot "Galactica" in November 2023. However, it was withdrawn just a few days later due to significant deficiencies. This incident makes it clear that AI bots are still at the beginning of their development.

ChatGPT's manufacturer OpenAI was founded in 2015 by Sam Altman, Elon Musk, and four others as a non-profit organization and only established a commercial arm in 2019. Microsoft announced at the beginning of 2023 that it would invest an additional 10 billion USD on top of its existing 3 billion investment.[4] ChatGPT is capable of responding to inquiries in multiple languages, engaging in conversation, and answering follow-up questions. Its texts read as if they were actually written by a human, with nothing suggesting that they are essentially the result of statistical predictions based on pattern recognition in the underlying data. Since I frequently use ChatGPT and Bard in parallel, I can assert that the former provides significantly fewer false information. These are still a real problem with Bard. ChatGPT can also act like a smart search engine, solve complex mathematical problems, generate meaningful social media posts, and write homework or reports for students. The start-up DoNotPay uses ChatGPT to help consumers cancel subscriptions, contest parking tickets, and generally stand up against large companies.[5] Recently, ChatGPT even passed an MBA exam presented to it by a professor from the renowned Wharton Business School. The bot performed very successfully in a bar exam in the USA and placed in the top one percent in the "Biology Olympiad," an international high school competition.[6] The impressive thing is that these are exams where previously only humans competed and only they had a chance of success. ChatGPT passes the so-called Turing Test without any problems. It is named after the aforementioned British mathematician and "father of computer science," Alan Turing. In his 1950 scientific paper "Computing Machinery and Intelligence," Turing postulated that machines must be considered "intelligent" if a human can no longer distinguish them from a human conversation partner based on their contributions to a conversation. The bot can produce more or less sophisticated digital art with its additional module "DALL-E" based on human specifications. The name DALL-E is a combination of the name of Salvador Dali and Disney's science fiction film "WALL-E." The version GPT-4, released in March 2023, is multimodal, meaning it can not only generate text but also, for example, suggest a recipe from pictures of ingredients. Its capabilities are truly impressive despite the early stage of development. The question of why Caesar crossed the Rubicon in 49 BC and what consequences that had was correctly answered by ChatGPT. Equally sensible was the requested procedure for detecting hidden malware on websites. My request to write a program to determine whether any given number is a prime number was promptly fulfilled. One can see the broad range of applications. Nevertheless, the provided statements should be taken with critical caution, as no sources are currently given, and the data used only goes up to 2021 (as of April 2023). Both are different with Google's Bard. It provides sources, its answers can be verified with a click from Google's search engine, and the database is also up-to-date. It was also not too difficult for me to trick ChatGPT. But that will also change. One thing the bot has already learned. When I asked if it had an idea of itself, it replied: "As an artificial intelligence language model, I have no self-awareness or consciousness. … I am able to understand and respond to user inquiries, but I have no ability for self-perception or introspection." Obviously, OpenAI is trying to avoid the trouble Google had with its LaMDA AI system, which one of the engineers claimed had consciousness and even told the *Washington Post*.[7]

A German federal state has consequently already allowed it in schools.[8] After all, it makes no sense to block such developments. The truth is: We and our children must learn to deal with AI critically, competently, and productively. Those who believe that AI or internet access must be excluded in lessons or exams are giving kids the wrong tasks and have an antiquated concept that misses the reality of our children. I have rarely seen my children doing homework or preparing for exams without using the web. Such possibilities also explain why I now prefer to communicate with bots on certain topics rather than with a human. Even much more modest chatbots than those from OpenAI or Google are far better than the phone announcements of some call centers, which antiquatedly inform me that all employees are in conversation and I should please have "some" patience. However, those who use intelligent chatbots must be aware that their words are processed and stored in the provider's cloud. This is particularly true for household assistants like Cortana, Siri, and Alexa. Numerous data privacy violations have been linked to Alexa, including instances where the device recorded and stored conversations even when not explicitly activated by a wake word like 'Alexa'. A similar-sounding term such as 'sister' was able to do the trick.[9] Smart homes are a good thing but still pose a challenge in this regard.

From these explanations, it becomes clear that potential job competition between humans and machines has already moved out of the factory halls. A study by Cornell University from March 2023 shows that "about 80% of the U.S. workforce could be affected by the introduction of GPTs in at least 10% of their tasks. About 19% could be affected in at least 50% of their tasks. The impact extends across all wage levels, with higher-paid jobs potentially being more significantly affected."[10] Behind this lies very good news: the shortage of skilled workers can be addressed with AI. I think, for example, of people who today struggle with our burgeoning bureaucracy and thus have less and less time for their actual tasks. A doctor who can delegate administrative tasks to an AI has more time for their patients. The extent of digitalization can generally be observed beyond AI. In the supermarket, I use a scanner that registers my purchases. At the checkout terminal, they are read in seconds, I pay with a credit card, and I'm already on my way. The time savings are enormous: I go through the payment process in no time, instead of unloading the shopping cart, placing purchases on the conveyor belt, having them scanned individually by the cashier, reloading, and paying. Everything happens in a flash and without the many people in front of you who have forgotten their credit card PIN, not to mention the not only older folks who, with exasperating persistence, place exactly counted money on the counter and then still have to search for the missing 2 cents. A similar direction was recently pointed out by the website of the English newspaper *Daily Mail.* It reported how robots are helping the owners of the restaurant "Bella Italia" in Cumbria cope with staff shortages.[11] The robots, in a charmingly quirky cat shape, move quite naturally, are multifunctional, can speak, and transport a lot of dishes. The remaining human employees thus have more time to take care of the emotional side of hospitality and the individual needs of the customers. This creates customer loyalty, which robots do not yet understand—not yet.

These different examples make it clear how IT-driven automation and assistance have spread in our daily lives. The interfaces between humans and computers exist not only on large or small screens; they are everywhere. However, less immediately tangible—at least for most of us—are the major changes that IT has brought about in the economy.

# Industry 4.0, 5G, and Digital Twins

Products like ChatGPT and other forms of AI can be something like an iPhone moment for many industries. Apple's smartphone, available since 2007, revolutionized the market for mobile phones and consumer electronics and elevated it to a new level. Similarily, businesses will have to deal extensively with Artificial Intelligence. Meaningful use cases include answering customer inquiries, supporting quality management, optimizing supply chains, material research, designing pharmaceutical products, and much more. What they all have in common is that they are based on the analysis of large amounts of data.

The Fourth Industrial Revolution, also known as Industry 4.0, historically describes the latest stage of a development that began in the second half of the 18th century with the First Industrial Revolution. This marked the transition from manual to machine production of goods, particularly using steam engines and water power. The new human ability to generate mechanical energy on a massive scale had an enormous impact on the further development of our species and led, not least, to a steep increase in the world population. It took about a century—depending on the country and region—for the First Industrial Revolution to fully take hold. The Second Industrial Revolution, roughly spanning from 1871 to the period between the World Wars, describes the triumph of industrial mass production, associated with the expansion of transportation routes, the use of division of labor production methods, and electrification, while the Third Industrial Revolution is already based on the extensive use of digital technology. The automation of increasingly complex tasks, the replacement of mechanical and analog processes with digital ones, and the selective replacement of human labor with computers are essential features of this third epoch. It began during World War II and extends into our present. These "powder-free" revolutions were not limited to purely technical changes. They were accompanied by profound social and political upheavals and deep, often painfully felt cuts in the world of work and people's lives. However, they were also accompanied by an enormous increase in productivity, the constant improvement of living standards for broad segments of the population, and the emergence of political-social movements aimed at social emancipation and participation. Without them, there would have been no social balance, the associated acceptance of changes, and political stability.

Currently, we are in the warm-up phase for an even larger upheaval, whose true dimensions are only gradually becoming apparent. While we are still perfecting automation, the gate to a new, fourth industrial age has already opened. The core of Industry 4.0 consists of the networking and coordinated interaction of all technologies and processes involved in a company's value creation. As a result, this means the establishment of digital business models. Unlike its predecessor, we are no longer talking about gradual automation and improvement of existing work processes, but about their redesign. Depending on the business object, business model, and industry, this new design can take on very different contours. An agricultural company has different production processes than an automotive manufacturer, and these, in turn, differ from the requirements of a digitally controlled smart city, where things like traffic or energy efficiency are in the foreground. What they all have in common, however, is the endeavor to realize operational efficiency and added value through the implementation of data-driven, AI-controlled processes. Therefore, the term fourth industrial revolution does not have a predominantly technological connotation, but it describes a completely new way of achieving the set business goals through digitalization. This also makes it clear that digital innovation should not be a technical issue in the first step, but must start with the company's goals. Technology is "only" the means to an end.

In the smart factory, the intelligent factory of the future, production organizes itself. People, robots, transport systems, facilities, warehouse logistics, and other company areas communicate with each other, if necessary also with external systems, such as those of suppliers. IT components and software are merged with mechanical and electronic systems to form so-called Cyber Physical Systems (CPS), which enable efficient control and management of the entire production process infrastructure. Unlike the traditional system of manual data collection and command input, delays during the production process are eliminated: data analysis, command transmission, and control of stationary and mobile systems take place in real-time via the IIoT. The Industrial Internet of Things refers to a large number of sensors that provide the necessary data for optimal control in real-time and, for example, indicate where a robot or a component is currently located, whether there is a problem with the technology or quality somewhere, and whether a human needs to intervene. Products and their components are controlled in the manufacturing process, e.g. via RFID (Radio Frequency Identification). This is a frequently used, unobtrusive technology for automatic and contactless identification and localization of objects using radio waves. Electronically labeled components for the end product "tell" the machines what should be done with them and into which variant of the end product they should be installed. In this way, individual customer wishes can be produced up to batch size of one, i.e., a single piece, without the need for a separate manufacturing process. This form of flexibility creates speed and competitive advantages, not to mention lower costs.

For this novel communication between the involved machines and product components, very fast networks are required. Data and command transmission must take place in real-time, otherwise, the precise availability of machines and components in the production process cannot be guaranteed. One of the keys to this is 5G networks, the successors of the current 4G mobile network. "5G" refers to the super-fast network of the fifth generation. Currently, peak transmission rates of 10 Gbit per second are already being achieved; soon it will be up to 50 Gbit.[12] The latency time—the time it takes for the device on the other side to respond to a request—is only one millisecond, which in reality means nothing other than real-time. Private users will realize its advantages primarily in the form of very fast internet uploads and downloads, which will prove to be a great relief for videos or games from the net. For the economy, however, 5G is likely to prove to be a quantum leap, which, in addition to the high speed, has to do with a few other decisive properties of these networks. They make it so attractive for smart factories, smart cities, smart logistics, and numerous other "smart" applications.

With 5G, many separate networks can be spanned side by side on the same physical mobile infrastructure (such as transmission masts), technically referred to as "slicing" and "beam forming." The parallel operation of many logical networks enables correspondingly many simultaneous applications side by side. This can be, for example, autonomous driving or the control of a factory. While current networks broadcast data in a spherical shape, with 5G, the data stream can be "beamed" specifically to a particular end device—such as a robot or a moving car. By the way, those who are worried about too much radiation exposure from mobile phones today can relax with 5G. While 2G still generated 2 watts of exposure, with 5G it is only about one percent of that.

5G also allows companies to operate their own logical networks, a kind of private mobile network. Particularly interesting in this context is the 5G feature of direct data exchange between numerous end devices—such as sensors. The data stream no longer has to run through a data center but takes place directly and accordingly quickly between the end devices, whose number is almost unlimited: up to one million devices per square kilometer are possible. As with radiation exposure, 5G also brings significant energy savings. It requires only about 1/100 of the energy of today's 4G network per transmitted bit.[13]

With so many advantages, it is clear that 5G also plays a significant role outside the Smart Factory. In 2021, the American consulting firm PwC attempted to determine the impact of 5G on global economic development as well as on individual industries, regions, and countries. According to their figures, the additional global GDP generated by 5G by 2030 will be $1.3 trillion. Of this, $65 billion is expected to be attributed to Germany. The five biggest beneficiaries among the industries include, first and foremost, healthcare, followed by so-called Smart Utilities, which can be used in the private sector to control light and heat. In third place are media applications for the consumer market, then the Smart Factory, and finally financial services.[14]

Anyone who collects as much data as an intelligent factory needs two things: first, a place to store, process, and analyze the data, and second, applications that implement the results in the production process. For the former, there is the in-house data center or the cloud; the latter is provided by programs, including Virtual Reality and Digital Twins. Both come into play whenever people want not only to analyze data but also to visualize it, thereby making it more useful for their own decisions or activities.

"Cloud is when I can access huge data and computing capacities from anywhere with my small phone." My friend Karsten's answer to the question about the meaning of "cloud" hits the nail on the head. When we check the weather forecast, convert current exchange rates, hold virtual meetings with colleagues from the home office, or use an app like Flightradar to find out the current position of an airplane we are waiting for at the terminal, we are doing exactly what Karsten described. Economically speaking, we are using the services of a cloud provider for very little money, which no private user could ever maintain cost-effectively. And the best part: thanks to the access we use via common browsers, we don't have to worry about the software being up-to-date. And if we access the cloud through an office suite like Microsoft's or the free LibreOffice from the Document Foundation, the same applies. Even sophisticated software is no longer purchased thanks to the cloud but subscribed to. It is thus always up-to-date and can be used by anyone at low cost.

For companies, it is not much different. Smart Factories and other applications collect and process their data in the cloud. The cloud, whether rented or self-operated, scores with virtually unlimited scalability. This is a significant advantage given the very rapidly growing volume of data. If more computing power and network capacities are needed due to increasing customer numbers or unforeseen peak loads, the existing resources automatically scale up. This process is called upscaling. If less capacity is needed, it goes in the opposite direction, called downscaling. Parallel to this, operating costs also rise or fall. Second-by-second and volume-accurate billing of the resources used is included. You only pay for what you actually use. However, while private individuals usually use a public cloud and share resources with others, such an approach is not always advisable for companies. This is partly due to data security reasons. After all, the company's know-how lies in the data. Therefore, they either operate their own cloud in their data centers or rent computing and storage capacities exclusively for themselves from a global provider like Microsoft and Amazon or a local provider like the german Hetzner, depending on their needs. In both cases, this is referred to as a private cloud. It is usually more expensive and, like the public cloud, can be distributed across a multitude of data centers around the globe, thereby accelerating data access for a subsidiary in Asia, for example. Companies also use hybrid clouds for cost reasons, which combine private and public access. In my own start-up, my partners and I have benefited from a high-quality IT infrastructure through the cloud, which would otherwise have been far beyond our financial reach. The cloud is thus also an economic factor for small businesses that rely on state-of-the-art IT infrastructure but cannot afford high investments. Modern IT makes the world of business more equitable.

Why do you need a digital twin? And what is it anyway? To avoid misunderstandings: this is not the usual avatar from internet forums. Digital twins do not depict people. They map objects in a digital model, such as a machine, supply chains, or an entire factory. The user can see this model in a Virtual Reality (VR) headset—or on a screen. The focus is more on the captured state data of the depicted object and less on how realistic it looks. The digital twin of an entire factory, for example, consists of the many sensor data that accumulate during a production process and are fed from the cloud. This can start with the delivery of components and end with the shipment of a finished product. The accumulated data allows for identifying weaknesses, simulating processes, exploring "what-if" scenarios, and discovering efficiency potentials. How long do certain processes take, where do errors occur, how can energy be saved, how do changed time specifications affect the process? The digital twin is thus essentially a big data application that avoids the operation on the open heart in the sense of an actual intervention in existing processes and still provides a realistic state model of an object.

The possible applications of virtual reality go far beyond the digital twin. Anyone who has ever played a computer game with a VR headset knows that they are dealing with a computer-generated "reality." A VR flight simulator gives us the feeling of actually sitting in a cockpit and controlling the aircraft, while a "shooter game" transports us to a battlefield and finally lets us become a hero. Depending on the quality and power of the hardware and software used, we immerse ourselves in the simulated environment and become part of it. This is called "Immersive Gaming." Virtual reality in the context of Industry 4.0 is essentially no different. However, the benefit is not generated through an entertaining game but through purposeful applications. Training is one of the frequently used applications. Anyone who can practice operating or repairing a machine immersively with a VR headset causes no damage and has a significantly better learning effect. The US Navy uses the technology to train its ship crews in a scenario of 300 virtual ships and 100 geographical settings.[15] Anyone who can virtually drill an emergency situation, such as fighting a fire in a factory, will be able to react better in a real emergency and will more likely know what to do. Anyone who is able to demonstrate a product to their customer using VR will not only make a better impression than with "death by PowerPoint" but will also save significantly on costs in the long run.

# Platform Economy and the Reinvention of Value Creation

Industry 4.0 allows us to rethink the way we produce products, engage in agriculture, or develop and market services. Despite this enormous impact, it is only one of the major pieces in the puzzle of current economic transformations. Another is referred to by the term platform economy. Behind this term lies a new type of IT-driven value creation. In a traditional company, added value is created internally by its own employees—for example, through the production of "tangible" products, consulting services of a management consultancy, or the management of investments by a bank. The platform economy works differently. Its value creation is fundamentally not carried out by its own employees and workers but externally by partners and end customers who use the digital services provided by the platform for their transactions with each other.[16] The operator of such a platform assumes "end-to-end" responsibility for the user by bringing together business terms, IT infrastructure, processes, cybersecurity, administration, payment systems, and compliance into a unified framework of internet-based, modular service offerings. It goes without saying that extensive use is made of artificial intelligence. With large amounts of data and the use of AI, platform operators help their customers find the right providers for their needs. They are the match-makers for business and the initiation of contacts for any purpose. As a result, end customers and partners flock to the platforms like bees to a honeypot. A good example of this is Amazon's trading platform.

In addition to the already described business model of social media, whose value creation arises from their users richly feeding them with data and then making this data available to their advertising partners, there are other well-known variants of the platform economy: the app stores of Google, Microsoft, or Apple, but also many other smaller stores with specific orientations. Examples of this are gaming platforms, SAP's virtual marketplace with its approximately 2,000 partner apps, or Salesforce's App Exchange. They offer developers of extensions and add-on modules for their own products an easy-to-use, worldwide sales forum. The more developers provide such modules—such as an AI application for evaluating SAP data—the easier it becomes for SAP to close its own offering gaps in an economically viable way. This external value creation makes SAP products more interesting for end customers.

At Apple alone, there are 4.8 million apps in the store, and at Google, around 2.6 million (as of 2022).[17] Through their platforms, they orchestrate sales and, to a certain extent, also quality control and competition. Anyone who wants to list an app as a developer at Apple must first undergo a kind of compliance test, for which Apple has defined the criteria. This ranges from technical minimum requirements to the handling of in-app purchases to "ethical" guidelines for the content. Google proceeds similarly but, in my personal experience, is less strict regarding the requirements. App approvals for the stores are by no means just an automated formality. Apps that do not meet the criteria can be returned with conditions for revision. The platforms also promote competition among app providers by allowing users to publicly rate their products. This creates a level of transparency that was previously not available in such a simple way—if at all. Anyone who receives a poor rating for their app has poor chances of selling it.

A look at Amazon, Tencent, Alibaba, Airbnb, Uber, Google, Rakuten, or eBay makes it clear that the concept works across products and industries and in many variations. All these companies have created immense value at a breathtaking pace. This also applies to smaller providers than the 800-pound gorillas of the industry. Grab Holdings is one such case. The company was called Grab Taxi in its Malaysian beginnings and still does not own any vehicles. Grab is a startup that is little known in the West but quite present in Asia, with its current headquarters in Singapore, a net revenue of 675 million US dollars, and a growth of 44% in 2021.[18] I have been able to convince myself of Grab's qualities during my numerous visits to our development team in Ho Chi Minh City. Grab was the first "Decacorn" in Asia. Unlike a "Unicorn," i.e., a startup with at least one billion dollars in company valuation, the hurdle in this category is ten billion. The people at Grab have clearly set boundaries for their competitor Uber in Southeast Asia with regionally adapted offerings and have evolved from the original ride-only provider to a supplier of groceries, an intermediary of insurance and mobile payment services, a package sender, a service provider for travel expense accounting, and much more. The ecosystem of its partners includes independent drivers, merchants, and other companies that offer their services via the Grab "Super App." With its service "Grab Maps" announced in June 2022, the company is even challenging Google. This example shows what can generally apply: The platform economy works particularly well for expansion into broad and diversified product portfolios.

Meteoric rises like those of platform companies are hardly found elsewhere. The Japanese Rakuten Ichiba was founded in 1997 and should still be known at least by name to fans of FC Barcelona and the Golden State Warriors from San Francisco as their sponsor. With its highly diversified portfolio, the "Japanese Amazon" achieved a revenue of 15.3 billion dollars in 2021 and is strongly on an international expansion course. Amazon was founded in 1994 and generated a revenue of 469.8 billion dollars just 27 years later. Google's founding was in 1998, and its revenue in 2021 was 257.6 billion dollars. Facebook was launched in 2004, and its revenue in 2021 was 117.9 billion. Microsoft first appeared as a classic IT company in 1975 and achieved a revenue of 168 billion in the fiscal year 2021. It took a comparatively long 46 years to do so. The difference between Microsoft and the platforms is more than remarkable from a growth perspective. The rapid development pace of the platforms becomes even more striking when comparing companies outside the IT sector. The three largest car manufacturers by revenue (fiscal year 2021), namely Volkswagen (founded in 1937/295.7 billion dollars), Toyota (founded in 1937/281.7 billion dollars), and Mercedes Benz (founded in 1926/178.9 billion dollars), appear like participants in a snail race compared to the major platforms.[19] It is no wonder, then, to hear the following sentence from a board member of a global car company: "The question is not how quickly technology companies become car companies, but how quickly we become a technology company." How to work like a technology company and keep up with their pace of innovation thus becomes the central question across almost all industries.[20]

Anyone who still sees IT as a necessary accessory or even as a "cost center" instead of an opportunity for growth and new business fields has missed the point. A look at the platforms—but also at companies that are turning their business model in this direction or complementing it in this way—can provide inspiration. Because: Well copied is always better than poorly invented. What enables such rapid successes? Beyond good and motivated personnel, there are essentially three things: technical infrastructure, network effects, and venture capital.

The production environment of the "platformers" consists largely of an IT infrastructure in the cloud. In the initial phase, it is usually rented from one of the commercial providers. Only over time do the successful ones among them acquire their own data centers (DCs). Google started with about 30 computers provided by the then DC provider Exodus in Santa Clara for 1200 dollars a month.[21] Only later did they build their own capacities. Cloud providers generally guarantee a contractually stipulated 99.9

percent availability of their technology. Since such services are usually held multiple times in geographically separated data centers, this is less spectacular than it sounds. If one fails, another seamlessly and ad hoc takes over the job. This allows even small companies to guarantee their customers the required high availability assurances. The same applies to the complex issue of cybersecurity. Anyone who looks at the long list of international security certifications of Microsoft's Azure Cloud or the DCs of Deutsche Telekom will quickly recognize how significant this advantage is. For many companies, such security standards are otherwise hardly maintainable with economically justifiable means, not to mention the specialized personnel and structural requirements needed for this. All this leads (not only) for the platform customers of the cloud providers to significantly lower initial investments and less capital commitment, which means more money is available for the acquisition of partners and customers. The cost structures of the platforms are therefore generally more advantageous than those of companies whose value creation occurs "internally." Anyone who wants to build a machine factory, a logistics company, or an airline faces entirely different investments, greater risks, and longer dry spells to success.

Platforms often prove to be stable ecosystems with high user loyalty, promising steady growth and continuously attracting new users. This applies—grosso modo—to their various business fields and scales. Good examples of this are social media (Snapchat, Facebook, Twitter, TikTok, …), online retail (Shopify, eBay, Amazon, Alibaba, …), ride and delivery services (Uber, Grab, Lyft, …), job search (LinkedIn, Indeed, Xing, …), and review portals (TripAdvisor, Yelp, Trusted Shops, …). This, of course, does not exclude economic downturns, such as those that occurred in 2022/2023. Especially for the big players, even customers—somewhat exaggeratedly put—are not a scarce resource. Nor are the partners who do business on the platforms. Their markets seem almost infinitely expandable, nearly unlimited. A key reason for this is network effects. What is meant by this?

Broadly speaking, network effects mean that with each additional customer or partner of a platform, its value increases for each of its users, as the example of Uber shows. The company is the world's leading platform for all forms of urban mobility and yet defines itself not as a transport business, but as a "Tech Company."[22] Uber was founded in California in 2009 and already achieved an annual revenue of $17.45 billion in 2021 with 29,300 employees in 72 countries. With just under four percent of the shares, the state investment fund of Saudi Arabia is the largest single shareholder. Uber does not employ drivers but relies on freelancers who sometimes use their own cars. This keeps costs low. On the other side of the chain are customers who want to get from A to B, looking for a driver and using the Uber cloud platform as a matchmaker. The more drivers there are in a city area, the faster the customer gets their ride, which increases Uber's attractiveness for them. The more customers use Uber, the greater the earning potential for the drivers, which in turn increases the platform's appeal for them as well. Due to the existing, cloud-based, and easily scalable IT infrastructure, the costs per new customer and driver grow only marginally compared to the added value achieved. This increases liquidity for Uber with each user. A classic win-win situation. Additionally, Uber has diversified its portfolio over time. It now includes, among other things, delivery services in cooperation with restaurants (Uber Eats), "same-day delivery" services for everyday items or documents (Uber Connect), supplementary offers for municipal transport companies (Uber Transit), and patient transport in collaboration with health insurance companies (Uber Health). This ecosystem is constantly growing. All services are handled over the existing IT infrastructure with a high return on investment (ROI) and optimized with artificial intelligence. It remains a mystery why traditional taxi companies in Germany and elsewhere have legally challenged Uber and tried to sue the company out of the market. Instead, they could come up with innovative business ideas themselves, which has not happened in the industry since the era of horse-drawn carriages. The words of Master Yoda, the chairman of the Jedi High Council, come to mind: "You must unlearn what you have learned." Without this willingness, there is only stagnation.

Despite the best prospects for success, platforms are not without risks. Alibaba, the Chinese counterpart to Amazon, makes the critical importance of network effects very clear in its annual report (2022) to the American Securities and Exchange Commission. Weaker network effects are equated with regulatory interventions by the Chinese government as one of the main business risks.[23] The money earned is also invested in diversification here. Alibaba was founded in 1999 by Jack Ma in Hangzhou. Due to impressive initial successes, the former English teacher was able to secure $25 million in venture capital from the American investment bank Goldman Sachs and the Japanese technology company Softbank in the same year. The turn of the millennium brought the rise of platforms in the USA and revealed a glaring gap in capitalist China—an almost ideal entry point for Ma and his 18-person team. Fifteen years later, Alibaba went public in New York. The Alibaba Group now generates around $134.5 billion in revenue (as of March 2022).[24]

Alibaba's activities are wide-ranging and demonstrate global ambitions, even though most of the money is currently still earned in China. With the motto "Meet, Work and Live at Alibaba," the company formulates a very ambitious claim. It aims to become the center of its customers' daily lives with its activities: "Our vision is that our customers meet, work, and live at Alibaba."[25] Alibaba has continuously broadened its scope and currently claims to be not only a diversified conglomerate of trading platforms but also the largest IT company in China with its cloud services for third parties. Other activities include venture capital, logistics, financial services, wholesale, collaborative working, brick-and-mortar grocery retail, and much more. With AliExpress, consumers can bypass retail and purchase a wide range of goods directly from Chinese producers and distributors worldwide. Alibaba's involvement with Evergrande, the struggling Chinese construction company, is an example that diversification does not always go well.[26]

Platforms not only change business models but also competition. Their tendency to diversify drives them beyond traditional industry boundaries and creates new competitors for companies from outside their established markets. The platforms themselves benefit from the grace of late birth. They were born as economic digital natives and can therefore expand without costly and painful transformations. Google Nest, a company that builds and markets products such as thermostats, smoke detectors, and surveillance cameras for the smart home, is a typical example of new platform competition in traditional industries. Even long-established industry leaders can get into trouble when suddenly confronted with the competitive advantages of platforms. "Caught off guard" sometimes even means the end for solid companies.

Another form of network effects can recently be well observed using the example of WhatsApp in India. There, customers of the online grocery retailer "JioMart" can browse its offerings and place orders within WhatsApp.

Visiting JioMart's homepage is no longer necessary. WhatsApp is becoming a kind of Lieferando with a broader portfolio and different means. What lies behind this is easy to guess: The parent company Meta is building another ecosystem for its subsidiary with the focus on "shopping".[27] Not everyone in this industry will be pleased with the new competition.

Venture capital, alongside infrastructural prerequisites and network effects, is the third essential factor for success. The providers of venture capital (VCs) invested incredible sums in IT companies of all kinds during the IT gold rush around the turn of the millennium in Silicon Valley and elsewhere, despite not always convincing business models. After the bubble burst in 2001 and billions in value were destroyed, they proceeded a bit more cautiously, though not hesitantly. Very high sums are still in play. In 2021, a new record was even set worldwide with investments in start-ups: 612 billion dollars, the highest sum ever. Of this, 311 billion flowed into the USA, with 105 billion going to recipients in Silicon Valley. Asia (175.9 billion) ranked second, and Europe (93.3 billion) came in third.[28]

Platform companies are popular with VC firms. They offer the chance for rapid growth and thus increasing company valuations. Both are what venture capitalists want to see because it makes the potential return on investment enticingly high. Facebook's first investor in 2004 was Peter Thiel, co-founder of PayPal, who put just 500,000 dollars on the table. That earned him 10.2% of the company at the time. In 2005, Accel Partners joined in, having to invest 12.7 million dollars to get 11% of the ten-employee company.[29] Compared to Facebook's current market value, these are pocket change amounts.

Unlike traditional economic forms, VCs in the platform economy focus more on growth than on profits. Grab Holding recorded around 3.5 billion in losses with its 675 million US dollars in revenue in 2021. Nevertheless, the team around founder Anthony Tan made it to Decacorn status. Not only the business model but also the valuation of a company follows different rules in the platform economy. Those who grow quickly have the prospect of becoming one of the big players in their industry. "Blitz-scaling" is the term used when companies grow significantly faster than their market and competition. In other words, they gain market share more quickly. Once you have become a kind of de facto standard in this way, revenue and costs can be balanced in favor of profits. This makes the game so interesting for VCs. WhatsApp, for example, became available in 2009 and was already bought by Facebook in February 2014. The price for the company with its 450 million users was 16 billion dollars. Not a bad result for five years of market presence. At that time, around one million new "WhatsAppers" were joining every day. Mark Zuckerberg, founder of Facebook, commented on the acquisition at the time with the words: "WhatsApp is on the path to connecting a billion people. The services that reach this milestone are all incredibly valuable."[30]

In 2016, Microsoft bought the social network LinkedIn, a forum for professionally oriented users, for 26.2 billion dollars in the largest deal in the company's history to date. That was 8.7 times LinkedIn's annual revenue, a steep price! The platform had entered the market in 2003 and had 433 million subscribers at the time of the acquisition. For the investor consortium around LinkedIn, this marked the end of very successful engagements.[31] For Microsoft, LinkedIn was not only a very favorable opportunity to enter a platform business with an interesting target group with a "big bang". After a series of loss-making acquisitions, the chance also arose to score points with investors once again. For example, the company had paid 9.4 billion dollars for Nokia's mobile phone division in 2014 and 6.3 billion dollars for the advertising company aQuantive in 2007. In 2012, the aQuantive acquisition was written off with 6.2 billion, and the cumulative write-downs for Nokia amounted to 8.55 billion—no small matter even for Microsoft.[32] However, Microsoft is not alone in such failures. Google, for example, sold its 12.5 billion US dollar acquisition of Motorola Mobility in 2012 to the PC manufacturer Lenovo two years later for a quarter of the sum. This made Lenovo the third-largest smartphone manufacturer in the world overnight.[33] It is obvious that the price for acquisitions like WhatsApp and LinkedIn was not based on the physical, "tangible" balance sheet values (tangible assets, such as buildings and inventory) of the acquired companies. The theoretical values (intangible assets) were paid for, which, depending on the situation, only appear on the balance sheet during acquisitions. These include values that are difficult to quantify monetarily and temporally, such as a company's brand, future growth expectations, and the hoped-for general effect on the buyer's future business. This intangible assets effect is particularly pronounced in the platform economy but is also a trend in traditional economic forms. The consulting firm Ocean Tomo demonstrated in a long-term study in 2021 that across all major regional market indices, the valuations of the companies captured therein have shifted very significantly towards intangible assets over the past 25 years. The authors of the study leave no doubt: "Data spanning more than a quarter-century clearly show that the economy has evolved from one where value was measured by 'touch' to one driven by 'thought'."[34]

The fact that some platforms are very large companies does not necessarily make them monopolies. Their end users have a choice and can switch to other providers if dissatisfied. The situation is different for their partners who use platforms as sales or marketing channels.

Switching is more difficult for them, and they are significantly more dependent on the well-being of the platform and the rules set by the operators.[35] Just think of the impact that Uber's expected strategic shift to self-driving cars will have on drivers. The Chinese tech and search engine giant Baidu is already experimenting with such taxis, where the driver is (still) present in the passenger seat for safety reasons.[36] A good example of potential problems between platform providers and their partners is the case of Epic Games against Apple. Epic Games is itself a "vertical" platform and offers games. Among gamers, the company is known for top sellers like Fortnite. In 2021, the Epic Games Store generated $840 million in revenue and had more than 194 million PC customers.[37] The legal dispute with Apple, which began in 2020, was about the presence of Fortnite in the App Store and the conditions Apple attached to it. Devices with Apple's iOS operating system were and are interesting target markets for game providers due to their widespread use. The same applies to Google's Android operating system. Epic had just introduced its new payment system "Direct Pay" for in-app purchases. With its help, it was able to bypass the hefty 30% commission that goes to Apple for such purchases in the App Store. Apple then accused its partner of breach of contract and removed its products from the store. Although Epic received support from industry giants like Microsoft during the subsequent legal battle, it lost the case. Apple was acquitted of the accusation of monopolistic practices on nine out of ten counts. Apple only had to make one concession: App providers are now allowed to inform App Store customers about alternative payment methods. Epic, on the other hand, was ordered to pay Apple 30% of the revenues generated in the App Store with Fortnite since the beginning of the dispute, amounting to over $12 million.[38]

The concept of the platform economy is—unsurprisingly—also appealing to innovative companies outside of IT. A prime example of this is Ping An Insurance, founded in 1988 and mentioned elsewhere, which today is more of a technology conglomerate with an attached insurance company. At the end of 2021, 647 million users were registered on its internet platform. With 227 million customers, at that time, one in six Chinese was a Ping An customer. The creation of a Ping An ecosystem and targeted diversification also play an important role in this case. In addition to the insurance industry, Ping An is active in areas such as banking, asset management, financial technologies (FinTech), healthcare, real estate, automotive services, and smart cities. In December 2021, Ping An Group employed 110,000 people in its technology sectors alone. That was about 11% of the total workforce of 950,000. How seriously technology is taken in the company is also revealed in the organizational chart: Jessica Tan, who joined the Ping An Group from McKinsey in 2013 as Chief Information Officer (Head of IT), became its Deputy CEO and Chief Operating Officer (Head of Operations) in 2018 and is also "Chairman" of Ping An Technology (as of July 2022).[39] It fits that Ping An defined the third decade of its existence under the overarching theme "Exploring Finance & Technology," and the current fourth with "Deepening Finance & Technology."[40]

But Ping An is no longer just a user of technology; it is also a driver of it. At the end of 2021, the entire group had filed 38,000 patents. Its business unit Ping An Technology serves over 3,000 financial institutions and more than 2,000 partner hospitals with its OneConnect Cloud. The platform offers them, for example, a range of interesting AI applications, including modules for analyzing and predicting future disease risks of patients, which can be used for prevention. It is not out of the question that this could also influence individual insurance rates. The creation of an ecosystem with third-party companies is the declared goal.[41]

For the end users of its platform, Ping An provides applications that aim to attract new customers on the one hand and support existing customers in their interactions with the company on the other. Cross-selling plays an important role in this context. Unlike acquiring new customers, it involves selling products to existing customers that they do not yet use.[42] This is associated with lower costs than acquiring new customers and is therefore quite lucrative. Anyone who orders from Amazon knows the principle: If you buy a product, a matching additional product is automatically suggested.

# The End of Centralization?—Crypto Economy and Blockchains

In a podcast by the American consulting firm McKinsey from 2018 on the topic of blockchain, the authors still appear quite reserved regarding possible use cases for this technology. I will explain them in more detail below using the specific example of cryptocurrencies, which should not be equated with the broader term of the crypto economy.[43] The caution of the people at McKinsey is understandable, as there were only a few companies in 2018 that used blockchains for their applications. The authors indicate that they themselves—as well as their clientele—were still in the exploratory phase. In 2018, the total size of the global market for blockchain technology was only 1.57 billion dollars.[44] The current figures on the expected market development look very different. Although they vary depending on the research institute, they all share the commonality that they anticipate a huge market volume with enormous growth opportunities. The Indian Fortune Business Insights sees the market at 7.1 billion dollars worldwide in 2022 and predicts an average annual global growth (Compound Annual Growth Rate, CAGR) of 56.3% to 163 billion by 2029. Researchers from Market Research Future in the USA are also optimistic: They expect a CAGR of 67.54% by 2030, reaching a total of 137.6 billion.[45] Given such expectations, it is not surprising that investors in young companies for blockchain technology and digital currencies have not been deterred by all the uncertainties and volatility of this market. The crisis of the "crypto winter" in the second half of 2022 will not change this permanently. It is characterized by the collapse of cryptocurrencies, mainly caused by scandals and irregularities at their exchanges.[46] In my opinion, this is a highly necessary market correction, and the topic of blockchain will not be entirely affected by it. In the first half of 2022, venture capitalists invested 17.5 billion US dollars. They are well on their way to surpassing the record value of 26.9 billion from the previous year.[47]

Whoever may be right with their numbers: The growth and opportunities are very high even for IT standards. How strongly blockchain applications have established themselves in the few years since 2018 becomes clear with a click on the websites of the major providers of blockchain-as-a-service platforms. Industry giants like IBM, Amazon Web Services (AWS), Oracle, SAP, Alibaba, or Microsoft Azure have discovered this business field for themselves. They offer their customers a cloud platform on a subscription basis for the development and operation of blockchain applications, similar to software-as-a-service, and present numerous reference customers.[48] The necessary hardware and software are provided and managed by the platforms. They also provide their customers with a legal framework that creates the required transparency and compliance for this not easy topic. This facilitates the entry into the crypto economy for companies and reduces financial and legal risks. For neither the technology nor the legal frameworks are easy to understand, nor can the highly sought-after developers for such projects be easily found." Here, IT is once again driving a paradigm shift that will further change our economy.

So what is a blockchain? The term is likely familiar to most of us in connection with cryptocurrencies. Bitcoin, Ether, Binance Coin & Co. are by far not their only applications. However, digital currencies have brought blockchains their media and political attention, pushing all other applications into the background. The extent to which digital currencies are just one of many possible use cases is demonstrated by Ethereum. This is the platform that issues Ether (short ETH). ETH is one of the best-known and second-largest cryptocurrency in the world right after Bitcoin. Quite "incidentally," Ethereum also operates thousands of other blockchain apps. "Welcome to Ethereum. Ethereum is the community-run technology powering the cryptocurrency Ether and thousands of decentralized applications," the company's homepage greets the visitor.[49] The wide range of these apps includes everything from music streaming services to art trading to computer games.

At its core, a blockchain is nothing more than a database with special properties. It is not centrally held—as for instance in a company's cloud—but there are multiple, always identical copies of it distributed across the computers of all participants in a blockchain network. To access one of these databases, each of them needs a cryptographic key. It consists of two mathematically connected parts:

First, a publicly viewable part (Public Key) that allows the individual user to encrypt data and legitimizes them to all others; second, a corresponding Private Key that is known only to the individual user and allows them to decrypt, modify, sign, and send data to other participants.[50] The legitimacy provided by the Public Key does not mean that the user's identity is revealed, which can be a significant advantage. These keys are mathematical masterpieces and are currently practically unbreakable. They ensure that only authorized persons can read or modify the contents of the database, and all others definitively know that the changes were made legitimately.

Every entry in the database—such as sale—builds on a previous entry, with which it is cryptographically linked via a so-called hash value in an immutable manner. Regardless of which participant conducted the sale, it must be confirmed as authorized by the computers of other participants in the blockchain according to a consensus procedure embedded in the algorithm. This could mean that a transaction only becomes valid after approval from, for example, at least 50% of the other participants and is then synchronized with all other distributed database copies. This procedure is called a "distributed ledger," i.e. a distributed accounting system with an identical ledger on all computers. If a change is not confirmed according to the specifications, it remains ineffective. Thus, not only is the storage of the data itself decentralized, but also the decision about its integrity and validity. In a central database in the cloud, a successful hacker could "simply" read or alter its contents. In a blockchain, however, only the hacked copy would be affected in such a case, but not all the others. To be equally successful as with a central database, the hacker would need to gain access to at least 50% of the participating computers in our example and meet some other, not exactly trivial conditions. De facto, this makes the manipulation of a blockchain impossible. There is no single point of failure as it exists in a central database. This makes it much more secure.

Blockchains store changes to their data chronologically in information blocks that are linked together like the links of a chain. This has a very important additional advantage. Every participant can view the entire history of its contents. Thus, blockchains have a kind of built-in auditing, which creates a high level of transparency. A simple example of this would be a blockchain-based real estate register, where every purchase and sale and even the smallest change in ownership can be easily traced. Imagine the amount of paperwork involved for parties distributed across multiple regions or countries—a time-consuming nightmare scenario.

Due to their decentralization and the special kind of trust-building among their participants, blockchains pose a challenge to institutions that have so far functioned as traditional intermediaries, central service providers, recording instances, or regulatory watchdogs for transactions. Why would you still need a real estate agent if the deal can be securely concluded on a platform equipped with the necessary documents in a commission-free, hierarchy-free peer-to-peer network (i.e., equals trading with equals) of a blockchain? Why would you still need a bank if you can transfer money directly worldwide? Why would you still need a notary if their antiquated, time-consuming certification with paper and fountain pen is not nearly as securely protected as a blockchain with its sophisticated "keys" and consensus mechanisms? On the topics of money and currencies, this raises fundamental questions about the role of the state and central banks.

Blockchains thus allow direct transactions to be processed transparently and tamper-proof without an intermediary central authority. They are not suitable for every application, but for many. Decentralized processes with many parties who do not know each other or do not know each other well enough are particularly suitable. In such an environment—unlike in a network with known companies and individuals—the "zero-trust principle" must apply. This means that there is no advance trust; participants must prove their trustworthiness anew each time, and the control mechanisms must be secure. A good example of this is a supply chain. As soon as a product leaves the factory, dozens of parties are involved: airlines, freight forwarders, customs authorities, port companies, warehouse operators, and last-mile delivery suppliers. Anyone who wants to know at any time who did what with their product, whether it was stored properly, or whether the pallet that arrived at the recipient still contains the original supplier's product has many good reasons to consider a blockchain solution. Vaccines are a particularly fitting example of this. For many other products, such as food or car parts, the security and control of supply chains are highly relevant.

A less obvious use case is the trade in intellectual property (IP). Anyone interested in selling or acquiring patents has to do a lot of manual work, pay fees and charges to lawyers and other institutions. There are now blockchain-based, AI-supported platforms that have set themselves the task of capturing the world's patents and making them searchable and viewable. This is associated with easily recognizable practical advantages. But ultimately, it is about much more. Behind this is the idea of a legally secure trading platform for intellectual property, which promises a potential trillion-dollar market that is still in its infancy.[51]

Anyone who is still not convinced of the disruptive potential of blockchain technology should consider applications such as identity management, electronic voting, digital health passes, or digital state money. The market seems unlimited. The topic of digital health passes as a blockchain makes it clear how decentralized systems can give individuals more power over their data. In contrast to the traditional data exchange between doctors and health insurance companies—where the individual must give their basic consent but is excluded from the data exchange itself—the decentralized identity architecture would give them the ability to decide for themselves how their health data is used and who is allowed to do so in each case.

With the release of Bitcoin as the first digital currency on January 9, 2009, the technology opened the door to the vast world of cryptocurrencies. Viewed soberly, they are nothing more than payment systems based on blockchain technology and have so far been issued almost exclusively by private issuers. Anyone who is technically capable can currently (still) do so. For example, a company or an individual could create their own currency using one of the blockchain platforms like Ethereum. Their value is set on "coin exchanges" like eToro, Binance, or Coinbase, similar to stocks. Supply and demand determine the price. There, they can be bought and sold and exchanged for euros, dollars, yuans, etc.[52] Bitcoin has remained a kind of leading currency among cryptos to this day, having prevailed over both earlier eCash attempts and newer versions due to a better overall concept.[53] The motivation for the development of this technology is described in a nine-page white paper by Satoshi Nakamoto, published in 2008: "What we need is an electronic payment system based on cryptographic proof instead of trust, allowing any two willing parties to transact directly with each other without the need for a trusted third party."[54] The paper is surprisingly light on mathematics and therefore easy to read.

Financial institutions may not have liked it at the time, although many of them are now looking for ways to take advantage of the underlying technology. This is also why there is a lot of investment in relevant start-ups. It is still unclear who the developer or developers were who signed the paper under the pseudonym Satoshi Nakamoto. If it was indeed a single person, one cannot deny them a portion of genius, especially for the simplicity of the basic ideas. There are now about 20,000 "cryptos," of which about half are dead, i.e., they are not used and are therefore worthless.[55] In industry jargon, they are somewhat disparagingly referred to as "shitcoins." An example of this is the digital bolivar. Venezuela is trying to use it in the fight against its hyperinflation and suppresses competing coins, but no one wants it.[56] Somehow, its advantages are apparently not clear enough, and somehow trust in the issuer still plays a role in digital currencies despite blockchain, deep in the heart.

The term cryptocurrencies easily leads to misunderstandings. The constant ups and downs of Bitcoin, Ether & Co. on the crypto exchanges occasionally end in severe crashes. They occur more frequently and thus appear quasi-systemic. One may therefore rightly question whether the term "currency," with all its associations of state oversight and targeted monetary policy by central banks, should be applied to them at all. At their core, they represent highly speculative and risky investments and are used as such. On June 18, 2022, the value of Bitcoin fell below one of the psychologically important marks for stock traders. In this case, it was 20,000 US dollars. Ten days earlier, it had been around 30,000 dollars. On January 1 of the year, one Bitcoin was still worth around 47,700 dollars. Thus, 60% of its value was lost in six months. In November 2021, Bitcoin had even stood at the record mark of 69,000 dollars.[57] According to the *Neue Zürcher Zeitung*, the approximately 10,000 active cryptocurrencies destroyed a staggering 1,200 billion US dollars in value in the first six months of 2022.[58] On August 9, 2022, the German crypto bank Nuri, with its 500,000 investors, filed for bankruptcy due to ongoing volatility. At least it participated in the German banks' deposit insurance system, which covers customer assets up to 100,000 euros in such cases, thus preventing the worst for less affluent investors. The collapse of the crypto exchange FTX and its ongoing criminal aftermath marked the tragic endpoint of the 2022 turmoil.[59] In my 35 years in IT, I have witnessed many crashes, although not all were as spectacular and consequential. Extremes and hype are characteristics of the IT industry, as is the fact that things eventually normalize. This usually cleanses the market and advances it technologically and economically. Unfortunately, normalization typically costs a lot of money. Therefore, it is wise to welcome and promote technical innovation while simultaneously separating the hype from the substance and keeping one's head above water.

Despite high risks, cryptocurrencies are enjoying increasing popularity among very different target groups. Their daily trading volume amounts to 107 billion US dollars, around 300 million people use them worldwide, and approximately 18,000 companies accept them as a means of payment (as of the end of July 2022). Initially, progress was slow; four years after the Bitcoin release, there were only about 70 equivalents. Back then—in January 2013—one Bitcoin cost 132 US dollars, by the way. It would have been a good time to get in.[60] The market exploded in 2021/2022 with a doubling of active cryptos to the mentioned 10,000, and the number of active and inactive together amounted to 20,703 at the end of February 2023.[61] The topic received a significant boost in attention in politics, business, and media not only due to the numerical development. Individual states are also warming up to it. El Salvador and the Central African Republic accept Bitcoins as a means of payment. In Honduras, it is being experimented with in a geographically limited area, the government-proclaimed "Crypto Valley." Guatemala also has its test area called "Bitcoin Lake."[62] The brave Ukraine accepts cryptos for donations to support its struggle for survival. Iran announced in August 2022 that it had—allegedly for the first time— conducted an import transaction with Bitcoins worth 10 million dollars.[63] Cryptos ensure anonymity, as participants in the blockchains remain unidentified due to sophisticated cryptography. This has advantages, especially if one wants to circumvent sanctions.

In light of this development, "Decentralized Finance," or DeFi for short, has become a serious economic reality that competes with the established, central bank-controlled financial system. Cryptocurrencies originated as a technology-driven idea with a limited objective (= payment transactions) and are increasingly becoming a topic for established currency regulators thanks to their own momentum. The parallel to other developments in IT is obvious. Just as Mark Zuckerberg, the founder of a network for college students, ended up with Facebook and Meta, or the Google founders Larry Page and Sergey Brin, who only wanted to improve internet search and quickly created a global corporation, Satoshi might be sitting at home today in front of the computer, rubbing his eyes in amazement at the consequences of his idea. Cautious contemporaries might feel a slight shiver at the thought of a financial system without state regulation and without central banks as the supreme currency guardians and guarantors of its integrity. Particularly with regard to Bitcoins, there is additional trouble. Their production

(English: mining) is extremely energy-intensive due to the complex and comprehensive calculations. The annual production of Bitcoins consumes as much electricity as the Philippines in the same period. Environmentally friendly is different, and anyone who uses Bitcoins should consider whether they should look for alternatives. Countries like China, Singapore, and Kazakhstan have already banned or restricted Bitcoin mining for this reason.[64]

In particular, illegitimate use cases, such as money laundering or extortion associated with the anonymity of cryptos, the extreme computational effort, and the associated energy consumption in the production of the coins, tarnish the image. How the topic will develop further depends on how the major economies and their governments will handle it in the future. They will set the agenda. The basic idea of a digital currency is certainly timely and attractive, and the solid technology for it exists. Once again, it depends on how it is used. A valid variant to solve the existing problems is the issuance of state cryptocurrencies. A prominent example of this is China with its advanced plans to introduce the digital yuan. It will literally pull the plug on the already banned private cryptos there.[65]

The EU has also responded and initiated important regulations that take into account the significance of the acceptance of state digital money by the public and the economy. The bait should taste better to the fish than to the angler. The created incentives and securities must be right; otherwise, state digital money will fare like the digital bolivar. The memory of the crisis years 2008/2009, in which central banks prevented the collapse of the world economy and German politics guaranteed savings accounts, clearly highlights the advantages of state money beyond everyday events. What would decentralized miners of cryptocurrencies have done or even been able to do in the face of the extremely dangerous crisis? Looking at the ongoing initiatives to regulate the market, one can assume that at least the developed economies have recognized the potential problems of private currencies and are striving for comprehensive regulation to protect users. In this case, too, the EU is "quite well on track." With the current proposal "Markets in Crypto-Assets (MiCA)" adopted by Parliament and the Commission, numerous aspects of digital payment systems such as crypto-assets, issuers of crypto-assets, and providers of crypto-asset services are receiving a binding legal framework for the first time.[66] The already cited study "Regulation of Cryptocurrency Around the World" by the American Library of Congress lists the current state of regulation in individual countries as of November 2021.[67]

# 5

# IT as Politics by Other Means

On February 24, 2022, the existing peace order in Europe disintegrated. The concept of "change through trade" and securing peace through the creation of mutual economic dependencies proved to be wrong. Today, such dependencies are considered a threat. The concept only worked as long as neither side was willing to prioritize imperial politics over economic well-being and peace. The EU model for post-war Europe has failed in dealing with Russia. For the Putin regime, the expected economic sanctions were secondary to the goal of subjugating the neighboring state of Ukraine through war. A policy of the West, which in hindsight appears naive, ended in disaster. Since then, Russia has been on the path to becoming the Soviet Union 2.0 economically and dependent on China. Contrary to Putin's promise made to the Russian population at the end of 1999, no free market economy that creates prosperity and is even remotely competitive on the world market (with the exception of weapons) will emerge under his

© The Author(s), under exclusive license to Springer Fachmedien Wiesbaden GmbH, part of Springer Nature 2024
J. Müller, *Turning Point*,
https://doi.org/10.1007/978-3-658-46079-2_5

rule. The country will continue to be stuck in raw material exports, as it will lack both foreign capital and free access to modern technologies. Before the war-related sanctions against the Putin regime, Russia imported high-tech goods worth about 19 billion dollars annually, with the largest part of these imports, 66%, coming from the EU and the USA, according to the Brussels think tank Bruegel. Even according to the Russian government, their domestic semiconductor industry is 10 to 15 years behind the current global standard. Skolkovo, the attempt to create their own Silicon Valley in the south of Moscow, launched in 2010 under then-Russian President Dmitry Medvedev, is now in decline.[1] The shift of its economic activities to India, China, Turkey, Brazil, and countries like Iran will not be able to compensate for the loss of Western-oriented democracies as import and export markets. Not to mention the "brain drain" of qualified IT workers, of whom an estimated 200,000 to 300,000 have already found their future abroad.[2] Germany in particular has risked a stark energy policy dependency on Russia over the years. By attacking Ukraine, Putin has renounced Germany's offer in return in the form of economic development, greater prosperity and peace for his country. The Federal Republic has thus exchanged its dependence for nothing; the second part of the equation has simply disappeared.

It is easy to be wiser in hindsight. Nevertheless, the events are remarkable. Putin did not act in secret. He waged wars to enforce his interests in full view of the world, which could not have gone unnoticed in Berlin: the war against Georgia in 2008, the extremely brutal wars against Chechnya until 2009, the occupation of Donbass in 2014, the almost simultaneous annexation of Crimea, interventions in Syria and Libya, not to mention the activities of the Wagner mercenary group in parts of Africa. The failed assassination attempt on Alexei Navalny on August

20, 2020, fits seamlessly into this scenario, perhaps also as one of the domestic political preparations for the later invasion of Ukraine. Despite all this, the German government still granted permission for the construction of the gas pipeline Nord Stream 2 in May 2018 and was willing to further increase our existing dependency on Russia. Americans and Eastern Europeans knew better and vehemently warned against it, only to reap paper-thin excuses and political trickery. A look into a European history book for the period from 1933 to 1939 could have helped and shown parallels. What does all this have to do with IT?

# Gray Areas Between War and Peace

The Prussian military scientist and general Carl von Clausewitz, born in 1780, saw war as the "mere continuation of diplomacy by other means."[3] Looking at the events of hybrid warfare in the first two decades of the twentyfirst century, one can say the same about the use of information technology.[4] IT has become an important means of confrontation between states in both hot and cold wars.

In general, it can be stated that it has significantly changed the way countries interact with each other. The West, here defined as a community of democratic states, has by now gained much experience with the fact that the use of IT has blurred the lines between war and peace. There are various reasons for this: The enormously increased importance of functioning digital infrastructures makes Cyber Warfare, also called Smokeless War, a decisive success factor. The war on the net forms an intermediate stage of escalation, which is cheaper and also carries lesser political risk domestically than Kinetic Warfare, its physical counterpart. The silent war on the net bypasses a large part of the population and therefore requires less public justification than a mobilization that is noticeable to everyone. Cyber War is also popular as a warning to the opponent, as it can be used to send a signal—for deterrence and marking red lines. When studying media coverage of internet confrontations, it is noticeable that it is extremely one-sided and therefore paints a false picture. Due to the flood of news about cyber-attacks on Western governments and companies, it conveys the impression that, apart from the Anonymous Group and a few others, hardly anyone in the West is concerned with cyber-attacks on Russian, Iranian, North Korean, or Chinese infrastructure, nor is preparing or conducting such attacks. Is that really the case? While conventional troop movements, patrols of the Chinese navy through the Taiwan Strait, large-scale NATO maneuvers, or North Korean missile tests are publicly staged, the efficiency of cyber-attacks depends on them remaining "undercover" in terms of targets and methods. The less the opponent knows about it, the worse he can protect himself. The West is by no means inactive, and Western attacks only occasionally come to public attention. The Stuxnet attack on Iranian nuclear facilities in 2010, the successful infiltration of a Dutch intelligence hacker group into the network of the Russian Foreign Intelligence Service SWR in 2014, or the cyber-attack by hackers on a database of the "Ministry of Public Security" in Shanghai in July 2022 are such examples of media resonance.[5] Given the imbalance of public attention, Western states appear to be in a defensive victim role. However, it can be safely assumed that this is not the case.

While NATO held back with direct attacks on Serbia's computers during the Kosovo War in 1998/1999 and formulated the possible targets of such an attack rather modestly from today's perspective,[6] the war in Ukraine shows the huge leap that IT has made as a means of confrontation since the turn of the millennium. The publicly visible activities of Ukraine alone make it clear how comprehensively Cyber War can be conducted in different areas. Two days after the start of the Russian invasion, Kyiv's 31-year-old Minister for Digital Transformation, Mykhailo Fedorov, launched an appeal on Twitter, calling for participation in the "IT Army of Ukraine." The operational instructions for (probably not all) attacks on Russian networks have since been given on a Telegram channel—publicly visible. The channel has around 260,000 subscribers (as of June 2022). The basic idea for this army had existed since 2020, originating from the—albeit defensively oriented and less IT-focused—Estonian Defence League.[7]

Its propagandistically effective part, which also appears on social media, launches attacks on Russian websites and similarly simple targets. The internal part probably consists of Ukrainian defense and intelligence personnel who operate increasingly complex cyber-operations against Russia.[8] The IT Army of Ukraine has powerful allies, even if they cannot be directly attributed to it. Just one day after Putin's invasion, a storm swept over Russian content on the web. Meta, Facebook's parent company, announced that it would no longer accept advertising money from Russian state media. This affected, among others, the propaganda heavyweights Russia Today and Sputnik. Twitter followed shortly thereafter, and on February 26, YouTube announced that it had blocked certain Russian channels.

But that was not all. Washington-based Cogent Communications, whose more than 77,800 miles of fiber optic cables laid through all the world's oceans and continents provide parts of the internet backbone, terminated their services for their Russian customers Rostelecom and TransTelekom as well as for three Russian mobile operators. Backbones, also called Core Networks, are the main connection routes of the internet made up of fiber optic cables that connect its subnets worldwide. Shortly thereafter, the fiber optic operator Lumen Technologies, also American-owned, followed Cogent's example. Google, Apple, Microsoft, Instagram, Spotify, Netflix, Mastercard, Visa, and many others also discontinued or significantly restricted their services. The Shorenstein Center at the Harvard Kennedy School has created a chronology of the back-and-forth of reactions and Russian counter-reactions for the first one and a half months of the war. The list is impressively long, especially when looking at the speed of the reactions.[9] The EU also participated in this type of boycott. Here, Russian propaganda channels, including Russia Today, were shut down. Technology companies around the world thus became a virtual part of Fedorov's army. Large tech companies usually take much more time to position themselves politically due to their own interests. In this respect, these events are already a kind of paradigm shift. After all, they had watched for years as Russia conducted its disinformation campaigns on their platforms. Given the severity of Putin's actions, a "business as usual" approach would have damaged their own image too much, and it can also be assumed that the revenue share from Russia were overall manageable and therefore easier to forgo.[10]

Until the Russian attack, Federow had been occupied with the digitalization of his country's administration and had created the app Diia for this purpose. In the meantime, Diia can also be used to report war damages, apply for financial support as an internally displaced person, or communicate Russian positions and troop movements. However, the minister does not see the activities of his "troop" as limited to operational-tactical and propagandistic areas. As part of his efforts, referred to as "digital diplomacy," he aims to position Ukraine as part of the Western internet world and to displace Russia from it. The latter has already been quite successful for Russia itself. Federow's digital diplomacy also led to tangible results: Two days after the invasion, he directly addressed Elon Musk on Twitter and asked him to make his satellite network "Starlink" available. Contacts with him had existed earlier. A few hours later, the network was available to Ukraine, and only days later, trucks with hundreds of satellite dishes arrived in the country. Elon is indeed a doer. Only those who do nothing make no mistakes. Even though his support through Starlink was less significant in the later course of the war, it was still very helpful. Since May 2022, more than 150,000 people in Ukraine, as well as the government and military, have been using the system every day. President Zelensky spreads his now-famous nightly addresses, among other things, via Starlink. After the liberation of Kherson in November 2022, thanks to Starlink, telephone and internet services could be resumed within a few days. The Ukrainian military uploads images of potential targets via a mobile network enabled by Starlink. The images are sent to an encrypted group chat of the artillery battery commanders. They then decide whether and from where the invaders will be fired upon. This procedure is significantly faster than the method used until then.[11] The satellite network also does not require cell towers, making it harder for its Ukrainian users to be located and targeted by artillery fire. Musk has done similar things for the protest movement in Iran, which began in September 2022. To break through the internet blockades of the mullahs, he provided the people there with around 100 Starlink connections.[12] Brad Smith, the president of Microsoft, promised Federow at the World Economic Forum in Davos to help with the digital reconstruction of Ukraine. In the search for war criminals and the identification of senselessly fallen Russian soldiers, the

New York software company Clearview AI, which specializes in law enforcement, cooperates. Their algorithms derive their ever-growing intelligence from the continuous analysis of a database of over 30 billion (as of the end of 2022) images. This makes it one of the largest worldwide. On March 1, 2022, Hoan Thon-Tat, CEO of Clearview, offered his help to the Ukrainian government in a letter. The determination of geographical origin, age, ethnic composition, and other characteristics of the Russian troops not only allows interesting conclusions for the military and the identification of war criminals. It also provides insight into Putin's domestic handling of the war and which ethnic groups from which regions of the vast country he believes he can most likely send into battle without risking much protest.[13]

Even we ordinary citizens can increasingly not escape the cyber war despite all the secrecy attempts by politics. "You may not be interested in war, but war is interested in you," says an article in the *MIT Technology Review*. The sentence documents the inevitability with which we are affected by the struggle for infrastructure and opinions.[14] The support of Donald Trump by Russian hackers and the disinformation campaigns of the trolls from Saint Petersburg in the 2020 US election campaign are well documented and proven. The head of the Wagner mercenary group also meddled with his troll factories as early as 2016.[15] The elections are a striking example of the activities of foreign services that manipulate the internal affairs of other states through fake news and fake accounts. Similar activities have occurred and continue to occur in other countries, including the EU. In Germany, for example, the network "Reconquista Germanica" is active, which operates disinformation on social media and YouTube channels. It is an alliance of right-wing net activists who were particularly active before the 2017 Bundestag election.[16] The name Reconquista is likely intended to draw a parallel to the gradual reconquest of Spain from its Muslim rulers since the early Middle Ages.

The Russian campaign of 2020 shows a significant increase compared to 2016 when Trump competed with Hillary Clinton for the presidency. According to a March 2021 investigation by the American Intelligence Community (IC), Russia's goal was to "disparage President Biden and the Democratic Party, support former President Trump, undermine public confidence in the election process, and exacerbate socio-political divisions in the USA." The term IC encompasses 18 separate organizations, including the NSA and the CIA.[17] Additionally, and this is remarkable for a report from March 2021, it was hoped that Trump's election would result in less support for Ukraine from the USA.[18] Drawing a connection to the events of February 24, 2022, is speculative, but it could also be, like the assassination attempt on Navalny, an indication of the long preparation for the war.

To a much lesser extent, according to the report, Iran, Venezuela, Cuba, and the Iran-sponsored Hezbollah also attempted to digitally influence public opinion in the USA. A website of the Digital Forensic Research Lab (DFRLab) of the Washington think tank Atlantic Council interactively displays manipulation attempts in the 2020 elections and shows their content and platforms (as far as known) from which they originated. A total of 18 source nations were identified, including Israel. Detours through third countries help with concealment. The recorded posts were shared a proud 29.5 million times.[19]

Attacks on the election infrastructure in terms of falsifying numerical results apparently did not occur. According to the IC's assessment, such manipulations would have been difficult and easily detected. China held back and did not make any visible attempts. Beijing saw no significant difference between the two candidates, so the risk of detection with all its consequences was too great. In general, it applies: Compared to the 2016 elections, not only has the number of "influencers" increased, but also the intensity. The authors attribute this, among other things, to the generally increased importance of such activities in international politics, as well as the use of social media with its easy access to the electorate.[20]

The IC report explicitly states that the attempts to influence the elections in 2016 and 2020 by foreign actors were not only about the elections as an obvious target but also about the long-term anchoring of politically exploitable opinions in public discourse. Popular topics include COVID-19 conspiracy theories, the ban on abortion, and the right to bear arms. The Kremlin orchestrates and coordinates its troll farms,[21] intelligence services, state television, and so-called proxies, who spread their pre-packaged opinions through their "private," unsuspecting social media accounts. Due to advances in "fake faces" technology, very realistic-looking, friendly, and trustworthy-appearing people who do not actually exist now appear on social media. The New York Times Interactive website provides examples of this, which are impressive in every respect and can serve as a warning.[22] Until then, such an appearance on Instagram, Reddit, or elsewhere would not have aroused any suspicion in me. Among the very skillful actors, a clear strategy is recognizable. They are not concerned with the difficult-to-achieve goal of "convincing" the recipients. Instead, the agenda is to sow confusion and doubt through long-term manipulations. Confronted with a cacophony of wild and contradictory claims, no one should know what is right anymore. If there is no longer even agreement on what facts are, then discussions on a factual level become very difficult. If enough doubt is present, people fall into decision paralysis and no longer believe even the credible actors.[23]

The USA is not the only country affected by disinformation campaigns. Its role as a top target results partly from its position in world politics and partly from the deep division of its political system and society. When politics is no longer about achieving constructive goals together but only about preventing what the other side wants, one becomes an easy prey for foreign and domestic actors. The creation of political enemy images, doubts about the legitimacy of democratic institutions, lies like the stolen election, or the defamation and vilification of individuals can be much more easily accomplished in such an environment than in states with moderation and balance. In Germany, there were also massive fake news campaigns in the run-up to the 2021 federal elections, primarily targeting the Green Party and the Christian Democrats (CDU). The investigative journalism network Correctiv has compiled numerous examples and backgrounds for this. One example is a photo of Annalena Baerbock (candidate for the Office of the Federal Chancellor, Green Party) with George Soros at the Munich Security Conference in 2019. Soros is an American billionaire and investor with Jewish roots, who is congratulated on the chancellorship in the text. In this way, a narrative about Soros is evoked, portraying him as a Semitic puppet master. On Telegram, a group called "Destruction of the CDU" founded its own channel, specifically targeting actions against the prominent party member Armin Laschet.[24] Wolfgang Schäuble, the gray eminence of German politics, aptly said in an interview with the popular ARD channel on December 12, 2022: "Technology has accelerated politics."[25] This applies to social media in general and especially to microblogging services like X, alias Twitter. Politicians who post or are mentioned there must have the resources to respond to comments promptly before they find their way uncorrected into the broad mass of users. "Fact-checkers" inevitably lag far behind.

# Big Tech as a Political Actor

As expected, extremists of all stripes extensively use social media platforms in the battle for opinion dominance in cyberspace. After all, they are the most effective carriers and multipliers of information. If false information, half-truths, or lies are repeated often enough, they eventually seem familiar, and "familiarity is not easily distinguishable from truth."[26] The corresponding likes and shares go viral due to their provocative content and gnaw at the foundations of democracy. Fake news and disinformation—whether shared by users consciously or out of ignorance—are not a new phenomenon. Modern disinformation campaigns adopt methods that were already established before the Cold War. What has changed is the mode of dissemination, its global reach, the diversity of topics, and above all, the number and diversity of the authors.[27] Today, right- and left-wing extremists operating on the web use controversial topics or acute concerns of the population for their political purposes, even without the need for foreign involvement. As the cat gets smarter, so does the mouse. The internet now offers good starting points if there are doubts about the truthfulness of information. The website of Correctiv is one such German-language instance. The English-language site Bellingcat falls into the same category.[28] Its operator is based in the Netherlands and has gained international fame for exposing lies related to the downing of a Malaysian airliner over the Ukrainian Donbass in 2014 by Russian-sponsored separatists.

De facto, the platforms have now attained the status of important political actors. At the latest, this has caused IT to completely lose its political innocence. A double-click on the term "platform" opens several windows at once. In addition to the well-known social media giants, they show image boards (forums that do not require registration), video and gaming sites, and messenger services. A special variant of this is the app Telegram by the russian brothers Nikolai and Pavel Durov, the founders of the social medium "VK" (VKontakte), a kind of Facebook, which is popular in Russia. Both were forced to give up their involvement in the service in 2014 because the Russian government had de facto taken it over. Pavel said at the time that Russia was "incompatible" with the internet business and fled the country.[29] On Telegram—also called "Terrorgram" due to its popularity among certain user groups—there is hardly any moderation and strong encryption with optional self-destruction of sent messages, reminiscent of James Bond. This offers participants solid protection from prosecution. Not least for this reason, it has meanwhile developed into a mix of messenger service and social medium. With the help of Telegram's Bot-API and the associated developer software Bot-Father—whose logo shows a stylized image of Marlon Brando—third parties can automatically distribute their content to Telegram users. These users only need to register with the bot with a simple message beforehand.[30] According to its own statements, the app of the company founded in St. Petersburg in 2013, with interim headquarters in Berlin and later in Dubai, is one of the five most frequently downloaded apps worldwide and has over 700 million active users monthly (as of August 2022). This growth, according to the company's statements, is solely due to personal recommendations, as Telegram refrains from promoting its service.[31]

Such unmoderated platforms cast a lot of light and a lot of shadow. An example of the shadow is from Myanmar. In February 2021, the currently ruling junta overthrew the democratically elected government and established a reign of terror. About 1,500 people have been killed and tens of thousands imprisoned in the country with a population of 54 million. A Facebook influencer and junta supporter, Han Nyein Oo, used Telegram for "doxing." This means that he called on junta supporters via various Telegram channels to send him private data of regime opponents. This includes their addresses, personal circumstances, or—for example, in the case of shop and business owners—information about their location. The information flowed abundantly, and Han Nyein Oo then distributed it to his over 100,000 followers. Subsequently, businesses were destroyed, and there were arrests and raids by the police.[32] A kind of modern orchestrated, permanently established Reichspogromnacht of November 9, 1938, when the Nazi mob in Germany raided Jewish shops and hunted Jewish citizens in the streets, among other things.

While moderated media more frequently exhibit errors and missteps, for the prevention and removal of which the platforms allocate considerable funds, the problem with Telegram is systemic and rooted in its fundamental principles. A lamentable condition. But there is also a lot of light. For the same reasons of secured anonymity and unmoderated expression of opinion, Telegram offers a communication platform for dissidents in autocratic regimes to communicate among themselves and with the outside world. A good "light example" of this is the 2022 uprising in Iran, which mutated from a protest to a freedom movement. Telegram informs about the events in the country through several channels with hundreds of thousands of followers. The opposition channel "Iran International," based in London, which also operates conventional television, alone has over 600,000 subscribers. The app was already an important medium during the protest wave of 2017/2018, at a time when it was still little known outside the country. According to statistics from the UN-affiliated International Telecommunication Union, Telegram already had 40 million Iranian users per month at that time. With a population of 80 million people, of whom around 48 million own a smartphone, that is an overwhelmingly large number.[33] It is therefore no wonder that Telegram is in the regime's crosshairs and attempts are being made to suppress its presence in the country.

A special variant is also the social media and microblogging platform Truth Social, which is owned by Donald Trump.[34] After he was banned from the major platforms Twitter, Facebook, and Instagram following the storming of the Capitol on January 6, 2021, he founded his own. It was first available on February 21, 2022. The posts on Truth Social are called "Truth," and reposting or forwarding them is called "Re-Truth." Truth Social is an example of how people with enough money and influence can easily found social networks for political motives and spread strange "versions" of the truth.[35] Elon Musk took a different path with the acquisition of Twitter. After much back and forth, he bought the platform in October 2022 and took it off the stock market to be able to remodel it more easily according to his ideas. It remains to be seen how the battle for the content orientation of the medium will turn out, after a lot of critical personnel either left on their own or were dismissed. However, the turbulence has already had one effect: alternative platforms, such as Mastodon, founded in Germany in 2016 and organized in a decentralized manner, are gaining traction as a result. Whether advertisers will follow the users, however, remains questionable.

The role as political actors is now more or less willingly accepted by the major platforms and blogs. As part of their business strategy, they prefer to position themselves as advocates of free speech, which leaves them with some leeway. However, due to increasing political and regulatory pressure in the USA, the EU, and China, they have decided to moderate their content. Being filters and commentators for news, which is perceived by traditional TV and print media as part of their genuine task, is foreign and burdensome to them. Mark Zuckerberg is not an editor-in-chief and does not write editorials for Facebook's Sunday edition. Eradicating hate messages, excessive violence, fake news, and other offensive content is also very expensive and ultimately can create more trouble than recognition for the platforms. The only question is from which direction it comes. Being part of a political debate is usually not a win but a lose position for a company. From an economic perspective, it is not in the operators' interest to drive certain topics, individual users, or entire groups away from their platforms. Their goal is rather that as many posts as possible go viral, i.e., that they are spread to a large audience by the algorithms and the users themselves, thereby increasing their engagement on the platform. Political correctness of the content is not the same as its ability to go viral. At this point, the interests of the regulators are not easily reconcilable with those of the Social Media companies. Annoyed users whose posts or accounts disappear easily end up with corresponding groups on Truth Social and the like. Are those good alternatives? The platforms live off as many users as possible and the already described network effects. The success of their business model is based not on exclusion but on inclusion. This makes them nolens volens "disinformation-compatible."[36]

Another factor comes into play. The line between extremist content and the right to free speech is not always easy to draw. This is true on the one hand technically, because it is a task not easily solved by the developers of a search or filter software. The alternative is expensive and far too slow human labor. By participating on the web, every extremist can become a publisher in their own way, not always to the delight of everyone else. Without extensive automation, the task is unmanageable given the flood of posts and blogs. Identifying and deleting inappropriate posts must happen very quickly, otherwise, they are shared many times and the whole mechanism remains ineffective. On the other hand, the question arises whether a commercial company is allowed to decide whose opinion is appropriate and whose is not? Where are the limits of this decision-making freedom? In view of these problems, it makes a lot of sense from a state perspective to reach reasonable and practical compromises with the platform operators and thereby strengthen their role on the bright side of power.

# Digital Arms Race

In 2020, the Belfer Center at Harvard University assessed the "digital power" of a total of 30 countries. The main criteria for the study were: offensive cyber power, i.e., the ability to harm the opponent through digital activities, the strength of a country's cyber defense, the maturity of its cyber security industry, and its ability to spread or combat propaganda. For the European Union, the authors had good news: in the overall ranking, three countries made it to the top 10 list: the Netherlands (rank 5), France (6), and Germany (7). In the subcategories "Offensive" and "Defense," Spain and Sweden are also found. Israel did not make it to the top 10, which is more likely an indication of discreet working methods rather than a lack of capability and success.[37]

The same can be assumed for North Korea, whose leader Kim Jong-un has a degree in computer science. It does not appear in the top 10 ranking in any of the three categories, which is unlikely to correspond to reality.

According to the CIA's World Factbook, the country has significant capabilities in the field of cyber warfare, contrary to its otherwise backwardness, and continues to arm itself. [38] Its activities are mixed with criminal machinations to finance the state budget, making North Korea one of the few criminal organizations that have a national flag and a seat in the UN. The authoritarian-led country has its own operational unit for the monetization of cyber operations. Unit 180 for Cyber Financial Operations, located in the Reconnaissance General Bureau (RGB), is tasked with stealing money from institutions and companies beyond North Korea's borders. The unit operates from overseas to better disguise its activities. The theft of cryptocurrency, credit card fraud, extortion with so-called ransomware, and plundering bank accounts are the main activities that yield considerable profits year after year.[39]

In the overall ranking of cyber war powers, the USA is predictably in first place, with China in second place. How long this order will remain so will be shown in the coming years. The battle for global digital supremacy is mainly fought between these two powers. It is a reflection of their general struggle for economic, political, and military supremacy. The "Critical Technology Tracker" of the think tank Australian Strategic Policy Institute (ASPI), which has been studying the global development of technological leadership between countries and regions for years, concluded in March 2023 that China is now superior to the USA in 37 out of 44 high-tech fields. In the IT-dominated category "Artificial Intelligence, Computing and Communications," the study sees America ahead in only three out of ten subcategories: integrated circuits (chips), high-performance computing, and natural language processing. In important fields such as artificial intelligence, machine learning, protective cyber security, and blockchains, China's lead is considered significant in some cases. The EU is technologically ahead of China only in the subcategory of integrated circuits. In contrast, Russia is hopelessly inferior to these three digital powers.[40] The Cold War and the arms race are repeating themselves in IT, only that things are more complicated than before due to the multiple mutual dependencies among the adversaries. The accompanying music is correspondingly shrill. In July 2021, Joe Biden, obviously addressing the usual suspects China and Russia, issued a clear warning: "If we end up in a war, a real war, with a major power, it will probably be as a result of a major cyber-attack."[41] A spokesman for the Chinese Foreign Ministry called the USA "the world's largest source of cyber-attacks."[42] The stage is thus set, the tone established.

The two leading cyber powers invest a lot of money in both the offensive and defensive aspects of cyber war. By the nature of the matter, reliable figures are difficult to determine, not to mention the comparability between them, which must remain unsatisfactory due to different measurement criteria. What can be ascertained should therefore be taken with a large grain of caution. This applies not only to autocratic regimes. There, the information situation is even more difficult than in democracies, where governments have to justify their budgets and have them approved by parliaments. They resort to black budgets in such situations, so their competitors do not get a complete picture of the direction and strategy behind their investments. According to the IT market research company International Data Corporation (IDC), global total investments in cyber security in hardware, software, and services amounted to $151.95 billion in 2021. They are forecast to rise to $223.34 billion by 2025, corresponding to a compound annual growth rate (CAGR) of 10.4%.[43]

The threat situation to which every state is exposed and the associated political implications can be illustrated by a very significant example. In 2014, the US government's personnel administration, in 2015, the health insurer Anthem, and in 2017, the financial service provider Equifax were hacked. All three fell victim to cyber-attacks, with huge amounts of personal data falling into the hands of the perpetrators. US security agencies suspected hackers on behalf of the Chinese government behind the attacks. None of these is an isolated case; they represent only the largest incidents that have come to public attention. On August 4, 2021, William Evanina, a former FBI special agent and later head of the National Counterintelligence and Security Center (NCSC), testified before a US Senate committee that China is likely in possession of about 80% of the personal data of US citizens. They came from the mentioned hacks, but also from attacks on 5G networks, according to Matthew Pottinger, a former security advisor to the Trump administration, in the same hearing. China has thus carried out the most successful criminal action "ever." He assumes that the People's Republic is capable of creating a dossier on "every adult American." With advanced data analysis and close links to other information, the door is wide open to "influence and intimidate, reward and blackmail, flatter and humiliate, divide and conquer." This is how spies and collaborators are recruited.[44] Anyone in Germany who still thinks that 5G technology from China can be used in our networks without concern should not ignore such warnings. The experience with Putin's Russia should serve as a warning.

In China, spending on cyber security is said to have amounted to around $10.26 billion in 2021 and is expected to grow to $21.46 billion by 2025. That seems quite low to me, despite a CAGR of a good 20%. For the US market alone was a substantial $65 billion in 2021.[45] This figure includes private sector spending as well as that of regional government agencies, but not Washington's direct spending, making it difficult to quantify the financial commitment of the USA. The same applies to the People's Republic of China, which relies on close integration between the party, state, and economy and prescribes minimum spending on cyber security for certain types of companies.[46] It occasionally provides money directly for individual sectors of the private economy. Government-mandated cyber security measures can be audited and reviewed by it.[47] Beyond all the numbers, the approach clearly shows how high China assesses its own threat situation and how much the country is striving to close the gap with the United States in the field of cyber security as well. As expected, it usually acts much less shrill than Russia.

## One World, Two Systems

Cybersecurity, however, is only one field in the battle for digital supremacy, as can be seen in the example of the Chinese internet giants. One does not need to be a China expert to notice that there are now respective national counterparts for the major American platforms. They serve the purpose of keeping America at bay and securing the Chinese state's dominance of opinion on the internet. Weibo replaces Twitter, Baidu takes the place of Google, WeChat combines WhatsApp and Instagram in one app, Alibaba is China's Amazon, and PayPal is Alipay there. For TikTok, there is, for a change, no American counterpart; the Californian platform Triller comes closest. In China, TikTok is called "Douyin". Both apps belong to the same parent company, ByteDance, headquartered in the Chaoyang District in the eastern part of Beijing. TikTok focuses on foreign markets and is very successful, while Douyin is for China. TikTok is suspected by some Western governments of spying on their citizens and posing a national threat. Indeed, the company has fired two employees based in Beijing after it became known that they had siphoned off user data.[48] Similar things are happening, albeit on a smaller scale, in Russia. TikTok, Instagram, and YouTube have local equivalents like Yappy, Rossgram, and RuTube. The state-controlled platform VKontakte tries to be Google, and the Russian app store is called RuStore.[49]

The partly long-standing independent existence of the Chinese tech giants in an otherwise tightly state-controlled economy and society does not fit into the government's concept. Specifically, President Xi Jinping prefers companies that are under the influence or in the hands of the state. Therefore, in 2021, the Chinese government publicly targeted, among others, the tech giants Tencent, Alibaba, the internet shopping and delivery platform Meituan, as well as companies in the gaming and cryptocurrency sectors, imposing high fines on some and tightening the legal framework.[50] However, the story has another aspect. At the end of March 2022, 261 Chinese companies were listed on the three largest US stock exchanges, namely the New York Stock Exchange (NYSE), the technology exchange NASDAQ, and the NYSE American. Among them were IT giants like Baidu, Bilibili, JD.com (all NASDAQ), and Alibaba (NYSE). The market valuation of these 261 companies at that time amounted to a total of 1.3 trillion dollars, which is a small proportion relative to the total market capitalization of all companies on the three exchanges.[51] Only eight of these 261 listed companies were state-owned, five of which have since withdrawn from the NYSE (so-called delisting, as of August 2022). They cited low trading volumes in New York as the reason for their withdrawal in similarly worded statements. According to the state Chinese regulatory authority China Securities Regulatory Commission

(CSRC), they took the step voluntarily. China's version of Uber, Didi Chuxing, left the New York floor on June 10, 2022, and moved to the Hong Kong Stock Exchange. A month later, Alibaba announced plans to upgrade and make its Hong Kong-traded shares more accessible to investors on the Chinese mainland.[52] This can be seen as a preparatory step for a future withdrawal of Alibaba from the NYSE and another indication of a trend that has been emerging for some time: the "repatriation" of the stock market activities of Chinese companies. Less well-known companies are also affected. In the summer of 2022 alone, four Chinese companies previously listed only in the US debuted on the Hong Kong Stock Exchange: the financial software provider OneConnect Financial, Tuya, a platform for artificial intelligence, the asset manager Noah Holdings, and the retail group Miniso Group. As early as 2021, the telecom giants China Telecom, China Mobile, and China Unicom were delisted from the US stock exchange after the Trump administration had previously decided to restrict investments in Chinese technology companies. The numbers are rising, even though Chinese companies saw little need for a (secondary) listing in Hong Kong as recently as 2019.[53] It is also clear here: Due to its great importance, the IT sector cannot escape the political trend towards "one world, two systems." The trend continues.

These events reflect a long-standing dispute between the USA and China. An important milestone was marked by the so-called Holding Foreign Companies Accountable Act of December 2020, which threatened all Chinese companies on American stock exchanges with expulsion by 2024. The reason: The People's Republic was unwilling to submit to American stock market regulations. It prohibited local auditing firms from accessing audit documents, allegedly because national security interests were at stake. As a result, private Chinese companies in the USA had no choice but to bow to pressure from Beijing.[54] However, since August 2022, this problem has been fundamentally resolved due to a compromise between the two states, although the implementation and clarification of details are still pending.[55] According to many analysts, this course reflects China's understandable desire to become economically and thus politically more independent from the USA. However, "more independent" does not equate to decoupling from the world's financial markets. Over a number of years, China has successively created facilitations for foreign investors that contradict isolation. Additionally, American investors are not prohibited from investing in the same companies on the Hong Kong stock exchange that they previously invested in New York due to the delisting. The world is disentangling (decoupling), the division into different spheres of influence is underway and will be further cemented by state regulations and legal standards on both sides of the Pacific. China also wants foreign capital in the future, but not on the terms of the USA, rather on its own.[56] Therefore, it is not expected that the movement away from US stock exchanges and towards Hong Kong or Shanghai will end with the agreement of August 2022. This goes hand in hand with China's emancipation from Silicon Valley and generally from Western IT. Leading the way is the Chinese city of Shenzhen with its 20 million inhabitants. Here, no one is dependent on America's Metas or Googles, and certainly not on Tesla, Mercedes, or BMW when it comes to e-mobility—and it is already the world capital of drones. The clustering of future industries, their dynamism, and the freedoms granted by politics there are impressive. The Chinese leadership once again demonstrates its pragmatism when it comes to achieving set goals.[57] It remains to be seen how the country will develop despite its downsides—such as the low birth rate and the suppression of personal and entrepreneurial freedom. High tech is not everything, but without high tech, everything is nothing in our modern world. The described events reflect a fundamental change in geopolitics. The West is no longer able to set the rules for everyone else, as it did in the last century—and for several centuries before that.[58] This message has also reached the global South, as evidenced by the stance on Russia's invasion of Ukraine. Therefore, in the coming decades, we will need to muster a lot of pragmatism and realism to avoid losing the rest of the world as partners. In the end, results count, not intentions. The opposite of "well-intentioned" is not ill-intentioned, but poorly executed.

# The Battle for Chips

The IT industry is closely intertwined worldwide. This is reflected, for example, in the flows of investment capital, the global outsourcing of product developments and IT-related services, or the internationalization of know-how and leadership personnel. Indian or Chinese CEOs are not uncommon in Silicon Valley and can be seen at prominent addresses like Microsoft, Google, NVIDIA, Blackberry, or Adobe. A case in point is the supply chains, particularly those of semiconductors, where the interdependence and fragility of the industry are especially evident. Without these memory chips, processors, and other types of ICs (Integrated Circuits), there would be no modern computers or cars, no medical technology, no satellites, no technical toys, not even a heating system that meets today's control requirements. One might think that whoever has the chips has the power. But it's not that simple.

What distinguishes chips from financial flows is primarily the fact that they are tangible. When money stops flowing due to sanctions, it eventually finds its way to the target like water. Dam breaches, as shown by the current conflict with Russia, occur repeatedly, and holes are hard to plug. In contrast, chip production requires factories and physical components; they are tested, packaged, and sent on a physical transport route after production. This makes them more susceptible to delivery blockages. Complicating matters is the fact that geographically dispersed suppliers with highly specialized know-how for the different stages of the design and production process are involved in their manufacture. They are mainly located in the USA, Europe, Japan, Taiwan, South Korea, and China and cannot be easily replaced. Not to mention that the number of manufacturers and suppliers, except for those of chemicals and gases, is very limited due to the highly capital-intensive manufacturing processes. Semiconductors are therefore a very good example of pronounced global division of labor and a multitude of potential breakpoints in supply chains.[59]

In summary, this means that each of the countries involved in manufacturing is dependent on each of the others, and (at least for now) none can simply turn off the proverbial oil tap without suffering massive damage itself. A finely balanced ecosystem in which, of course, the weights in the global power poker of chip manufacturing are unevenly distributed and which cannot be said whether it will not be hollowed out and destroyed in the future by targeted autonomy efforts of some participating states.

In 2021, the global revenue from semiconductors, depending on what is attributed to the sector, ranged between 595 and 616 billion US dollars.[60] To better understand the magnitude: The draft of the German

Finance Minister from March 2022 for the German federal budget was significantly lower, namely at 457.6 billion euros.[61] Chip manufacturers can be roughly divided into three categories that reflect market activities: foundries, fabless, and integrated device manufacturers (IDM). Foundries are companies that produce semiconductors on behalf of their customers according to their specifications. Fabless, literally "factory-less" chip manufacturers, are those that focus on the very demanding design of their semiconductors and outsource production. IDMs themselves cover the entire manufacturing process, i.e., design, production, as well as testing and packaging. Many of the involved companies operate in more than one of the three categories, so they are not pure plays.

Taiwanese companies accounted for a proud 64% of the global foundry revenue of 107.5 billion dollars in 2021. According to the assessment of the Director of National Intelligence of the USA, Taiwan dominates global chip production.[62] At the top is the giant TSMC, based southwest of Taipei, which alone accounted for 48% of the capacity and 53% of this revenue.[63] South Korea accounted for 18%, China for 8%, and the remaining 11% was divided among the USA and other countries. In total, this means that 89% of global foundry production is located in a geopolitical hotspot between China, South Korea, and Taiwan. In this region, Washington and Beijing are fiercely competing with each other, with China repeatedly threatening Taiwan with military force. The significance of the conflict becomes even clearer when looking at who TSMC produces for. Customers include Apple (with more than 25% of TSMC's revenue in 2021) as well as the American chip giants Qualcomm, AMD, NVIDIA, and Broadcom, to a lesser extent also Intel and the German Infineon. However, this select group also includes manufacturers of cars and consumer goods. If Taiwanese chip manufacturers were crippled, it would have enormous consequences for the availability of semiconductors and thus for the global economy. It is not for nothing that the "U.S.-East Asia Semiconductor Supply Chain Resilience Working Group," abbreviated as Fab4, was founded under the leadership of the USA in September 2022. It consists of companies and governments from Japan, Taiwan, South Korea, and the United States. Its goal: to ensure stable supply chains from the Indo-Pacific region. The President of the Republic of China (Taiwan), Tsai Ing-wen, referred to the initiative as "Democracy Chips," which makes the direction more than clear.[64] We are at a point that the *New York Times* rightly called the "Tech Cold War."

The semiconductor revenue of fabless companies amounted to over 177 billion dollars in 2021. On the global ranking list, American companies play a much more significant role with a 68% market share than Asian ones, yet their supply chains are also heavily dependent on Asia.[65] The US companies Qualcomm, Broadcom, and NVIDIA occupy the top three positions, with the Taiwanese MediaTek in fourth place, and the rest is essentially shared by America and Taiwan.[66] Building a modern chip factory requires investments of up to 15 billion US dollars; this does not even include the not easily available know-how. This explains the fabless companies' enthusiasm for outsourcing to foundries. Among IDMs, as with fabless companies, US manufacturers dominate. Their global market share was almost half in 2021, at 47%, of a total revenue of 332.8 billion dollars.[67] The major US players are Intel, Texas Instruments, Micron, and ADI, as well as the South Korean Samsung, which is also very active in the foundry business. Infineon from Germany is also noteworthy. However, this does not mean that these market giants are autonomous, as they also need suppliers and partly have production done by foundries.

The complex relationships and mutual dependencies in the chip market between countries, manufacturers, and suppliers can be illustrated by the example of Electronic Design Automation (EDA). This involves a bundle of highly specialized, complex software tools for chip design and the corresponding chain of work steps, the design flow. Simply put: the design determines how a chip must be structured to have the desired properties and do exactly what it is supposed to do according to its specification. Depending on the application, such as in a car or a mobile phone, these specifications can be very different. EDA tools are thus an important part of the supply chain. Without them, manufacturing is not possible. The centimeter-sized semiconductors can contain billions of individual components. The design process is highly modular. This includes, for example, the simulation of transistor behavior and chip performance, verification for compliance with the given specifications, preparation for production, and much more. EDA tools provide corresponding software modules, which are smaller, functional units of programs—called libraries in technical jargon—that can be activated depending on the work step. The complexity of these tools can be seen in the fact that their manufacturers spend around 35% of their revenue on research and development and are characterized by a constant chain of technology acquisitions.

The market for EDA tools is dominated by three major manufacturers: Synopsis, Cadence Design Systems, and Mentor Graphics, which has been part of Siemens since 2016. All three are based in the USA.[68] Against this background, it becomes clear what the Trump administration did when it blacklisted the largest Chinese chip manufacturer, SMIC, and 60 other Chinese companies in 2020. This was intended to prevent American companies from supplying necessary equipment for the production of technologically advanced semiconductors to Chinese firms. As a result, SMIC's shares fell by 5.2% on the Hong Kong stock exchange.[69] According to statements from the market research company Gartner, the semiconductor manufacturer HiSilicon, which belongs to Huawei, lost 81% of its revenue due to the Trump sanctions and ended up with only 1.5 billion dollars in 2021.[70]

The measure has the potential to thwart China's Five-Year Plan for developing its own semiconductor industry. The Biden administration went a step further. In August 2022, the president signed the "Chips and Science Act," which aims to further promote the domestic semiconductor industry and make it more independent from foreign suppliers. The scope amounts to $280 billion, of which a substantial $52 billion is for direct subsidies to American manufacturers.[71] That this measure is explicitly directed against China became evident when the US Department of Commerce announced in August 2022 that companies receiving grants from the Chips Act would not be allowed to make investments in China for ten years.[72] It can now also be expected that new American chip factories will no longer be built in the german state of Saxony-Anhalt, but rather in Arizona or Ohio. One can be curious about the $80 billion investments in Europe, including a chip factory in Magdeburg, announced by Intel's CEO, Pat Gelsinger, in March 2022.[73] Less than a year later, he preemptively demanded significantly higher subsidies to start their construction.[74] This can probably be interpreted as a reaction to the Biden administration's "Inflation Reduction Act," with which the USA massively subsidizes the domestic economy—and especially high tech.[75] The decree hits another technological field in the same vein. It is about keeping companies in the USA or attracting them from other countries in the emerging market of "green technology." The EU will have to counter these measures, which are easily recognizable as protectionism.

China has launched a whole series of initiatives to reduce its dependence on Western technologies, particularly in semiconductors. The reason for this is not only the high sums it has to pay annually for such imports. Much more important is the strategic aspect. The USA is trying to block China's access to these high technologies, as is evident from the efforts of Trump and Biden. Accordingly, President Xi Jinping accused the USA and the West of suppressing his country at the opening of the Chinese National People's Congress on March 4, 2023.[76] Beijing's master plan "Made in China 2025" (MIC 2025) is a strategic imperative in this segment. As early as 2015, the government set the goal of increasing the share of domestically produced semiconductors from 10% at that time to 40% by 2020 and to 70% by 2025. For this, it spent a lot of money and also participated in more than 70 relevant domestic companies. So far, it has failed miserably. In 2021, it only reached 16%.[77]

Nevertheless, a chip is not just a chip, and it's not just the quantity that counts. Until mid-2022, it was thought that the 16% ready for series production were only products of the order of 24 nm (1 nanometer = 1 billionth of a meter) and upwards. These are still far from the state of the art of today's 5 and 3 nm chips from advanced manufacturers in other parts of the world, which are used in artificial intelligence and, of course, in the military.[78] Why are these size games important? Simply put: The lower the nm value, the smaller the distance between the transistors on the wafer, the more fit on it, and the less energy is consumed, despite a significant increase in performance. The nm number is thus also a measure of miniaturization, scalability, and efficiency. TSMC delivered the first 5 nm chips to Apple for the A14 Bionic processor of the iPhone and iPad Air in October 2019. The M1 chip of the MacBook from 2022, with which I wrote this book, is a 5 nm chip with 16 billion transistors on an area of only about 125 mm². In the summer of 2022, there was a big surprise. The Chinese manufacturer SMIC presented a new powerful 7 nm chip to the astonished professional world. The analysis team of the Canadian company Tech Insights concluded after thorough investigations that these are 7 nm chips manufactured using a process that largely corresponds to the manufacturing process of the Taiwanese world market leader TSMC. This similarity is no coincidence. For years, TSMC has complained about poaching by Chinese companies that lure engineers and managers with a lot of money.[79] Those who, like TSMC, also produce in a competing country should not be surprised by this.

We have become accustomed to seeing our Western dependence on China as "unidirectional" and only bleak for the future. The West as a victim, fear, and drama sell well in the media. The strategically very important chip market shows that this is not the case in all areas. However, it is also true that none of the European semiconductor manufacturers made it to the list of the world's top 10 in 2021. Incidentally, no Chinese company did either. The field is dominated by the USA, South Korea, and Taiwan. The first European, Infineon, landed in 12th place, followed by STMicroelectronics (Switzerland) with its French-Italian roots in 14th place and the Philips spin-off NXP (Netherlands) in 16th place.[80] In this world of interdependencies, Europe generally faces the choice of whom it wants to be more dependent on: China or the USA, which, unfortunately, raised doubts with Donald Trump about whether they will continue to be a reliable partner in the future, as they have been in the past.

In this situation, the EU launched an ambitious project in 2013. By 2020, Europe's share of global chip production was to be 20%. In fact, it was a meager 10%, even less than in 2013.[81] As if that weren't bad enough, Europe currently produces none of the most technologically advanced chips used in mobile phones or data centers. Half of the semiconductors manufactured in Europe are 180 nm and larger.[82]

This is strongly reminiscent of the fate of China's ambitious goals from 2015, which were also missed by a wide margin. After 2020, the EU's problems became even more apparent in the context of the "chip shortage". The crisis began with the anti-Corona measures in many countries and a simultaneously sharply increased demand for electronic devices. Companies and authorities switched to home office, schools switched to home schooling. Additionally, a drought in Taiwan caused companies like TSMC problems in procuring water for the production of their semiconductors. European key industries such as the construction of cars, medical devices, machinery, and electronics suffered and continue to suffer from a stalling supply of semiconductors. As a consequence, the EU Commission initiated a very detailed monitoring of supply chains. "Caught off guard," as in 2020, should no longer happen, in the future, potential weak points should be anticipated and addressed. The question is how efficient such monitoring can be by an authority that relies on second-hand information, and whether it would not be better organized privately.[83] But one way or another, monitoring is definitely a good thing.

In her State of the Union address to the European Parliament on September 15, 2021, Ursula von der Leyen, the head of the EUs Commission, declared "European Tech Sovereignty" to be a priority goal, particularly highlighting the semiconductor industry.[84] As she had announced, a proposal for a "European Chips Act" followed in February 2022. Its goal is to "strengthen Europe's competitiveness and resilience in the field of semiconductor technologies and applications." It is to be supported by a budget of €43 billion, consisting of private and public contributions. More than two-thirds of this sum are intended as direct subsidies for the construction of chip factories.[85] The EU is thus following the American, Chinese, and South Korean examples and is giving up its reservations about direct subsidies in a strategic area.[86] As expected, this commitment has drawn criticism from "free traders."[87] However, dying principled and beautifully is not an alternative in a technology issue that is vital for Europe's economy. The complex supply chains of the industry will continue to pose a major challenge for the EU—as well as for the USA, China, and others. The European ecosystem of chip production demanded by the Commission President is the right path but can only be achieved in close cooperation with the involved companies and within the framework of a transatlantic-asian partnership. It will be interesting to see what the concrete implementation will look like. One thing is clear: it will take time, and the clock is ticking faster and faster.

## Splinternet—The Fragmentation of the Digital World

The breathtaking success story of the internet has many reasons: the constant advancement of its technology, the fundamental simplicity of its design, the general, worldwide accessibility and availability. Essential also are and were the commercialization of the World Wide Web and the fact that it is not monopolized in the sense of a political orientation. The "tweeting" on the internet represents a multitude of voices, to which even the most eccentric birds can contribute. Beyond bits and bytes, tolerance ranks at the top of its list of success reasons. There is no global censorship authority on the web, and even countries that have such within their jurisdictions do not manage to suppress all tweeting. The net is lively and interesting because it is tolerant. If tolerance dies, the web itself dies.

Henry Kissinger, former US Secretary of State and presidential advisor under Richard Nixon and Gerald Ford, Nobel Peace Prize laureate of 1973, 99 years old and still a sharp observer of geopolitics, sees globalization "under severe pressure." What once began with the opening of China in the era of Mao Zedong and Nixon is now in danger due to tensions between the two world powers as well as between China and other Asian states. The challenge lies in interrupting the dynamics of this development. According to Kissinger, the world is undergoing a profound change, "comparable to the Enlightenment centuries ago." Technological development places higher demands on the leadership abilities of politicians. This applies, according to Kissinger, also to domestic politics, not just in relation to other states.[88]

Two things are remarkable about this statement. On the one hand, it is the demand for technological competence as part of the requirement profile of politicians. Similar sentiments were echoed when Wolfgang Schäuble noted that technology has accelerated politics.[89] Such statements would have elicited puzzled looks at the beginning of my IT career over 30 years ago. It shows the political shift in significance that the industry has undergone. "Technology is the engine that powers superpowers," says a contribution from the Carnegie Foundation.[90] Symptomatic of this is that Big Tech companies like Meta, Google, X and others are much more present in public discourse today than Microsoft, Intel, or IBM were in the last millennium.

In a world where systemic conflicts and societal developments are increasingly co-determined by technology, such competence from politicians would indeed be desirable. Even more important, however, is Kissinger's almost anachronistic demand to interrupt the dynamics of "decoupling"—understood as the opposite of globalization. The disentanglement of the economic and geopolitical landscape hits the IT industry very hard. For example, the American-imposed ban on selling chips with special AI capabilities to China and Russia caused the stock prices of AMD and NVIDIA to plummet by 3.7% and 6.6%, respectively, in one day.[91] The process will take many years and—regardless of its pros and cons in individual cases— will ultimately be of great disadvantage to the world economy.

Naturally, the internet is massively affected in the battle for opinion dominance and informational control. Just like the economy, it is impacted by decoupling. Primarily, it concerns two aspects: first, the censorship and targeted blocking of websites with undesirable content, and second, a complete "shutdown" of the network, which also includes communication tools such as messenger services and mobile communications. Both aspects are—like the battle for chips—a variant of decoupling and part of the digital arms race. Authoritarian regimes are prepared to block their citizens' access to politically undesirable information and to cut off their communication with the outside world. In this way, China has created not only a system of alternative facts but a veritable alternative reality in the national web environment. A parallel universe of propaganda, in which web surfers are forced members. The complete shutdown of the network also has the advantage for dictatorships that in crisis situations—such as mass demonstrations—the coordination of protest movements is made more difficult. Iran demonstrates a particular "artistry" in this regard. Protests against high gasoline prices in 2019 were met by the government with a very successful shutdown, where only four to five percent of external connections remained open. The specialists at NetBlocks described it as "the most severe shutdown" they had "observed in any country in terms of its technical complexity and scope."[92] As a consequence, 80% of Iranians now use VPNs and other tools, even though these have been banned since 2009 and their use is punishable.[93] The Internet Society tracks which states have shut down and who is currently doing so.[94] According to a report by the UN Human Rights Organization from May 2022, there were a total of 931 shutdowns in 74 countries between 2016 and 2021, the majority of them in Asia and Africa. Twelve countries have shut down the network more than ten times during this period; among them, the junta in Myanmar is the worst offender with a total of 15 shutdowns in 2021. It can be assumed that the aim was to cripple protest movements, while censorship may have played a lesser role.[95] Those interested in the technical methods of shutdowns and wanting to learn how to maintain an internet connection even as a layperson are recommended to visit the "KeepItOn Coalition" website.[96] The difficulties governments face in filtering content as a graduated form of shutdown are reminiscent of the problems social media platforms have in fishing out hate messages and other inappropriate content. The isolation of the internet as the ultimate escalation stage has another very significant aspect. Splinternet is the term making the rounds as a threatening future description.

On March 2, 2022, Göran Marby, President and Chief Executive Officer of the Internet Corporation for Assigned Names and Numbers (ICANN), wrote a letter to Mykhailo Fedorov, the aforementioned Minister for Digital Transformation and Deputy Prime Minister of

Ukraine.[97] Behind the cryptic-sounding name of ICANN stands one of the most important organizations worldwide for the administration of the internet. It was created in the late 1990s by the US Congress and belonged to the US Department of Commerce until its privatization in 2016. Its main task is the administration and operation of the Domain Name System (DNS), without which the internet in its current form would not exist. The DNS translates the clear names of web addresses, such as www.amazon. com or www.wikipedia.org, into a structured sequence of numbers. These are the already discussed IP addresses, through which websites are accessed. One can think of the DNS as the phone book of the internet.

Shortly after Putin's invasion of his country, Fedorov asked ICANN to cut off Russia's access to the internet. For this, certain country-specific top-level domains operated from Russia, along with all the country's IP addresses, were to be deleted. Top-level domains (TLDs) are, for example, *.com, *.info, *.biz. A variant of these are geographic TLDs, such as *.de for Germany or *.ru for Russia. If these TLDs are blocked, it means that servers with the corresponding domains are no longer accessible. Additionally, Fedorov had also demanded the deletion of all SSL certificates issued within these domains, among other measures. SSL stands for Secure Socket Layer and is a protocol that encrypts traffic over the internet, making it much more secure. It is also used for emails and other applications. Servers equipped with SSL certificates transform the simple HTTP protocol for communication with them into the encrypted HTTPS. If Marby had fulfilled all the requests, Russia would have been cut off from the internet, and secure communication with Russian servers would have become impossible. Marby rejected Ukraine's request, citing the limits of his capabilities within the highly decentralized administration system of the internet and ICANN's "mission." For Russia, the lack of internet access would not only have been militarily catastrophic. Apart from international payment flows and credit card services, which were later partially blocked by sanctions anyway, parts of the Russian industry, science, healthcare system, and service sector would have been significantly affected. Any company that—perhaps unknowingly— relies on software components hosted on foreign cloud servers for its operations would have been paralyzed. Furthermore, software maintenance, necessary bug fixing, and access to technical documentation and industry forums would no longer have been possible. The fact that these servers are operated by entities in the USA and Europe does not make the situation any more pleasant from a Russian perspective.

The West would, in principle, be able to block the Internet for certain countries without those countries being able to block the Internet for the West. This variant of a shutdown is a powerful weapon in cyber warfare. What the nuclear option represents in conventional warfare, the externally imposed shutdown of a country represents in the Smokeless War. Nevertheless, there would be retaliatory options for states whose Internet would be shut down against their will. The aforementioned fiber optic cables on the seabed, through which data traffic flows between continents, are a very vulnerable target. When the Russian Navy demonstratively planned "maneuvers" off the coast of Ireland in dangerous proximity to the transatlantic submarine cables during their country's military buildup in Belarus in January 2022, Western militaries were extremely concerned. They feared an attack on the fiber optic cables between Europe and the USA. When Putin spoke of unprecedented consequences at the beginning of the invasion, should NATO intervene, he probably did not only mean a possible nuclear escalation but also the severing of the main arteries of global Internet communication.[98]

In light of such scenarios and the rightly or wrongly assumed influence of the USA on ICANN and similar organizations, it becomes understandable why states of different colors declare their desire to have a web administered by themselves. For them it is not only about censorship and the repression of dissidents but also about protecting a critical infrastructure. Should they succeed in building a national network or should the West disconnect certain countries from the Internet, the Iron Curtain once denounced by Winston Churchill would descend in a modern version as a digital Iron Curtain 2.0, be multipolar, and stretch not only through Central Europe but across the entire world. The Internet would become a victim of geopolitics and transform into the Splinternet, the digital version of decoupling. This would be the end of the world computer, the dream of a globally available network. For the world economy, for science, and for general access to information of all kinds, this would be a serious problem. A good example of this is the effect that China's "Great Firewall"—a noble term for the system of state Internet censorship—has on the attitudes of young people there. Their views are becoming increasingly nationalistic because they lack access to international media and communication with the outside world.[99]

Russia and China have been trying for years to build a national network that functions independently of the global web, and other countries are doing the same. North Korea, for example, is even a step further with its own Internet called Kwangmyong (Bright Network), but it also has nothing to lose. While the population is cut off, only a few strictly monitored institutions enjoy access to the global network.[100] Almost all of Kwangmyong's traffic is routed through China, to a lesser extent also through Russia. The only permitted search engine is of North Korean origin. China also relies on its own means in this regard, with voluntary or involuntary help from the Chinese tech giant Baidu, after Google apparently proved too defiant. Controlling a company based in Beijing is much easier than controlling a company based in Mountain View, California. Google publishes its Transparency Report annually, listing government requests to remove content by country and year, along with the reasons for them.[101] The reading is interesting and insightful.

In contrast to disconnecting from the Internet, building one's own data infrastructure is easier to understand. For example, Russia's precaution to ensure that the data of its authorities is provided exclusively via Russian servers results from a legitimate national security interest. The EU is also pursuing similar efforts. With the GAIA-X project, a European cloud infrastructure is to be built, which implicitly also aims for more independence from American cloud services. Its explicit claim is to enable European states to make self-determined decisions about where data is stored, how it is processed and used, and who has access to it under what conditions. All this is to be done in accordance with "European values" and data protection regulations.[102] Not all experiences with the USA have been positive. Trump's behavior towards Europe is a clear and hopefully lasting warning signal.

# Backbone of the Internet

"Spying among friends, that's just not done." The famous quote from Angela Merkel in 2013 refers to a wiretapping scandal in which the American National Security Agency (NSA) tapped the Chancellor's cell phone from the US embassy in Berlin. The uproar was great, especially because it later emerged that her predecessor Gerhard Schröder was also allegedly on the intelligence agency's wiretap list.[103] Who else in Europe had uninvited eavesdroppers remains speculation. According to research by a group of German media, high-ranking politicians from Sweden, Norway, the Netherlands, and France were likely affected.[104] If Angela Merkel was not quite as among friends as she believed, she was not alone. She was in the company of millions of Americans and citizens of other countries who were spied on by the NSA and probably still are. However, not everyone enjoys special treatment like a chancellor. For us ordinary people, eavesdropping is fully automated and without an individually focussed approach. What the affair teaches, however, is that in the world of espionage, everyone can be both perpetrator and victim, friend and foe.

Anyone standing in front of 33 Thomas Street in New York's Lower Manhattan looks at a 29-story high, ugly concrete block without windows. It could be standing on the Death Star of the Empire, as seen in "Return of the Jedi." If a Sith Lord with his red lightsaber were to be seen among the many satellite dishes on the roof while passing by, it would not really be surprising. The building is apparently so fascinating that you can play with its 3D model on the Internet.[105] It has functional sisters around the globe. So, it is not the only one of its kind, although some of them look more attractive.

There is something special about the building, as will soon become clear: The backbone of the internet consists of 486 active undersea cables (as of 2021), which are operated both privately and by public institutions, including the military. Through their fiber optics, 98% of the world's total internet traffic flows. Their length is 1.35 million km, and with the exception of Antarctica, they connect all continents with each other. The network is geographically roughly divided into Trans-Atlantic, Trans-Pacific, America, Intra-Asia, EMEA-to-Asia.[106] Until companies like Elon Musk's Starlink with their thousands of satellites in low Earth orbit can compete with the cables, a lot of time will probably pass. Satellites are more gap fillers and suitable for applications with specific purposes.

Among the major private cable operators, besides many others, are Deutsche Telekom, the Japanese NTT Communications, British Telecom, and especially US companies like AT&T, Lumen, Verizon, Cogent, and Zayo. Meta, Microsoft, Amazon, and Google are also active. They have recently been considered strong market drivers and are involved in this segment as investors.[107] In February 2021, Google commissioned another of its own fiber optic cables for its global Google Cloud. It connects Europe and the USA with a record-breaking capacity of 250 terabits per second. In 2022, Google's "Grace Hopper" fiber optic cable was put into operation. It connects North America, Spain, and the United Kingdom.[108] The market for traditional operating companies, i.e., telecommunications companies, thus gets wealthy competition. Anyone who enters "Connected to United States" as a search term on the interactive "Submarine Cable Map" can see at a glance which country is the center of global internet connections and where their traffic converges.[109] Edward Snowden wrote in his book *Permanent Record* that the "internet is thoroughly American." The infrastructure of the internet is under American control, and 90% of global data traffic runs over technologies that the US government and American companies have developed, operate themselves, and own, "in most cases on American soil."[110] Even though states like China or Russia try to develop alternatives, America, according to Snowden, still maintains its dominance "as the guardian of the main switches, who can turn them on or off almost at will." This could be understood as good news. Worse would be a web controlled by dictatorships. Nevertheless, the finding has left an uneasy feeling since Donald Trump. What does all this have to do with Merkel's phone, the ugly building in New York, and the NSA?

The codename of the skyscraper on Thomas Street is TITANPOINTE. It was given to it by the NSA—it is written in the typical uppercase letters for the agency. AT&T operates one of its largest installations of network switches and routers in the building. This directs data traffic and phone calls between the United States and many countries around the world over the backbone of the internet to their destination. When a data packet is sent, such as an email, it usually passes through several switches on its way to the recipient. An ideal place for an intelligence agency whose task, among other things, is to conduct signal intelligence, i.e., to tap electronic data traffic and phone calls. The NSA has set up an impressive eavesdropping machinery in the building in cooperation with AT&T, which scrutinizes vast amounts of data flowing through its facilities.[111] Of course, official bodies remain silent about this. But from Edward Snowden, we at least know which technical methods are used.[112] AT&T is not the only major internet service provider that closely cooperates with the NSA and other intelligence agencies. The "partner network" and thus the NSA's tapping points span the entire world and consist—voluntarily or involuntarily—of telcos like AT&T, technology companies, large platforms, and authorities. TITANPOINTE has siblings.[113]

Despite all high technology, the backbone of the internet is physically bound. Not everything is wireless. As described, it consists of fiber optic cables laid through oceans and reaching or leaving land at certain endpoints.

This involves very high investments. Even the now seemingly antiquated undersea telegraph cables could only be afforded by the economically and technically leading nations. In the second half of the nineteenth century, Great Britain already laid underwater cables to its overseas colonies like India, New Zealand, and Australia. The first transpacific cables in the early twentieth century led from the USA to Hawaii, Guam, and the Philippines. Canada, New Zealand, and others followed shortly thereafter.[114] These basic structures still determine the ownership and course of the major fiber optic routes today.

The cooperation of intelligence agencies, as in the case of spying on Angela Merkel, when the Danish service assisted the American one, is also not new. British and American intelligence agencies had already cooperated during World War II. Later, this close cooperation was extended to three Commonwealth countries: Canada, Australia, and New Zealand. The group is known as the "Five Eyes." The global infrastructure of the internet is literally on their doorstep. A look at the world map and the docking points of the backbone cables shows that they all have direct access to major fiber optic connections. Each of the five countries is therefore able to tap these on its own territory and make an important contribution to the signal intelligence of the five Western agencies.

The internet is sometimes unpredictable in the routes it uses to direct individual data packets to the recipient. Here too, the NSA can use so-called traffic shaping, a technique for controlling data streams, to help its cause. The Five— and of course other intelligence agencies of different origins—fish enormous amounts of data from the net daily at tapping points like the one in New York. If a preliminary screening indicates interesting content, the corresponding file is forwarded and analyzed in more detail. Depending on the intention, it can be altered or left unchanged and sent back into the large data flow of the net within a few hundred milliseconds. No one notices anything! For example, files can be attached that allow direct access to the recipient's computer or mobile phone as soon as they are opened by an unsuspecting person.

The NSA and its four allies differ from other intelligence agencies in one respect: no one else is so well positioned. When they combine their data, it does not always result in a complete picture, but it does provide a very comprehensive view of global communication content. Through special applications, the services' employees can, for example, enter mobile phone or credit card numbers. As a result, they are shown all collected content and activities of people associated with them. Fortuitous geographical locations along the oceans and historical-economic conditions come together here to their advantage.[115] Even a seemingly ultra-modern phenomenon like the backbone of the internet is overshadowed by history.

"Just plain awesome," enthused an employee from the Five Eyes circle about their data collection and analysis capabilities. Technology can evoke pleasure and enthusiasm. However, both are significantly dampened when one considers the political implications and data protection aspects of monitoring the world's population without concrete suspicions. The mass searching of internet traffic, referred to in industry jargon as upstream collection or passive data collection—as opposed to targeted surveillance of individuals or groups—constitutes a legal violation in many democratic countries or is at least situated in a gray area. Which citizen would like to come under the scrutiny of law enforcement just because they used a term flagged as suspicious by the intelligence service in Google's search engine or in their emails, or clicked on the "wrong" video on YouTube? Who wants to get into trouble because an intelligence service tracks their cookies and sees that visits to websites deemed suspicious are accumulating? The undoubtedly legitimate interest of the state in tracking terrorists, drug cartels, money launderers, child abusers, and extremists can entail dangerous risks and side effects for our freedom.

But should it be that criminals and dictators can use IT capabilities at will to manipulate elections or persecute dissidents, while constitutional states are not allowed to fight back with the same weapons? Democracies perish if they are not determined and resilient in their self-defense. European history after the First World War offers enough teaching material for this, by far not only from Germany. Long past and recent events line up in a long chain of related evidence. Setting an appropriate legal framework with expertise in the spirit of a resilient democracy and ensuring that it is adhered to is an important legislative and executive task.

# 6

# New Hackonomy—The Alternative Platform Economy

Anyone who still exposes themselves to the risk of cracking safes today is not quite up to date. The gang of thieves from the movie "Ocean's Eleven" is a thing of the past. A personal experience of a special kind illuminates why this is so.

Until Wednesday, February 10, 2021, the topic of hacking was rather a marginal phenomenon for me personally. When I reached for my phone in the morning, a message appeared on it, telling me to update the banking app of my financial institution. The subsequent update process and the appearance of the screen seemed quite normal and matched the look I was used to from my bank. However, during the process, which lasted only a few minutes, there were a few small things that seemed "strange" to me. Therefore, I started taking screenshots, just in case I would have to explain to my bank later what had happened. Shortly thereafter, I cut off the internet connection and logged into my bank accounts via my laptop. Result:

© The Author(s), under exclusive license to Springer Fachmedien Wiesbaden Gmbh, part of Springer Nature 2024
J. Müller, *Turning Point*,
https://doi.org/10.1007/978-3-658-46079-2_6

Someone had managed to put on an almost perfect show for the supposed update on my iPhone. About €8,000 was missing from the company account and a small amount from my personal account. The withdrawals were still in progress. Only a call to my financial institution ended the spook, and a few weeks later, they reimbursed me for the damage—also thanks to my screenshots, which proved that I had not acted negligently.

Hacking is increasingly attracting public interest. On the one hand, because more and more spectacular cases of cybercrime are being covered in the media and it is gaining visibility against the backdrop of the now every-day cyber war. On the other hand, because more and more people are personally affected by it. My own experience illustrates this as well as the numerous hacked email accounts of private users. The search term "hacking" produces a list of almost 700,000 websites, videos, and blogs on Google. On Telegram, there are channels like "The Hacker News," which informs its over 122,000 subscribers seriously and up-to-date about the latest events in the scene. Articles in American magazines with headlines like "How to talk to your kids about cybersecurity"[1] also stand for the ubiquity of the phenomenon. A study by the German Association for the Digital Economy (Bitkom) from August 2022 provides insights into the extent and structure of cybercrime in Germany. Theft, espionage, extortion, and sabotage caused a total damage of 223 billion euros to the German economy in 2021. To better contextualize this number: In the same year, the tax revenue of the german Federation only was 313 billion euros. Just two years earlier, the total damage was "just" 110 billion.[2] Cyber-attacks have become a kind of pandemic, prompting the Swiss Zurich Insurance to classify the associated risks as no longer insurable.[3] This rapid growth is also due to improved case recording, but the threats have also actually increased significantly. Notably, attacks from Russia and China have recently surged. 43% of the affected companies identified at least one attack from China, 36% from Russia. At the top of the list of perpetrator typologies, however, are organized crime and gangs. In 51% of the affected companies, the attacks came from this environment. According to Bitkom, the distinction between criminal gangs and state-controlled actors is becoming increasingly difficult. Worldwide, the estimated total damage in 2021 was more than 6 trillion dollars, with not only the number of damages increasing but also the methods becoming more sophisticated.[4] The annual State of Cybersecurity Report by the consulting firm Accenture found in 2022, based on information from more than 4,700 companies worldwide, an average of 271 attacks per company annually. This is an increase of 31% compared to the previous year. Attacks that originated in their supply chains recorded the highest growth rates at around 61%. Why this is the case, we will see later. Christoph, a neurologist and friend of mine, once told me: "If the doctor tells you that you are healthy, he hasn't examined you thoroughly enough." Anyone who believes they have never been attacked just hasn't noticed it. The more sophisticated the know-how and technical resources an attacker must have to penetrate a system, the greater the security. Therefore, the best protection remains prevention and investment in cybersecurity.

# Black Hats, White Hats

A typology of hackers remains an approximation due to the complexity of the phenomenon. The "industry" is roughly divided into two groups: Black Hats and White

Hats. The former ideally represent the bad guys, the latter the good guys. What makes the difference?

White Hats often work on behalf of companies, institutions, or governments to find vulnerabilities in their systems. IT manufacturers use the help of these service providers, who are occasionally referred to as "Ethical Hackers." Some of them publish their results for free on relevant developer sites and internet forums. Here, fame counts, not money. White Hat customers want to protect themselves from hackers and make it more difficult for them to penetrate by specifically eliminating vulnerabilities. This happened in Microsoft's widespread collaboration software "Teams" in September 2022, where White Hats proved their capabilities.[5] Lucky that the discoverers were not others. An example of the targeted search for vulnerabilities on behalf of a customer comes from my own business practice. When I was with my colleagues trying to acquire the first customer for our very young start-up, the customer wanted to play it safe. Building trust takes time. Before signing the contract, he demanded a penetration test. Such tests determine how secure the offered product is against hackers. The customer hired a White Hat company which specializes in such pen-tests. All tests were passed, a weight was lifted off my shoulders, and the deal could be signed. We had proof of quality in hand.

Black Hats use their skills for criminal activities but essentially do nothing different from White Hats. The difference lies not in the technique but in the purpose of their actions. Once they have found a vulnerability, the next step is to write a piece of code that allows them to exploit the "leak" for their intrusion. This code is called an "exploit." There are famous examples of exploits, such as the WannaCry worm, which caused a worldwide stir in 2017. A worm spreads itself automatically from computer to computer within a network, encrypting data in this case. The key to decryption was only available upon payment of a demanded sum. Estimates suggest that up to 300,000 computers in more than 150 countries were infected by WannaCry. A code of this type is called ransomware. The sums paid to hackers in such cases can cumulatively reach billions of dollars. If payment is not made, the complete deletion of all encrypted data is threatened. One can easily imagine what this could mean for a company. In December 2017, the USA and the UK blamed the Lazarus hacker group for WannaCry, which they suspected acted on behalf of North Korea. The group appears under various names such as Dark Seoul or Hidden Cobra.[6] Canada, Australia, and New Zealand joined this suspicion shortly thereafter. Thus, the Five Eyes were once again in agreement.[7]

According to Christopher Krebs, who was responsible for the security of national IT networks in the USA under Trump, 90–95% of hacker attacks are based on known techniques.[8] Hackers are similar to scientists. Most research builds on known methodology but still produces new results. Real breakthroughs, on the other hand, usually come from entirely new methods. If these are not yet known to cyber defense, they can be more easily outsmarted. This is one of the reasons why the legal cyber security community regularly updates each other at global industry events, such as the "Black Hat" conference. The same applies to cyber security: Learning is like rowing against the current; as soon as you stop, you drift back.

Hackers form stable or fluctuating groups with sonorous and changing names that reveal something about the people behind them: Masters of Deception, Fancy Bear, Maze, Legion of Doom, Lizard Squad. The frequently changing names serve, among other things, to confuse law enforcement. Sometimes their forums simply disappear from the Dark Web and reappear under a different name some time later.[9] Hacker communities at the time of their emergence at the Massachusetts Institute of Technology (MIT) in the 1950s and 1960s, around ARPA[10] and the still very young internet, were ambitious about research innovation compared to their current forms. A "hack" at that time referred to a programming achievement that demonstrated inventiveness, style, and technical virtuosity. The individuals involved, who populated the halls of the buildings at Tech Square in Cambridge even at night, proudly called themselves "hackers." That they also had the reputation of technical eccentrics and nerds at MIT did not bother them too much. They organized themselves into "clubs," such as the Tech Model Railroad Club, and saw themselves as a technical elite. Steve Levy aptly titled these early hackers "Heroes of the Modern Computer Revolution" in his cult book published in 1984.[11] How much the meaning of the term has changed!

# Business Models of a Parallel World

Modern hackers are not amateurs; they have sophisticated technical methods and business models. The cliché of lone wolves who roam the web at night in hoodies in their childhood bedrooms, producing green text on a black screen, reflects only a very small part of reality. The scene has become highly professionalized, grown into a lucrative economic sector, and developed highly efficient organizational structures as well as technical and human resources. The business models of the legal economy are often copied and transferred to the shadow world. For example, there are business partnerships, direct and indirect distribution channels for malware, non-profit organizations, and even something like public-private partnerships and much more. Marketing sometimes operates less quietly than one might expect in this milieu. Unlike the legal economy, hackers almost exclusively use cryptocurrencies, which are tailor-made for them due to their anonymity.

In the following, selected cases will be used to examine business models, procedures, and motives, providing insights into the diverse phenomenon of hacking. Given the highly complex reality, it is not always possible to clearly distinguish between the individual models. Black Hats and White Hats occasionally merge into shades of gray.

Some White Hats end up working for an intelligence agency. An example of this is Vupen, a group founded in 2004 that originally came from Montpellier in southern France and later moved to Washington D.C. They won a whole series of hacker awards and were contracted by the NSA, and according to Der Spiegel magazine, also by the German BSI (Federal Office for Information Security).[12] Their founder, the Frenchman Chaouki Bekrar, launched another company called Zerodium in 2015. According to their own statements, they have 1,500 researchers, mostly freelance hackers looking for vulnerabilities in IT systems, who count as their suppliers. Zerodium defines its business on its homepage as follows: "We pay high rewards. Zerodium is the world's leading exploit acquisition platform for advanced zero-day research and cybersecurity capabilities."[13] The term "zero-day" refers to nothing other than the discovery of a previously unknown vulnerability in a system or application somewhere on the web. On Zerodium's homepage, one can read about the types of exploits the company is particularly interested in and which purchase programs are available. Since its founding,

Zerodium has put a total of $50 million on the table for the purchase of vulnerabilities by the end of 2021 and then sold these exploits to interested companies.

One of the competitors, HackerOne ("where hackers learn and earn"), describes itself as the world's largest platform for vulnerability acquisition and claims to have paid out more than $150 million through its numerous bounty programs since its founding in 2012.[14] Viewed soberly, these "payouts" over such long periods are not all that high. However, it is not known how much the platforms have earned from reselling them. The long list of interested customers for the exploits published by HackerOne includes a wide range of companies such as the cloud service Go Daddy, the logistics company UPS, the machinery manufacturer Caterpillar, and the social media platform LinkedIn. They all want to find their vulnerabilities before others do. What benefits trading platforms like Zerodium, HackerOne, or the also significant Bugcrowd is the fact that modern applications are often used millions of times around the world. Operating systems like the iPhone's iOS or Microsoft Windows, applications like Outlook and Office, browsers like Firefox, Chrome, Safari, and Edge are therefore explicitly listed by Zerodium as interesting objects for the purchase of exploits. The greater the distribution, the higher the potential revenues.

The antipodes of these platforms are the criminal market makers. For obvious reasons, reliable facts about their business practices are harder to obtain than for the White Hats. The most significant difference in the business model between them and the "Whites" lies in who they sell their goods to. According a new scientific study, the prices for exploits on both the black and white markets average just over $100, although there are significant surcharges for spectacular vulnerabilities, reaching six- to seven-figure sums.[15] For example, Microsoft offers bounties of up to $250,000 on its own exploit platform. Particularly high-priced are those exploits that affect its mission-critical Hyper-V system. Still, $20,000 can be earned for tips on vulnerabilities in the Xbox Live online gaming platform.[16] Microsoft points out in its Digital Defense Report 2022 that criminal hackers typically develop new exploits only 14 days after discovering vulnerabilities.[17] It is a race against time. If hackers manage to exploit vulnerabilities faster than software manufacturers and their customers can patch them, then the attackers have won.

# Crime as a Service

Offers like Software-as-a-Service (SaaS), Platform-as-a-Service (PaaS), or even Infrastructure-as-a-Service (IaaS) are popular business models of cloud providers. The "As-a-Service" principle is familiar to many end users through the popular Office 365 products from Microsoft or Workspace from Google. They can be rented as cloud services for a monthly or annual fee. The same applies to storage space, such as Dropbox or Apple's iCloud. Hackers have long since adopted this business model. Two of their most successful variants are phishing and extortion as a service.

Phishing is an English portmanteau word that combines Password and Fishing. This already roughly describes its direction. With phishing attacks, criminals try to obtain user information such as passwords, addresses, phone numbers, and other valuable data through fake emails or SMS. Their messages often pretend to come from a known sender. This could be a bank, an authority, or even an internet provider. Sometimes hacked email accounts of private individuals are also used for this purpose. The recipients are, for example, asked to update their user account data on the website of the supposed sender by clicking on the link sent with the message. A popular tactic is also to point out an expiring credit card, whose data needs to be confirmed again, or the information that an account has been locked and one must log in again. The links lead to a website of the supposed sender, often very professionally imitated. If the victim enters their information, it is saved by the perpetrator. In some cases, the affected individuals are then redirected to the legitimate login page of the pretended sender to avoid arousing suspicion.

No one notices anything. Providers of Phishing-as-a-Service (PhaaS) offer their criminal customers "phishing kits" that include everything needed for raids through the internet. Such packages can be purchased for impersonating senders and websites of well-known brands like Amazon, American Express, or PayPal. Among other things, portals for creating and configuring phishing campaigns, cloned websites, and sophisticated security measures that protect the perpetrator from detection are offered. A kind of "one-stop shopping," as is very common in the legal world. Well-known players in this market are the groups BulletProofLink and 16Shops. While the former is from Malaysia, the latter is associated with the Indonesian Cyber Army. In 2021, they offered their kits for $70 per month. Meanwhile, counterfeit payment apps are also part of the portfolio. Not least for this reason, it makes sense to generally download apps only from the app stores of well-known providers like Apple or Google, who review them before they are available in the store. 16Shops is so successful that their PhaaS kits are sometimes used in the dark web just one day after release.[18]

Despite all security measures, Crime-as-a-Service providers occasionally get caught. This happened with the

PhaaS service Robin Banks. Its services were paid for in bitcoins and cost between \$50 and \$200 per month.[19] As can be easily seen, it specialized in the banking market—it counted famous names like Citibank, Santander, and the Commonwealth Bank among its targets. After the American internet and security service Cloudflare caught on to it and blocked it, it switched to the servers of the Russian DDos-Guard. This company is not very critical of its customers' activities and offers "bulletproof" hosting according to its own statements.[20]

Services like Robin Banks always have to live with the risk of being discovered by companies whose websites they have cloned. To avoid negative publicity, the latter try to discreetly get rid of the threat. For this, there is a considerable number of cyber security firms that offer so-called take-down services. The name says it all. Once commissioned, they do everything to block and neutralize the fake website or app. An example of this is Netcraft, which claims to be responsible for around 30% of the worldwide blockades of fake websites, apps, and other fraud methods.[21] Netcraft is an example of the ecosystem of legal firms and business models that have developed due to the growing cybercrime on the web.

The second successful variant of the "As-a-Service" business model is extortion, which continues to be on the rise. This is referred to as Ransomware-as-a-Service (RaaS). More well-known players in the market are the groups Conti, REvil, DarkSide, Lockbit, and DoppelPaymer. The Russian group Hive has gained particular prominence. In June 2022, specialists of the German state of Baden-Württemberg managed to hack their network. As a result, it was dismantled by an international consortium of law enforcement agencies, including those from the USA and Germany, in early 2023. It is said to have extorted and earned more than 100 million

US dollars with RaaS offerings.[22] The price for extortion as a service consists either of a one-time payment, a leasing rate, or a success fee. It's a bit like selling cars: the more often a model is sold, the higher the manufacturer's margin rises. It's no different with exploits. How does it work concretely?

The service is provided by the operator of the RaaS platform on the dark web. They develop or procure the exploit, provide the technical infrastructure, including computing capacities and network, and offer support in case the customer, called "affiliate" in industry jargon, has a technical problem. The malware, short for malicious software, often comes with numerous tools that allow buyers to customize it to their needs. The service also provides the key to decrypt the data after the ransom has been paid. The affiliate has access to the ransomware through a registration portal, which they can download and then inject into their victims' systems. Newer full-service providers also take care of money laundering and ransom negotiations with the victims of the attacks.[23] Avos Locker, a customer of the notorious Russian XSS hacker forum on the dark web, specalizes on the North American market and formulates its services as follows: "We take care of negotiations with the company, hosting the stolen data, payments, and ransomware software. Everything is accessible through our panel. Contact us to apply for access."[24]

Support in ransom negotiations is particularly in demand because these often overwhelm the abilities of the affiliates. Specific job profiles have developed for these services. The IT security firm Kela has specifically scoured the Dark Web for job offers from RaaS forums and achieved interesting results. Not only technical but also other competencies are in demand. Individuals who can conduct negotiations with the victims are particularly well-paid. To extract the highest possible sum, the extortionist must understand the business model, the key players and their interests, the IT landscape and its architecture, as well as the damage potential of the ransomware as precisely as possible. Since most hacker groups do not speak English as their native language, negotiators with very good English skills are indispensable and highly paid. After cyber insurance companies began to employ professional negotiators, the perpetrators quickly followed suit. The offered compensations for intermediaries can exceed one million US dollars or amount to up to 20% of the ransom sum.[25]

The RaaS platforms, similar to the PhaaS groups, offer a starter package that allows buyers to become active with significantly reduced time investment. Besides the quick availability of all resources, the model has another advantage. Even less technically skilled hackers can attack more complex targets with ready-made ransom software and rented infrastructure. The advantages for the operators are also clear beyond the financial aspects of multiple marketing of their software. For example, they do not have to select and evaluate potential targets, approach victims through phishing emails, infected websites, or malvertising. The term is a composite of malware and advertising. It refers to infected advertisements that are usually presented to the user on legitimate websites or in an email in the form of images. If the user clicks on it, their data is lost. The affiliate also takes over the procurement of email addresses and other tasks. This reduces the provider's costs, creates more capacity for acquisition, and expands the addressable market.

RaaS as a service has fueled the market and is partly responsible for the fact that ransom extortion is a very rapidly growing segment.[26] "Extortion Industry" is the term that accurately describes the situation. In 2021, there was reportedly a ransomware attack every 20 seconds worldwide on average. This development has led to some ransomware insurance companies having to cease their business and the prices for policies exploding.[27]

Not least because of this, there is a high willingness on the victim's side to comply with ransom demands. This is nothing but an expression of helplessness and pragmatism, based on a simple calculation. It is generally cheaper to come to an arrangement with the hackers than to invest huge sums in building a new IT system with all its collateral problems. Those who no longer have access to critical data and must manage the resulting business damage are running out of time and their options become very limited. IBM quantifies the damage in a study based on hacker attacks on 550 companies in 17 countries (March 2021 to March 2022): It averages 4.35 million dollars per company. The range varies significantly from country to country. For example, the damage for companies from Turkey was 1.1 million (rank 17) and for companies from the USA 9.4 million (rank 1). Germany ranks fifth in this list with 4.85 million.[28] The following example shows that mutual exchange about threats within an industry would at least help in prevention. Deutsche Windtechnik AG was hit by a cyber-attack in April 2022. It was the third German company in the wind power industry to become a target of extortionists within a few months. Enercon had already reported an incident in February, followed by Nordex at the end of March. In all three cases, the IT systems were up and running again very quickly. No ransom payments have become known.[29] Three months, three hacks within the same industry. That sounds like a wake-up call. If there are not already industry-specific early warning systems for cyber-attacks, it would be high time to establish them. Industry associations are traditionally politically oriented and primarily see themselves as interest groups. Such an alarm system could be a useful digital addition to their service portfolio. Because hackers like to use their methods multiple times for efficiency reasons, especially when the business model involves comparable systems at their victims.

# Cyber Mercenaries

In February 2023, the Israeli company "Team Jorge" claimed to be able to successfully manipulate elections on behalf of politicians and wealthy private individuals through social media, email campaigns, and other electronic means. Allegedly, up to that point, 33 national election campaigns and referendums had been affected, primarily in Africa, Asia, and Latin America. According to Jorge, 27 of these were successful, however that may be measured. For this type of service, the company charges between 6 and 15 million dollars, with account hacking available for as little as 50,000, preferably in cryptocurrencies. Its employees are former Israeli intelligence agents and elite soldiers. A team of investigative journalists named "Forbidden Stories" uncovered the case. Since its founding in 2017, more than 60 media outlets and over 150 journalists from 49 countries have occasionally collaborated within it. In the "Jorge" case, the Israeli daily newspaper *Haaretz,* Radio France, *Le Monde* and the British *Guardian* were involved, among others. From Germany, ZDF, *Der Spiegel* and *Die Zeit* conducted joint research.[30] The reporters posed as potential clients. Some, but not all, of what the owners claimed in conversations with the supposed clients can be verified. Here, as is occasionally observed in sales conversations, the offer and reality do not seem to be congruent.[31] Nevertheless, the incident is very remarkable, as "election manipulation on demand" on this scale and with this approach by privately organized cyber mercenaries with sophisticated technical skills is a new frontier. I also find it disturbing that these are former members of the Israeli security services, whose training was financed by the state and who must have lost their sense of right and wrong due to the lure of big money.

In contrast, since May 2022, a group named A.I.G. has been drawing attention to itself in relevant forums and on its own Telegram channels with a more traditional business model. This is not the well-known American insurance group, but the Atlas Intelligence Group (alias Atlantis Cyber Army). It offers its criminal clients a comprehensive range of tools and exploits as well as services. Stolen information is also part of the portfolio. A.I.G. also carries out commissioned hacks, the targets of which are specified by the client. The group, due to its business model and organization, is a good example of the New Hackonomy and the professionalization of the hacker scene. When a job is secured, it searches on its Telegram channel for the most suitable cyber mercenaries. Information about the project is disclosed on a "need-to-know" basis, similar to intelligence agencies. The individual mercenary knows only what he needs to know. He is neither aware of the big picture of the project nor the identity of the A.I.G. people. A.I.G. itself coordinates among the hired talents. Once the job is done, the mercenary is free for the job market again. This distinguishes the business model from that of many other hacker groups, whose members are more permanent parts of a team.

The Israeli security firm Cyberint has scoured the Dark Web, Telegram, and other information sources, resulting in a report on A.I.G. that provides interesting insights.[32] The group is hierarchically structured and consists of a small core of administrators led by "Mr. Eagle." Their marketing and partly their sales are conducted through easily findable and openly accessible websites, such as the italian Sellix, without the need to dive into the Dark Web. This is different from "normal" hackers. Sellix is one of the secure, anonymous shops specializing in digital products on the Clear Web, where, according to Cyberint, A.I.G. products can also be purchased with a range of accepted cryptocurrencies.[33] A.I.G.'s marketing occasionally takes quite curious forms that one would not associate with hackers. For example, on October 27, 2022, Mr. Eagle advertised the exclusive VIP area of his company on Telegram. VIPs then receive access to, for example, stolen information or exploits before they are offered on the market. A kind of "sneak preview," like in the cinema. The customer can thus get an idea of the value of the information and decide without competitive pressure whether to buy. Mr. Eagle simultaneously informed his audience that his company would raffle three free tickets for the VIP area among the commentators of his post. Two days later, it was announced: "We have contacted the winners of the raffle. Thank you to everyone who participated. Don't be sad if you didn't win; we have decided to give you a special discount. Buy access to Atlas VIP for only $20 instead of $30. Contact @v49m49 for more information."[34]

After successful projects, A.I.G. sends a brief message to their "soldiers" (sic) on Telegram. Communicating successful project completions is important in any company. The posts are adorned with a specially designed icon: "Hacked by AIG." The icon is reminiscent of Intel's former advertising logo "Intel Inside," which was found on numerous Windows computers. A member of the group seems to have once worked in consumer goods marketing. Mr. Eagle proudly and openly advertises his business connections, for example, to a police organization in Germany. Such specialists on-site with access to the right databases—if the claim is true—are valuable and save work. This makes A.I.G. more attractive.[35]

Like some legal companies, A.I.G. operates a form of "giving back to the community." It gives back some of its profits to the public by locating child abusers on the Dark Web and publishing their data—such as name, address, and phone number. Among them was once a German. The group supports the protest movement against the Iranian mullah regime.[36] A.I.G. ees itself as part of the global cyber army that helps Ukraine in its fight against Russia.[37]

Cyber mercenaries are generally on the rise.[38] The A.I.G. group stands out only in terms of organization and style, but not because of its business model. Among the Nation State Actors, i.e., states that hack institutions, companies, or private individuals of other states for various motives, cyber mercenaries are also popular. These often endanger and monitor dissidents, human rights activists, journalists, and representatives of a disfavored civil society on behalf of the state. This model is more dangerous for potential victims than that of permanently employed state hackers because it opens up a much broader spectrum of hacker tools and skills for the clients. In an already very opaque market, security agencies are thus faced with further challenges. Additionally, tracing back to the clients becomes more difficult than if they were acting directly. With this model, the hacker scene has arrived in the era of modern mercenarism.

## Money Heist and Golden Data

Hacks are legion in the financial world. A particularly spectacular case began in the Sultanate of Oman. Although it happened some time ago, it can still be seen as exemplary of the organizational talent and creativity in the New Hackonomy. What happened? In 2013, a very well-organized group stole a total of 45 million dollars from ATMs in over 25 countries almost simultaneously. The hackers acted much more cleverly and with correspondingly greater success than conventional thieves who use explosives. They infiltrated the IT systems of Bank Muscat, stole the data of prepaid credit cards, lifted their withdrawal limits, and produced hundreds of counterfeit cards with the stolen information. These were passed on to accomplices in the USA, Canada, the United Arab Emirates, Japan, and several European countries, who were thus able to withdraw money from numerous ATMs.[39]

Although the operation was highly organized, human fallibility resulted in the identification and conviction of eight 'cashiers,' while the masterminds remained elusive. Two young men found their act so impressive that they posted a selfie of themselves and the counterfeit debit cards on the internet with a boastful text, thus leading investigators to the right track.[40] Without posting on social media, nothing works anymore.

Other hackers have technically further developed the plundering of credit cards as a business model, eliminating human interaction as a weak point and source of risk. The Brazilian Prilex group is exemplary of this, having evolved over time into an APT, an Advanced Persistent Threat, to point-of-sale systems. In 2014, they were behind one of the largest attacks on ATMs in Brazil. More than 1,000 ATMs were emptied with over 28,000 cloned credit cards at that time. Two years later, the group was already significantly more advanced procedurally and in terms of their targets. They now had the entire range of electronic payment systems in focus. This included, among other things, mobile readers for settling bills, such as in restaurants. With their new orientation, they no longer targeted just one aspect of the money flow but the heart of cashless payments. According to an analysis by the internet security firm Kaspersky, Prilex's practice is based on a high level of knowledge about credit and debit card transactions as well as the software used for payment processing.[41] This can be taken as an indication that hackers occasionally recruit from the industries they later target. Due to insider knowledge, their methods become more sophisticated, and even well-secured, more complex targets are thus endangered—a real problem for cyber defense.

Even the pillars of the New Hackonomy are not spared by hackers. This refers to attacks on cryptocurrencies. While the blockchains of Bitcoin (BTC), Ethereum (ETH), and others are very secure, their infrastructure and the trading with them offer large attack surfaces. In terms of infrastructure, the so-called bridges between different blockchains are particularly vulnerable. What is meant by this and what are they needed for? Their technology is complicated, but the principle is simple. Bridges between blockchains function like currency exchange in conventional FIAT currencies such as Euro, Yuan, or Dollar. If a BTC coin owner wants to convert them into ETH coins, they need a connection between the blockchains. Since each of them is based on its own complex ecosystem of different rules and consensus mechanisms, it is not as simple as exchanging Euros for Yuan. This is where the bridge comes into play, which handles the desired transfer along with the associated technical processes. The same mechanism applies if one wants to use multiple blockchains, such as smart contracts, or develop applications that can interact with more than one blockchain. As already mentioned, cryptocurrencies are just one of the many application forms of blockchains.

In August 2022, 190 million dollars in crypto assets were stolen through an exploit of the bridge of the start-up Nomad. The company had touted itself as particularly secure and had outperformed many competitors with this claim. As recently as April 2022, Nomad had raised 225 million US dollars from investors.[42] In its desperation, Nomad published an appeal to the hackers on its website and on X (then Twitter). "Dear White Hat hackers and friends of ethical research who have secured the ETH/ERC-20 tokens. Please send the money to the following wallet address on Ethereum: 0×94A84433101A10aEda762968f6995c574D1b F154."[43] With this euphemistic description of a significant crime and the characterization of the perpetrators as White Hats, a different kind of "bridge" was presumably intended to be built, allowing repentant sinners to undo their actions. Whether this was successful remains to be seen. Attacks on bridges have certainly increased significantly, due to the growing economic attractiveness and practical advantages of interoperable blockchains. A few months before the attack on Nomad, 625 million US dollars were stolen through an exploit of the Ronin Bridge, and shortly before that, 300 million through a hack of the Wormhole Bridge.[44] In June 2022, the crypto bridge Horizon was hit, this time with 100 million dollars in damage. In total, the ten largest registered crypto cases in the first eight months of 2022 alone amounted to well over two billion dollars, although these were not only attacks on bridges.[45]

The increase in criminal energy and creativity since the case of Bank Muscat in Oman had already been evident in the attacks on blockchain bridges. It continued, as a third example of an incident shows. Crypto fraud through deep fake videos has now reached a whole new dimension. Deep fakes are synthetic media in which real existing people are depicted in actions they were never involved in, using artificial intelligence and machine learning. China was the first country to comprehensively respond to this emerging "epidemic situation" and enacted laws to prevent and prosecute deep fake offenses.[46] The typology of these crimes is long and ranges from fake pornographic films with celebrities to financial fraud. In one such case, the world's largest crypto exchange, Binance, was involved to make matters worse. The Brazilian company BlueBenx positions itself on its website as an ecosystem of "blockchain accelerators" that offers its customers regular interest payments on deposits and the provision of liquidity.[47] The company wanted to list its own cryptocurrency "Benx" on Binance and sought direct contact with the spokesperson of Binance to expedite the process. This contact was allegedly established through an intermediary in August 2022, and the Binance representative appeared in a video call with the BlueBenx managers. He agreed to the listing and demanded the immediate transfer of 200,000 dollars and 25 million Benx to the exchange. What happened next caused great dismay among the Brazilians. The supposed intermediary immediately exchanged the 25 million Benx into dollars. All BlueBenx customers were then prevented by the company from withdrawing their deposits, as insolvency would have otherwise threatened.[48] The Binance spokesperson was able to credibly assure after the incident became known that he had not participated in the video call. What appeared on Zoom were images based on old videos of him.[49] These events cast a poor light on the crypto industry. Its mantra of the security of coins leads to the public perception that the fragility of its infrastructure and the risks of human misconduct are overlooked. However, its technical and organizational environment demonstrably still offers large attack surfaces.

At the beginning of 2022, the American bank Morgan Stanley settled with its customers for 60 million

US dollars because it had not adequately protected their data from hackers. Almost 15 million clients participated in the class action lawsuit against the bank. In addition to the loss of image, there was also the—albeit manageable—financial damage.[50] In October of the same year, a court in San Francisco convicted the former head of security at Uber, Joe Sullivan, because the judiciary believed he had covered up a major data theft from 2016. At that time, data from 57 million Uber customer accounts, including about 600,000 driver's license data, were stolen. The manager, who had previously worked for the prosecution of cybercrime at the San Francisco District Attorney's Office and had held responsible IT security positions at Facebook and Cloudflare, had, according to the court, secretly made a non-disclosure agreement (NDA) with the hackers with the backing of then-Uber CEO Travis Kalanick and paid them 100,000 dollars in return. The manager took the money from a fund that the company used to pay White Hat platforms that sold it information about zero-day exploits. The affected customers were not informed by Uber despite the sensitivity of the data. The court considered the agreement with the hackers as aiding in the cover-up of a crime. When Joe informed Travis's successor, Dara Khosrowshahi, about the incident, he fired him.[51]

Both cases show how dangerous a negligent handling of hacker attacks can potentially be for companies and for the responsible individuals. The case of Uber is particularly noteworthy because the allegedly responsible person was personally convicted, even though he apparently acted with the approval of his company. However, his employer did not remain unscathed for long either. In 2018, it was fined 148 million dollars for the same offense.[52]

Data theft is also carried out on behalf of the state, and it is not just about espionage. The MABNA Institute of the Iranian Revolutionary Guards is a well-known player in this field, operating under such resounding names as "Silent Librarian" and "Cobalt Dickens."[53] In 2018, nine members of the group, known by name, appeared under the headline "State Sponsored Data Theft" on the FBI's Most Wanted list. The accusation was: severe identity theft. By that time, 144 American universities and another 176 institutions in 21 countries had already fallen victim to this group.[54] The Verfassungsschutz (Office for the Protection of the Constitution) of the German state of Baden-Württemberg, in a 2021 report, sees MABNA as an actor with high threat potential, through which Iran, alongside Russia and China, has established itself worldwide in the scene.[55] MABNA uses and trades stolen login data from predominantly academic and other scientific research institutions, which it obtains through phishing attacks. MABNA practices spear phishing, a variant that targets selected victims with personally tailored messages, aiming to strengthen their trust through this form of personal address. In some cases previously stolen email accounts of other academic institutions are used in the attacks, further increasing the recipient's trust. The obtained information is sold to third parties and passed on to other Iranian actors.[56]

In the Dark Web, which we will explore more extensively in the following chapter, there are numerous forums that trade in stolen data. It is not just about logins but a whole range of information such as driver's license data, credit card numbers, personal addresses, and bank accounts, all of which can be found in the traders' portfolios. A good example of this is Breach Forums with its telling name. It boasts over a billion stolen data records and does not shy away from attacking competing hacker forums in the Dark Web and stealing their data.[57] Attacks by hackers on hackers are generally not as rare as one might think.[58]

The perpetrators have various ways to monetize or use the data themselves. Besides fraudulent schemes, buyers use them for phishing campaigns, email spams, or brute force attacks. In the latter, users' accounts with known email addresses are systematically and continuously "bombarded" with password combinations until a hit is achieved. No question, brute force is an old-school hacker method, but it is still frequently used. The success is more likely the more personal data is available about the attacked person. Anyone who thinks passwords with their own name, supplemented by the numbers 123 or the children's birth dates, are secure should urgently reconsider their precautions. Such combinations are part of the systematic approach of the attacks.

# Classics of State Hackers: Sabotage and Espionage

Yehida Shmone-Matayim, Unit 8200, is an elite unit of the Israeli army. It got its name from its former address at 8 Haharash Street and 200 Uziel Street in Herzliya, about 30 minutes north of Tel Aviv. It is responsible for "Signal Intelligence," cyber warfare, threat analysis, and decryption, commonly referred to as hacking. Thus, it is the Israeli counterpart to the NSA of the United States. Only much smaller in number, with an estimated tenth of the NSA's budget, but better, according to experts. Unlike the NSA, which was massively hacked by the Shadow Broker group in 2016, the "8200" has never been massively hacked itself.[59] Its approximately 5,000 soldiers are talented young people, mostly aged 18 to 21, who have undergone a rigorous selection process. The selection of recruits begins during their school years. Numerous successful IT company founders were once members of the unit.[60] There are venture capital firms that exclusively invest in start-ups whose founders come from it.[61] Renowned security firms such as Check Point, CyberArk, and the controversial NSO Group, known for its scandalous Pegasus software, emerged from Unit 8200. My long-time Israeli friend Shaul, serial start-up founder, told me a little anecdote about the unit. When he was seeking capital for his young cyber security company, a potential investor asked him where in the 8200 he had served. His answer was: "Bill Gates and I, we were both not there." The matter-of-factness with which he was asked about 8200 shows that the unit is a kind of quality seal and incubator for Israel's very successful tech scene.[62]

As of November 2022, 126 of the over 3,600 companies listed on the American high-tech stock exchange NASDAQ came from Israel. This is quite remarkable for a country with just under nine million inhabitants. The business fields of the Israelis are, with few exceptions, computers, software, telecommunications, and bioscience, with a bias towards cyber security.[63] In 2021, Israel exported cyber security technologies worth 11 billion US dollars—almost ten percent of the world market—and had more unicorns per capita than any other country in the world. A 2018 study of Israeli cyber security founders estimated that 80% of respondents had experience in military intelligence.[64] It is reminiscent of the early days of the modern American computer industry after World War II. There, too, the military had a significant role in building the now globally dominant American IT industry.

The aforementioned Stuxnet espionage and sabotage attack on the Iranian nuclear facilities in Natanz in 2011 is probably the most famous known work of Unit 8200. Another example of successful cyber espionage is the malware "Flame," which, like Stuxnet, is probably also a joint project with the NSA. The similarities between the two viruses in the code are all too obvious. Flame secretly mapped and monitored Iranian computer networks and produced a constant stream of information that could be used for a cyber warfare campaign.[65]

The hacker attack on the SolarWinds Corporation is a case of particular sophistication and a then new methodology. The company from Oklahoma produces an IT monitoring and management software called Orion, which is used by more than 30,000 companies and government agencies worldwide. According to its purpose, Orion has access to IT systems to collect log and performance data. This privileged position and widespread use among large companies and especially American government institutions have made Orion a very attractive target for hackers. It was not difficult for them to obtain the corporation's customer list, as it was available on their website for marketing reasons. Prominent victims of the hack included giants like Microsoft, Intel, and Cisco, consulting firms like Deloitte, the US Department of Commerce, and—embarrassingly—the American Cybersecurity and Infrastructure Security Agency (CISA). This is the agency of the Department of Homeland Security tasked with protecting the US government's computer networks from cyber-attacks. The list can be extended indefinitely. It also includes other American government institutions and private companies where espionage is worthwhile.

What was new about the case was that the hackers were able to insert an exploit into an update of the Orion software in September 2019, which opened the door to the world wide open with a single coup. More than 18,000 SolarWinds customers installed the infected update.[66] According to a report by the Cyber Security Forum Initiative (CSFI), which works closely with the US military and parts of NATO, access to the SolarWinds update server was secured by the password "solarwinds123"—a special kind of negligence.[67] Additionally, it was not until December 2020 that the problem was discovered by the cybersecurity firm FireEye, which was also a victim and aptly named their discovery "Sunburst."

The time from the release of a virus to its discovery averaged 95 days worldwide in 2019. With a long 16 months of "dwell time," as this period is called, Sunburst set a negative record. This gave the virus plenty of time to spread worldwide. Alex Stamos, director of the Internet Observatory at Stanford University and former chief security officer of Facebook, even described the hack as "one of the most effective cyber-espionage campaigns of all time." According to a specialist involved in the investigation, Sunburst was based on new methodology and technology and was very innovative. The technical and organizational details of Sunburst read like a dissertation in the field of hacking.[68]

SolarWinds is a striking example of a supply chain attack. The same applies to the attack on Kaseya, a manufacturer of remote maintenance software, by the REvil Group. However, the goal here was not espionage but extortion with a demand of 70 million dollars. The FBI managed to hack the perpetrators' infrastructure and apprehend one of them. Such attacks are popular because supply chains often involve companies with which their customers have long-standing relationships and whose security measures are sometimes taken more lightly. This was also the case here. A seemingly harmless software update from a well-known supplier for prominent companies and government agencies was unsuspected. It shows once again that Zero Trust, a principle I have already discussed in connection with blockchains, is more than necessary in IT. Even if it contradicts the basic trust we have in dealing with well-known suppliers and their personnel.

Due to the overall picture of this attack, it was suspected early on that the SolarWinds case involved large-scale espionage and that a state-supported group from Russia was at work. Based on its own analyses, Microsoft suspected the Nobelium group (aka UNC2452, aka Dark Halo, …) close to the Russian state as the perpetrator, which later carried out similar attacks.[69] The Biden administration came to similar conclusions after completing its investigations and imposed sanctions on Russian institutions. Research of this kind is not easy, but it is not hopeless either. Every hacker inevitably leaves traces in the network. In the scene, they are called bread crumbs. An example of this is the source code of the virus, which contains technical details that allow conclusions to be drawn about the programmer's language, location, and connections to other known hacks. In the case of SolarWinds, however, the hackers were very good at sweeping up their crumbs, which is why the question of the perpetrators has not been definitively clarified to this day. Given the objective, the selection of victims, the pronounced technical know-how, and the resources used, a purely private group as the perpetrator is quite unlikely. A private-public partnership for criminal purposes or special units of the military or intelligence services are more likely. Often, states are behind it, with the denials of the affected governments usually not long in coming. Even if it is possible to identify hackers in state service, as the FBI regularly does, it is very difficult to apprehend them. For example, on October 15, 2020, an American federal court indicted six named and pictured officers of the Russian military intelligence service for their alleged role in the targeted damage to computer systems around the world. The defendants were accused of a conspiracy to hack aimed at "spreading destructive malware and other disruptive actions for the strategic benefit of Russia" through unauthorized access to the victims' computers.[70] To my knowledge, none of them have been arrested.

# Hacking for a Better World

Hacktivists are people who engage in hacking from their perspective with pure motives and refer to their vision of a better, fairer world. The word is a combination of "Hacking" and "Activist." The portfolio of their activities is very broad. Hacktivists pursue a variety of cyber activities and do not limit themselves to attacks on computer systems. They use IT to ensure freedom of speech and human rights, organize protests online, disseminate information on the internet, or enable opposition members to communicate with each other or with the outside world despite an internet shutdown imposed by unwanted rulers. Namely, maintaining communication is of very high importance for opposition groups, for easily understandable reasons. This works in various ways, such as by providing proxy servers like Psiphon, portable satellite modems like Fallback, unblockable, blockchain-based websites, or peer-to-peer messaging (P2P) apps that, like satellite connections, still function even during a complete shutdown.[71] P2P apps are like WhatsApp, only without a central server. Each individual device that has such an app installed becomes a network node and forwards messages to the next device or all devices with the same app nearby. Even blocking mobile networks does not help against this, as it works via Wi-Fi and Bluetooth technology. Obviously these connections are limited in their range.

One of the best-known hacktivist groups is Anonymous, which, unlike other hackers, seeks public attention due to its ideological and political motivation. Anonymous describes itself as a collective[72] and acts as an apparently loose, worldwide association of hackers with moral claims and not always consistent communication. Central control is not discernible. Anonymous first appeared in the context of the imageboard 4chan, which has been active since 2003. It offers a wide range of topics, from cooking to video games to politics. Registration is not required, and posts are usually made anonymously.[73] Even today, contributions from users who do not want to give their names are referred to as "anonymous." *TIME Magazine* included Anonymous in its 2012 list of the "World's 100 Most Influential People." Dozens of alleged members have already been arrested around the world.[74]

From their statements on the web, an anti-authoritarian, grassroots democratic, egalitarian, anti-capitalist, libertarian, and socially just worldview emerges. One can imagine Anonymous as a kind of moral court with an attached executive. Despite their contrary claims, the group has a tendency towards conspiracy theories. They want to hold companies, governments, and institutions accountable for their allegedly or actually disgraceful deeds, as numerous statements on their Telegram channel and in a kind of manifesto on X (Twitter) demonstrate.[75] There, Anonymous publicly keeps track of their activities on one of their own news channels with over 8.1 million followers (as of November 2022). Their trademark is well known; it is the black-and-white Guy Fawkes mask with its distinctive mustache. Fawkes had unsuccessfully attempted to blow up the House of Lords and King James I of England in 1605. The group is characterized by a high level of cyber activities, ranging from simple shutdowns of websites to targeted attacks on the operational capabilities of institutions, companies, and governments. For example, on October 28, 2022, Anonymous claimed on Twitter in a message to Iran to have hacked the control of Iranian drones. Whatever that exactly means, not much impact has become known at least. The tweet demonstrates the group's enormous self-confidence, but unfortunately, they did not provide proof for the claim.[76] On YouTube, they posted a theatrically made video to Vladimir Putin on the occasion of his invasion of Ukraine. In it, they threaten him with cyber attacks and make the consequences of his actions clear. A YouTube message to the late Iranian President Ebrahim Raisi regarding the oppression of his people is similar in style and content.[77] Both videos are unlikely to have been well received by their recipients; whether they are useful is, however, questionable. For private hacktivists of this kind, it will always be very difficult to inflict serious damage on a highly armed power in cyber warfare.

# The Enemy in Your House

When media report on hacks, they are usually directed against companies, governments, or other institutions. We ourselves generally do not feel truly threatened. This is based on three false assumptions. The first relates to our perception of security when we use "harmless" electronic devices that are connected to the internet. Those who own devices such as a baby monitor, a television, a webcam, a refrigerator, remote heating control, or an alarm system rarely assume that a hacker could take over these devices and gain access to their home network. And yet, they are gateways for black hats. The most popular smart home devices among hackers are televisions and intelligent voice assistants, such as Amazon's Alexa. The AI software is found in countless speakers from the company, all of which bear the model name "Echo."[78]

In some cases, consumers make it more than easy for hackers. Those who do not change the initial password provided by the manufacturer on devices—such as the popular and complex "0000"—are leaving the doors wide open. All a hacker then needs to do is search for the password in the device's user manual on the web. If consumers even consider the security question at all, the second false assumption might be that the manufacturers of the devices have provided sufficient protection. Asking a few precise questions to the seller or critically reading the product descriptions should be part of the standard repertoire when purchasing. If the answers are vague, unsatisfactory, or the topic is entirely missing from the product information, then one should steer clear and look for better alternatives. Often, the devices do not even have antivirus protection or a firewall that can offer some protection against intruders. This makes them attractive and vulnerable to hackers. Finally, one intuitively associates "hacking" only with computers. This is the third false assumption. Anything connected to the web is a potential target. Even an internet-connected coffee machine can be hacked. "If you connect it, protect it," what you bring online, you must protect.

What can happen through hacking of smart home devices, I would like to illustrate with two examples. One night, Ellen and Nathan Rigney, a couple from Texas, woke up. They heard vile curses coming from their young son's room. When they jumped out of bed and turned on the light, the camera of the baby monitor in their room, which had been off until then, was activated. The hacker spoke through the camera: "I will kidnap your baby, I am in your baby's room." The parents ran upstairs to their child but found it safe and alone.[79] They immediately turned off the Wi-Fi in their house, and the spook was over. The story was so gruesomely interesting that it even made it to NBC News.[80] This was a Wi-Fi hack, i.e., intrusion into a house's wireless network. The method seems to have become so popular that you can take courses on it on the internet for under 100 €. More than an undefined "basic understanding of computers" is not required.[81] Nest, the company that made the Rigney family's baby monitor, is quite a big player in the market for smart, connected household devices. Since Nest has been a subsidiary of Google since 2014, the company should also have easy access to advanced security technology. Nevertheless, the device obviously did not have sufficient protection mechanisms. What in this example can still be considered a consequence-free but very nasty attack does not apply to our second example. It goes back to a 2020 project in the IT security course at the University of Applied Sciences Emden/Leer in northern Germany. There, students were given the practical task of hacking a specific type of surveillance camera. The project lasted four months, with the result that the hack worked well, and they could even have built an interface through which anyone—even without good computer knowledge—could attack the targeted camera model.[82] No one wants a hacker to eavesdrop or observe them through their own camera or read stored recordings. But there is another essential point to the project's outcome. Whoever hacks the camera is automatically in the victim's network and has access to everything that is connected: from the door lock to the window security system. Zero trust towards offered smart home devices is an urgent imperative. Not only the camera but also connected refrigerators or the aforementioned coffee machine are good entry points, even if you can't do much with these devices themselves.

The range of possibilities for hackers would be very incompletely described without taking a look at the dark web. It appears in media reports about hackers as a lawless space. But that is only one of its many sides. What lies behind the term dark web, where does it come from? What is it used for and by whom, what is its significance in the big picture of the internet, and why does it evade any regulation?

# 7

# In the Basement Vaults of the Internet

The Roman god Janus looks with his two faces in the first month of our calendar year into both the past and the new year. In ancient Rome, he was the symbol of the duality of future and past, of good and evil, of light and darkness. If one were to search for a symbol for the Dark Web, one could not imagine a better one than him. The Dark Web has a bad reputation. This is no wonder, as many shady characters with their websites lurk within it: drug and arms dealers, child abusers, providers of ransomware and stolen data, counterfeiters, and organ traffickers. However, it also has another, largely unknown side. It is bright, it means for many people the possibility to communicate with the outside world without fear of persecution and to express their opinions freely. The Dark Web is the thorn in the flesh of dictatorships. Anyone who googles "Dark Web" will find almost exclusively negative portrayals. This is not only due to Google's search algorithm. As is often the case when it comes to evaluating technological

© The Author(s), under exclusive license to Springer Fachmedien Wiesbaden GmbH, part of Springer Nature 2024
J. Müller, *Turning Point*,
https://doi.org/10.1007/978-3-658-46079-2_7

achievements, media coverage lacks balance. But what exactly is the Dark Web and how does it differ from other variants of the internet?

# Origins of the Dark Web

The Dark Web (also called the Dark Net) is a so-called overlay network, i.e., a layer of the World Wide Web. It is one of three. The other two are the Clear Web and the Deep Web. We navigate the Clear Web when we visit news portals, hunt for bargains, or watch videos on YouTube. Its contents are unencrypted and clearly visible, hence its name. The Deep Web is often mistakenly equated with the Dark Web. Simply put, everything that requires a login belongs to the Deep Web. If I want to check the status of my bank account or make an online transfer, I have to log in to my bank's website. The same applies if I access one of my data storages—like OneDrive or Dropbox—in the cloud. Once I have logged in, I pass through the door to the Deep Web. The contents beyond this threshold do not always have to be harmless and legal. Everything in the Deep Web cannot be captured and indexed by search engines like Bing or Google. The necessity of logging in keeps them outside the door. The Deep Web is estimated to represent over 90% of the data on the World Wide Web.

The third layer of the web, the Dark Web, is somewhat different. Its contents are always encrypted and thus "darkened." For this reason, they also cannot be indexed and elude search engines. It requires special technology to bring them to light. The common browsers we use for the Clear and Deep Web do not work in the Dark Web. The adjective "dark" actually derives from "invisible," not from "dark" in the sense of dark dealings —analogous to the dark matter of space, which we cannot see but know is there.

When I look at german advertisements for medications, the phrase usually appears: "For risks and side effects, consult your doctor or pharmacist." The side effects of the Dark Net were knowingly accepted at its inception in a weighing of pros and cons. However, the package insert with the corresponding notes came only later. As is often the case in the history of modern computing, the American military stood at the beginning of the Dark Web, more precisely the United States Naval Research Lab (NRL), founded in 1923. It serves the U.S. Navy and its forces for amphibious and land-based operations, the Marine Corps.[1] In the mid-1990s, with the growing popularity of the internet, it became clear that its openness to everyone and its still weak security were not compatible. The activities of its users were easy to track, personal data was poorly protected by today's standards, and communication over the web was anything but secure from eavesdropping and manipulation. Anyone who wanted to change this needed an additional layer to the Clear Web—which was not yet called so—that allowed the advantages of the existing IT infrastructure of the internet to continue to be used while eliminating the described security problems. But why would a government create such a web if it would offer the same advantages to its enemies and ordinary criminals as it would to itself?

Michael Reed, one of the three scientists who developed the technical foundations for the Dark Web at the NRL, answered the question in an email dated March 22, 2022, as follows: The purpose of the Dark Web—which also received its name later—was of an intelligence nature. The idea of being able to communicate from one point of the internet to another point somewhere in the world without being able to find out who was exchanging with whom, when, from where, and about what, was highly attractive to the American military and its intelligence services. In this way, not only would messages and data be securely transmitted, but also informants, agents, and spies, and all those referred to in military jargon as "Forward Deployed Assets," could be protected. The disadvantages of the communal use of such technology with numerous uninvited guests would have been outweighed by the advantages, according to Reed. Moreover, the many other users of the web would give the military more "cover" in the large data stream, which only made things better.[2]

# Journey Through the Night

The new foundational technology by Michael Reed, David Goldschlag, and Paul Syverson was based on the earlier idea of Onion Routing, which was developed to maturity at the beginning of the millennium and will be presented in more detail later. The result was TOR, The Onion Router. TOR is a technology for secure and anonymous data traffic in the Dark Web. To surf in it, you need the TOR browser, which can be downloaded from the Clear Web. The websites in the Dark Web all have the ending "onion," just like those in the Clear or Deep Web have endings like.com,.de, or.info. However, the difference in naming goes further. Its servers and websites do not have meaningful names. They consist of a string of numbers and letters with 56 characters and the domain designation *.onion. The reason for this is, on the one hand, that unlike in the Clear Web, there is no central authority like the aforementioned ICANN with its Domain Name System (DNS) that assigns and manages domain names. On the other hand, Onion addresses are the result of a cryptographic calculation that ensures anonymity. A good example is the web address for downloading the TOR browser. It is in the Clear Web: https://www.torproject. org/download/. The equivalent page in the Dark Web is not so easy to remember. Its address is: http://2gzyxa5i-hm7nsggfxnu52rck2vv4rvmdlkiu3zzui5du4xyclen53wid. onion/. Instead of establishing the connection to the target server as directly and without detours as possible, as in the Clear or Deep Web, TOR does the exact opposite. For the journey through the Dark Web, the Onion network sends the data from the user's computer encrypted to an entry server (Entry Node), also called a guard. The Entry Node encrypts it again and sends it to the next server. This process continues over at least three stations, including the guard. The last station, the exit server (Exit Node), finally sends it to the server where the desired website is running. Each individual computer only knows the address of the computer to which it forwards the data. In this way, the path back to the sender remains in the dark.

Thus, the data has already been encrypted at least three times by the time it reaches the Exit Node. If the website on the target server has a web address that starts with https://—like for example https://www.wikipedia.org/– they are encrypted once more; then even the Exit Node cannot read them when sending. But: If the target site uses the http:// protocol, the data is visible in plain text to the Exit Server. Since you do not know who operates the Exit Server, this poses a risk. It is generally advisable to avoid websites that only use http://. The routing and encryption process makes it clear why it is called Onion technology. Like the layers of an onion, the encryptions cover the data traffic. Because all currently around 9000 TOR nodes are publicly listed (as of November 2022),[3] an Internet Service Provider knows from the address of the guard that its customer is using TOR, but nothing more. The way TOR works means that accessing a website in the Dark

Web can take longer than one is used to in the Clear and Deep Web. Security has its price, "there is no free lunch," as the Anglo-Saxons say. For the sake of completeness, it should be mentioned that besides the Onion network, there are other subnets that are based in the Dark Net, but their significance is less.[4]

# Good and Evil in Virtual Space

Some may be surprised by the fact that Dark Web pages are also operated by such popular institutions as Facebook, the *New York Times,* Deutsche Welle, or the investigative journalists of ProPublica. It may be somewhat less surprising that there is a freely accessible server of the CIA. Why is that so?

If you read the brief history of the TOR project on its website, you might get the impression that Onion Routing technology and the TOR browser, as its most well-known product, were developed exclusively for such noble purposes as protecting dissidents, preventing mass surveillance by intelligence agencies like the NSA, or supporting protest movements, such as the Arab Spring in 2010.[5] This falls under the term "legend formation." Michael Reed explicitly stated in his above-quoted email that such application purposes "were irrelevant to the actual problem we were trying to solve."[6] However, it is true that the applications of TOR have significantly developed in this political direction beyond their original secret and military service orientation. An expression of this is also that the US government—in addition to direct co-financing—has granted the project the tax-exempt status of a non-profit organization.[7]

TOR is a real support for individuals and groups who want to keep an eye on governments of all kinds in very different ways, organize protests, or stand in opposition to "the powerful." This is also evident in the fact that its use is banned in countries like China and Iran. To circumvent these restrictions, the TOR team has, of course, developed a clever technique in the form of a so-called Poison Pill, which upsets the censors. IT is like water; it always finds its way. Facebook has been offering secure access to its platform via the Dark Web since 2014.[8] This also has very practical reasons. Anyone using TOR as their standard browser, i.e., wanting to navigate both the Clear and Deep Web, may encounter problems with a Clear Web page like Facebook's. Facebook and many other websites have security mechanisms that can automatically lock an account as suspicious. For example, if an account is accessed from Paris at 9 PM and from Buenos Aires at 10 PM, it is not unlikely that Facebook will lock it. No user can operate from both locations in such a short time. However, this can easily happen with TOR, with its changing paths from the client to the target server. For a website genuinely programmed for the Onion network, this behavior is completely normal and not suspicious. But even more important is: Anyone who wants to use Facebook as a platform for free expression, communication with the outside world from a dictatorial state, or organizing political protests is poorly served in the Clear Web due to the risks of persecution. Here, the platform's website in the Dark Web helps.

The presence of the CIA in the Dark Web has further reasons.[9] When the intelligence agency published its Onion address in 2019, it justified it as follows: "Our global mission requires that people can access us securely from anywhere. Setting up an Onion Site is just one of many ways we go where the people are." Everything possible on CIA.gov, from the very useful CIA World Fact Book to sharing information to applying for a job at the agency, is also possible on the Onion site.[10] So, anyone who wants to pass documents or other data to the CIA without fear of discovery, send messages, or contact them for any other reason can turn to their secure Dark Web server. Investigative journalists like those from ProPublica have a similar motivation for their presence in the dark web. For their informants, the whistleblowers, Dark Web sites like SecureDrop or BlackCloud[11] are of great importance. SecureDrop is the community site of a number of well-known publications, including the *Washington Post, The Guardian* and *Al Jazeera.* It is maintained by the Freedom of the Press Foundation, on whose board Edward Snowden sits.

Finding websites in the Dark Web is not as easy as we are used to in the Clear Web. Since classic search engines do not work in the Dark Web, one can alternatively search for Onion addresses in the Clear Web. There are several ways to do this. A simple Google search, for example, for "Dark Web Links," brings a long list of different directories and registers of equally varying quality to the screen. However, to access the found addresses, you need the TOR browser. A specific page in the dark web can also be searched directly without the detour through a directory. Anyone who enters "CIA onion site" or "CIA Dark Web Portal" in the search field of Chrome or Safari, for example, will find the dark address of the intelligence agency. However, an operator must want it to be findable in the Clear Web. Another way to access the Dark Web is through chat groups, such as those on the social media platform Reddit, which pays some attention to the topic.[12] However, all these variants are nowhere near as efficient and broad as a normal Google search.

If the search in the Clear Web does not lead to the desired result, surfers can access the directories and databases in the Dark Web directly with the TOR browser, especially since these are often not censored. This means that completely legal Dark Web sites are listed along-side those of terrorists or organ traders. Sometimes the mentioned Onion Sites no longer exist; currency can be a problem. The "Onion Index" and the search engine "Torch," which claims to have indexed over 1.1 million Dark Web pages (as of December 2022), are the most up-to-date.[13] The found links should generally be treated with caution, as one can quickly end up on an illegal site. For example, on one of the illegal Black Markets listed by the Onion Index, you can buy a Swiss Corona vaccination certificate for $199 or the data of a Mastercard for care-free online shopping for $60. Anyone navigating the Dark Web should know exactly what they are doing and how to take appropriate security measures. One of the directory operators puts it this way: "I am not responsible for the content of the websites linked here. 99% of all Dark Web sites that sell anything are scams. Be careful and use your common sense. Every week I get 2–5 emails from people who desperately wanted to make money and fell for scam-mers. Don't be one of them!"

Not every directory service is as clear with its warning as Daniel's. He also censors the captured links and, for exam-ple, states that he has removed 4,445 pedophile and 16,600 fraudulent sites.[14] The Clear Web-accessible site "Dark Web Wiki" has also made it its mission to publish known scam sites, maintaining a user-commented, somewhat updated, and fairly long directory.[15] However, one can assume that this list only captures a small part of the "dirty" sites. But the risk of fraud is not the only concern. In the dark web, one can quickly catch a nasty virus or come into contact with people one would rather avoid by clicking carelessly or downloading files. Chat rooms are explicitly discouraged. Some operators of illegal sites communicate their server addresses directly to the contacts they want to see on their site for security and efficiency reasons. Therefore, they are hardly findable. A kind of "by-invitation-only" method, where access to the sites is also password-protected. One way to contact the operators is through the mentioned chat rooms, some Telegram channels, or Onion email programs like the swiss-based Proton Mail.

# Cracks in the Web

"There is a crack in everything, that's how the light gets in," sings Leonard Cohen in his song "Anthem." Finding such cracks in the Dark Web and bringing light into its dark alleys is no easy task. Given the increasing sophistication of the Onion network, law enforcement agencies face significant challenges. Nevertheless, there are frequent reports of the shutdown of criminal websites, whose operators could be identified and, less frequently, arrested. For example, on April 5, 2022, the german Federal Criminal Police Office (Bundeskriminalamt, BKA) announced that it had shut down the "world's largest" and oldest illegal Dark Web marketplace, the Russian-speaking trading platform "Hydra Market," and seized the server infrastructure located in Germany. Dmitry Olegovich Pavlov was identified as the operator, whom the Russian judiciary arrested in Moscow in the same month.[16] Bitcoins worth the equivalent of 23 million euros were secured on Hydra's servers. Hydra had been active since 2015. The platform's main focuses were the trade in drugs, stolen data and documents, as well as the provision of "digital services," such as the processing of stolen passports, into which a desired passport photo could be inserted for an additional fee. The enormous scale of Hydra is revealed by a look at the numbers. It had 17 million buyers and over 19,000 seller accounts registered. In 2021, the turnover was estimated by investigators to be at least 1.23 billion euros. A kind of Amazon of the Dark Web.[17]

Anyone comparing these sums with those of legal trading platforms on the Clear Web should consider that Hydra's target audience was much smaller and turnover was, of course, tax-free. The coup was achieved by BKA investigators from Wiesbaden, the Central Office for Combating Cybercrime (ZIT) in Frankfurt, and six American agencies working together. The US Department of Justice also praised the major investigative success. The Department of Justice estimated that in 2021, around 80% of all Dark Web sales based on cryptocurrencies were processed through Hydra. The investigators expertise in "Crypto Tracking," i.e., tracing payment flows in cryptocurrencies, was crucial for the success.[18] The expertise resulted from collaboration with major crypto exchanges like Coinbase or Kraken, which are legally required in the US to provide relevant information to tax authorities. There are also specialized companies like Chainalysis that professionally analyze and trace such money flows on behalf of their public or private clients.[19] As already shown in the chapter "New Hackonomy," the blockchain coins themselves are very secure, but not their technical environment and human actors.

A year before this success, investigators from Oldenburg and Koblenz shut down a Dark Market with more than 500,000 customers and 2,400 providers. The total turnover was a comparatively modest 140 million euros. Drugs, counterfeit money, and stolen data were also in the portfolio here. Police and intelligence agencies from Germany, the USA, Australia, Great Britain, Denmark, Switzerland, Ukraine, and Moldova cooperated. Europol was responsible for coordination. In this case, the arrest of the Australian operator was even successful.[20] This is very important because otherwise, the same business might have been reopened elsewhere. The number of customers and shops on the market was much smaller than Hydra's, but not insignificant. Both incidents show the dimensions of the criminal platforms and the broad spectrum of their user base. The case is also another example that only global cooperation among law enforcement can lead to success.

Child pornography is one of the darkest variants of criminal activity on the Dark Web. It ranges from the free exchange of images and videos to paid streaming services, where customers can express wishes in real-time during the "performance" about how the children should be tortured. Between 2006 and 2018, 256 Australians used such a service before it was exposed. The viewers were mostly between 50 and 60 years old and male, the majority had no prior convictions. The youngest was 27 years old, the oldest 82. They represented all strata of society and spent a total of 1.3 million Australian dollars on the provider based in the Philippines.[21] The service was exposed through the analysis of payment flows, in this case by the Australian government agency AUSTRAC, which is responsible for detecting criminal abuse of the financial system.[22] When it comes to child pornography without money flow, but "only" the exchange of images and videos, combating it becomes more difficult. In such cases, undercover investigators come into play, posing as interested parties. Due to the caution of the perpetrators and legal restrictions for undercover investigators, such operations are a game of patience. In the child pornography scene, it is common to first exchange image material among each other—this is part of the vetting of aspirants. However, the exchange is considered a criminal offense and is therefore prohibited for investigators. Nevertheless, they repeatedly achieve investigative successes, as the notorious cases "Lüdge," "Bergisch-Gladbach," "Münster," and "Wermelskirchen" in Germany show. The vast majority of cases against child abuse come from tips from abroad, mostly from the USA. This is another way to track down the perpetrators. The reason is simple: Internet services, such as for storing data in the cloud, are still dominated by American companies. In the USA, such clouds are regularly filtered for child pornography, and the results are reported to the National Center for Missing and Exploited Children. This agency then forwards the information to affected countries, such as Germany.[23] International cooperation is thus crucial, as with the pursuit of other crimes on the web.

Just like the internet as a whole, the invisible world of the Dark Web has its light and dark sides. Its spectrum ranges from unrestricted access to millions of scientific papers, articles, and books, to free expression and the exposure of corruption by whistleblowers, to wikis with instructions for bomb-making and the websites of other criminals. In the end, investigators might have the advantage due to better technical resources, provided they are not subjected to overly strict regulations. The further technical development of the internet, which we will discuss along with other future topics in the following chapter, will play a decisive role in this. It will determine the scope for preserving freedom and human rights on the web as well as that of criminal actors and investigators. Past and current successes in investigations speak clearly regarding the methods to be applied: Crime is increasingly shifting to the internet, and anyone who is active there—whether in the Dark Web or Clear Web—automatically has a global presence. Therefore, the placeless society needs placeless law enforcement with appropriate international cooperation and competencies.

# 8

# Digital Border Shift

The history of IT offers good examples of the normative power of facts. It is an industry that must reinvent itself at a high frequency like few others. With each reinvention, new technologies emerge that bring forth new business models as the basis for further innovations. Where is the journey of IT headed, what can we expect, what possibilities will it offer us, and what practical impacts will it have?

Providing answers to such questions would be material for a book of its own. Therefore, selected, concrete cases that meet three criteria will be discussed here. First: The relevant technology is still in an early stage of development but already shows long-term potential for significant applications in social, scientific, or economic fields. Second: Its practical application must be realistically achievable. Third: The required time frame should not exceed approximately 10 years. In a very fast-paced industry that has undergone surprising turns more than once, it is important to give more space to justifiable projections

© The Author(s), under exclusive license to Springer Fachmedien
Wiesbaden GmbH, part of Springer Nature 2024
J. Müller, *Turning Point*,
https://doi.org/10.1007/978-3-658-46079-2_8

than to speculation. Frequently found, not uninteresting thought experiments and more or less well-founded visions of a technical future in 50 years or more are thus deliberately excluded.

# Metaverse—Surfing the Web is So Yesterday

Nothing exists without history. This also applies to a highly modern high-tech matter like the Metaverse. Ideas for it with initial technical implementations date back to the 1950s and early 1960s when Morton Heilig presented his largely mechanical virtual reality machine called "Sensorama." It combined elements of the physical world such as videos, sounds, vibrations, fans, and smells, all without a computer-generated environment.[1] His invention was based on the idea of "experiential theater," not a technical vision with high potential to change the economy and social interaction. By chance, it coincided with the emergence of the Internet and its precursor ARPANET.[2] No one could have guessed that both ideas would converge into a new concept of a virtual world about 60 years later.

The Metaverse is a virtual, three-dimensional space on the Internet, consisting either of a purely digitally created environment (Virtual Reality) or a real existing one enriched with digital elements (Augmented Reality). In these spaces, we will be able to interact socially and professionally in the future. We immerse ourselves in them, hence they are called "immersive." Just surfing on the surface is a thing of the past. We will meet there for coffee, sit together virtually at a table, play soccer, attend a rock concert together even if we are thousands of kilometers apart, shop, hold business meetings, and negotiate contracts.[3]

The user experience will be—if we believe the predictions—that of a spatial presence that feels real. We will be represented there by an avatar of our choice, our proxy and alter ego on the web. Avatars are already a reality. We use them in a very simple form as small icons that represent us on Facebook or in a messenger like Signal. Advanced computer games give an impression of what is currently technically possible. At peak times, they can handle 10 million users simultaneously, and their manufacturers know what a sustainable IT infrastructure with very high data throughput and large processing speeds must look like. Gamers can also already choose their avatars from a range of characters and equip them. They then take them into a sports arena, a battlefield, a racetrack, or pilot an airplane. Those who have children of the right age can watch this together with them on platforms like PlayStation, Xbox, Roblox, Epic Games, or Rockstar and simultaneously strengthen the bond with their daughter or son.

In the future, our avatars will be holograms, digital images of ourselves. Star Wars fans can easily relate to this. Just think of the Jedi Council meetings where Obi-Wan Kenobi participates as a hologram from somewhere in a galaxy. The holograms will look like us and behave like us, as they will be controlled and configured by us. Such a Metaverse experience is still a promise for the future today. How the issue of haptics will be solved is also still open. Anyone playing soccer in the Metaverse will want to feel the ball. A foretaste of what is to come is provided by special virtual reality or augmented reality headsets. The required monster glasses already give us the 3D impression needed for the Metaverse experience. According to the industry, in about five years, it should work with normal glasses and in more than 10 years even with contact lenses. Especially for the merging of computer-generated and physical spaces and the necessary energy supply, the even smaller contact lenses are currently hard to imagine.

The concept of the metaverse will not necessarily, but with high probability, be successful. A good indicator of this is the behavior of large IT companies, institutional investors, and especially major users in the economy. On October 28, 2021, Facebook announced that it had renamed itself "Meta." Meta is, on the one hand, the holding company for a number of companies, including Facebook, WhatsApp, and Instagram. This part is referred to as FoA, Family of Apps—in other words, the parts of the company that generate revenue today. On the other hand, Meta consists of companies that are assigned to the RL, Reality Labs, division. It includes consumer hardware, software, virtual reality, augmented reality, and corresponding content. There, the future of the company is being created at a financial loss. In 2021 alone, Meta invested more than $10 billion in the metaverse and has already developed a number of technologies and available, practical applications for it. Since the summer of 2023, they have been promoted by Meta in a large-scale advertising campaign in the form of customer examples under the slogan "The Impact is Real."[4] The company is serious about the metaverse, and the first customers are joining in. But even government organizations are beginning to warm up to it tentatively. As one of the first institutions worldwide, a Colombian court held a trial in the metaverse in February 2023, which involved a traffic dispute. The parties were represented by avatars. According to Judge Maria Quinones Triana, whose avatar wore a black judge's robe, it felt significantly "more realistic" than a video call.[5] Not good prospects for Zoom, TeamViewer & Co.

In January 2022, Microsoft announced its intention to buy the game manufacturer Activision Blizzard for a staggering $68.7 billion. After long antitrust negotiations, it was finally completed in October 2023. In addition to the obvious strategic advantage for its Games Division, the metaverse was also a strong motive.[6] Other tech companies like Google, NVIDIA, Qualcomm, or Shopify, as well as institutional investors, have followed with billion-dollar investments.[7] By mid-2022 alone, they had put $120 billion on the table for it, more than double the $57 billion in the previous year, according to a McKinsey study.[8] The investment bank Morgan Stanley sees the revenue potential in the metaverse for e-commerce and advertising in the US alone at $8.3 trillion. Consumers could spend another five trillion "in the not too distant future" in the metaverse to test drive new cars immersively, walk through the results of a planned home renovation in advance, or take a sneak peek at next year's vacation destination.[9]And as is often the case with digital transformation, the sportswear manufacturer Nike is also ahead in the metaverse with "Nikeland."[10] Nikeland is a virtual, immersive 3D playground that is partly a life-size replica of the real Nike headquarters and can be entered with a headset. The environment was created in collaboration with the game manufacturer Roblox. It has a lobby where you can familiarize yourself with all the features or just meet up, a basketball court, a soccer field, a showroom, a future lab, and an area aptly named "My Playground." When the company offered virtual sneakers in Nikeland that visitors could design themselves as collectibles using designer templates, it sold 600 pairs for a total of $3.1 million within six minutes. Since its launch in November 2021, around 20 million people (as of June 2022) have visited Nikeland.[11] How seriously Nike takes the metaverse as a business field is also shown by the acquisition of the Web3 developer

RTFKT Studios in December 2021. RTFKT combines technical and artistic expertise in the development of NFT artifacts with the ability to produce them as physical products. The process is called "forging." What could be a better fit for Nike? No wonder, then, that you can now have digitally created sneakers called "Cryptokicks" sent to your home as IRL (In Real Life) and thus physical products.[12] The example of Nike shows one of the early, significant adaptations by the private sector, which many others have since followed. John Donahoe, President and CEO of Nike, summed up the strategy: "This acquisition is another step that accelerates Nike's digital transformation and enables us to serve athletes and creatives at the intersection of sport, creativity, gaming, and culture."[13] Hardly any more foresight is possible. Nike is building on an intertwining of virtual and physical businesses and prioritizes the shopping experience in the metaverse with unique products over immediate sales. This creates brand loyalty instead of succumbing to the results of price comparison portals. The customer decides through which channel the purchase is made, whether in a physical store or online.

The metaverse is all about platforms. They provide the space in which we will no longer access web resources two-dimensionally but three-dimensionally in the future. Whether the "spatial" metaverse will become the next major development stage of the internet, as the World Wide Web did three decades ago, depends on a number of factors in addition to the necessary investments and business cases. The more attractively its spaces are designed, the more intuitively they can be used, and the better they are accessible, especially mobile, from different devices, the greater the chance that it will gain broad acceptance. Game manufacturers, with their extensive technical know-how and particularly their experience with user behavior, can also help in this regard. Interoperability is an additional important success factor for the metaverse. This refers to the seamless interaction of systems from different manufacturers—in this case, the platforms—with each other. If I pay for an avatar in Game A from one provider today and customize it to my liking, I cannot take it into Game B from another game manufacturer. If I want to use the same avatar in Game B, I have to recreate and pay for it again, if that is even possible. Both systems are not interoperable. It is as if I bought a black and yellow fan scarf from my favorite soccer club Borussia Dortmund and could only use it in the club's stadium. The possibility of taking it to another stadium would be closed to me.

The same applies to any other type of fan accessories, which is why fewer companies would be interested in producing such products. The market for jerseys, caps, and bags would shrink, and their prices would rise. An ecosystem with network effects could not emerge. If we spend more time socially or business-wise in the metaverse, we will invest more money in the appearance of our avatars, especially in that of our holograms. Such virtual assets are therefore increasingly important and are by no means limited to clothing, even though in the virtual space, equipment and appearance are part of one's identity, a community, or the messages we want to send.[14] The same applies to software and hardware solutions for the metaverse. The larger the market, the more companies will develop applications for it. The more attractive products are available, the more customers will enter the metaverse. That it works cross-platform and interoperably is one of the important prerequisites for its long-term success. Not every platform operator will be thrilled by the idea that their customers can easily switch between different worlds. Achieving a high level of customer loyalty in this environment will pose challenges even for resourceful sellers.

The technical challenges for a metaverse, which is understood not only as a computer-generated, artificial environment but as a digital extension of the real world, are still enormous. If I e.g. want to navigate it confidently somewhere, it means nothing less than mapping spaces on a level that reflects the detailed perspective of a pedestrian. Additionally, I need to recognize the direction of gaze of the wearers of metaverse headsets or glasses to show them the correct environment. This requires gigantic amounts of data. Google's "Street View," which selectively offers views of street scenes, is just a modest beginning here. Questions about the internet connectivity of glasses that can display such data volumes, as well as their battery and computing capacity, are still open. Fast internet, i.e., 5G with universal availability, is another topic. In comparison, Web 3.0 is already more tangible. Especially in topics like interoperability and virtual possessions, its technology can be crucially helpful. Therefore, the metaverse and Web 3.0 – to an extend f- orm a kind of community of fate.

# The Internet as Blockchain: Web 3.0

In the beginning, there was the web, more precisely Web 1.0. In the early 1990s, it still consisted of a relatively manageable collection of static web pages that allowed little interaction with the user. It was limited to the publication of documents and other information. It was "read-only," as it is called in IT jargon. Over the years, it evolved into Web 2.0, as we use it today. It is characterized by media richness in the form of movies, documents, or games, etc. Above all, it is characterized by the interaction and the own content contributions it allows users on its web pages. It is "read and write" and allows millions of people to contribute content, quite different from Web

1.0. The best examples of this are the numerous social media platforms with our likes and posts. How does Web 3.0, as the future third evolutionary stage of the internet, differ from this?

Web 3.0 extends the chain of Read Only and Read and Write with the ability to own a virtual good on the web: "read, write and own." Here lies one of the essential connections to the metaverse. If, for example, I create my own avatar in Nikeland and equip it for money or design my own virtual sneaker, there must be a form of proof that I am the owner and only I can freely dispose of it. If I also want to use this avatar on other platforms and possibly modify it there, then I must be able to transfer both the avatar itself and the proof of ownership. The solution for both lies in the already discussed blockchain. How does it work?

In a blockchain, so-called tokens are created, a kind of digital vouchers that are proof that I am the owner of a virtual good. These tokens come in two forms. One for crypto money and one for other virtual goods, such as my avatar, the mentioned sneaker, or a piece of virtual land in the spatial web. In the case of bitcoins, 100 tokens prove that I own 100 bitcoins. It does not matter which bitcoins they are. It is similar to our familiar money. Which of the many euros that exist in Europe belongs to me does not matter. Like euros, the tokens of crypto money are interchangeable. The other type of token is called NFT, Non-Fungible Tokens. Each token represents a specific virtual good that is wholly or partially owned by a specific person or organization. This can be a sneaker or a piece of art. Such and other information is stored in the NFT block-chain.[15]There is now quite a lively trade in NFTs on the web, for example, for digital art. NFTs can be acquired, traded, and ideally transferred from one platform to another on platforms like OpenSea or Binance. In August

2022, Meta announced that its digital goods could be used on both Facebook and Instagram.[16] As long as cross-platform NFTs, like those from Meta or Microsoft, only move within the world of one provider, not much is gained. More exciting are projects where NFTs serve platforms across manufacturers.[17] First solutions from young companies like Ocavu, which have recognized the economic potential, are already on the market.[18] This proves once again: Whenever there is an attractive business case, a solution will be found. For the Nikeland avatar and its sneakers, this would ideally mean that I can play sports with them on an Adidas platform.

So much for the theory. For it to become practice, Nike and Adidas would have to agree to make their platforms interoperable with each other. If this does not happen, the depicted transfer cannot function either. It can be assumed that the major platforms will initially establish interoperability only within their own app ecosystems. However, the counter-movement is already here, as the example of Ocavu shows. The implications of Web 3.0 go much further. The operators of websites—such as social media, streaming and messaging services, and forums—determine within a legal framework who is allowed to do what on them and what happens to the collected data. They can use it themselves, resell it, or delete it. When we upload a photo file to a platform like Facebook or a video to TikTok, we relinquish the rights to it. The operators do with it as they please. The antithesis to this centrally organized network is a network organized decentrally with the help of blockchains, where each user determines their own data. In crypto-money, there is no bank that handles the transactions. The exchange of NFTs also does not necessarily require an intermediary. It can take place directly from the seller to the buyer. Decentralized blockchain apps (so-called DApps, Decentralized Apps) belong to no one, and you do not necessarily need an Apple or Google store to make them accessible to everyone. They are created and made available in a worldwide network of thousands of private or institutional computers. The most prominent platform for developing decentralized apps is Ethereum, whose crypto-money Ether—as already elsewhere explaineded[19]—is also an established currency on the net and is used for payment on the platform. Blockchain-based data and DApps escape a centrally organized internet and the control of a few large companies. This raises the question of the viability of business models of major platforms like Google or Facebook and, more generally, the question of power on the web. Those who can no longer arbitrarily access user data can no longer monetize it.

How this struggle will end and whether cross-platform interoperability on the web will ultimately prevail is still open. Proponents of a decentralized "free" internet of the future are working on solutions to correct the "misdevelopments" of the centralized Web 2.0 that they criticize. An interesting metaverse project of this kind is Pavia, a gaming platform that has been designed for interoperability and compatibility since the beginning of its still ongoing development.[20] Like many blockchain-based web solutions, Pavia is also being developed as open-source or "free software." This means that anyone can use its source code to improve the product, extend its functionality, or write applications for it. Hence the name "open-source". The condition attached to this is that the developer must make the usage rights for the program code they create available to all other developers free of charge under a special license. Open source software is a powerful movement in the software industry that has gained many followers over the years. The resulting pressure, but also the resulting advantages, are so great that even giants like Microsoft or Oracle make parts of their code available as free software.

The concept fits perfectly with the idea of the "free" Web 3.0. The future will show what will become of it and thus also of the metaverse and how the struggle of the antitheses will turn out. The most likely scenario is the coexistence of a centralized and a free internet, as we already know in part from Web 2.0.

Web 3.0 and the metaverse will place very high demands on network and computing speeds. Added to this is the rapidly growing data hunger, which is continuously increased by the Internet of Things or topics such as Industry 4.0 and artificial intelligence. In science, the questions are becoming increasingly complex, such as modeling the behavior of molecules with their very large number of variables in materials and material research. Processing much more data in conjunction with increasingly complex questions requires new computer architectures and processors that follow a fundamentally different approach than we have today. The answer to this challenge is currently being developed in the laboratories of science and the IT industry. One of them is the development of quantum computers, whose current state makes them the most likely winner in the competition for the practical application of alternative computing technologies.

# Computing with Quanta and the Reinvention of the Computer

At the end of 2019, Google and NASA announced that, in collaboration with the Oak Ridge National Laboratory (ORNL) in Tennessee, they had experimentally demonstrated the superiority of quantum computers, the so-called Quantum Supremacy. A specific mathematical task was solved with Google's Sycamore quantum computer in 200 seconds, while even the largest and most modern supercomputer in Oak Ridge would have taken thousands of years.[21] This was the preliminary culmination of a development that dates back to the work of physicist Paul Benioff at the Argonne National Laboratory, a facility of the US Department of Energy, in the 1980s. Once again, an organization of the US government was instrumental in the birth of a new, significant development in IT.[22]

However, we are still years away from a universal use of Sycamore and comparable machines. According to optimistic estimates, the realization of a universal quantum computer will still have to wait until well into the 2030s. The situation is comparable to the early days of modern IT, when machines like ENIAC were also not yet universal computers but had to be reprogrammed and rewired for each task. Nevertheless, the experiment demonstrates the impressive progress that can be achieved with the young technology. Incidentally, not only in the USA. In 2021, a Chinese research team announced that it had successfully conducted a similar experiment with a comparable result. For science, this was a gratifying, independent confirmation of the future viability of quantum IT, but it was predictably less well received by American politicians. China has meanwhile established itself as a serious player in the race for dominance in the field of quantum computing. It seems as if we are experiencing another modern version of the former competition between the USA and the Soviet Union in space, only this time the goal is much more terrestrial and America has a much stronger competitor in China.[23]Beyond all politics, two practical questions remain, the answers to which clearly highlight the differences between classical computers and quantum computers. One is why the computing power of today's computers cannot be increased indefinitely, and the other is why quantum computers do not have this performance limit.

The performance of modern computers depends significantly on the capabilities of their processors, in addition to their overall architecture. Their potential can mainly be increased through three measures: parallel processing with multiple cores[24], higher clock rates, i.e., the speed at which they can execute commands, and ever further miniaturization, meaning more transistors on a chip. However, their potential is largely exhausted. On the one hand, the increasing heat development with ever higher density of transistors on the chip is a problem, and on the other hand, quantum mechanical effects set limits to this density. These are referred to as "quantum tunneling" and occur when the distances between the transistors are in the range of only a few atomic lengths. Their current flow and behavior can then no longer be reliably controlled. The validity of Moore's Law from 1965, according to which the computing power of processors doubles every two years while costs decrease, is expected to end in the 2020s, according to Intel and many experts.[25] When that happens, it will be difficult to economically justify the immense investments in chip research and production. The benefits of miniaturization shrink, while the costs of advancing it against adverse effects such as heat development and quantum tunneling rise. So, in the foreseeable future, we have a technical and an economic problem with the further development of conventional processors. Peter Lee, head of Microsoft Research, once jokingly put it this way: "Every two years, the number of people predicting the death of Moore's Law doubles."[26] Therefore, the IT industry, together with science, must think about alternative computing systems if it wants to economically satisfy customers' thirst for solutions to increasingly complex questions and ever larger amounts of data. "If you can't beat 'em, join 'em," says a song by Queen from 1978. This precisely characterizes the alternative approach of research on quantum computers. If the problems from quantum mechanical effects in the further development of our current processors cannot be prevented, then they must be utilized.

Regarding the second question, namely the much higher performance limit of quantum computers, it helps to first look at the way we perform calculations today. At the heart of modern computers lies the processing of binary digits, or bits, which form the fundamental language of computing. The basis for the bits is the binary number system, which consists of the two digits zero and one. They represent the charge states zero (= power off) and one (= power on). With a combination of zeros and ones, all numbers and characters, including letters and special characters, can be represented. Why is it done this way? Because it makes computers much simpler, cheaper, and less error-prone to build than with electronics based on the decimal system with its ten numbers (= charge states). For that, each digit from 0 to 9 would have to be represented by a minimally different charge state, which would be easily misunderstood by the electronics. For example, with a total voltage of three volts, zero would be 0.0 V, one would be 0.3 V, two would be 0.6 V, three would be 0.9 V, and so on. The two states "power on" and "power off" are much easier to handle. The bits zero and one are processed by the transistors of the processor, they are the basis of all computers.

In contrast, quantum computers calculate with quantum bits, also called qubits. Quanta are the smallest units of energy and matter, such as an electron or a photon. Since this subatomic world does not align with our macroscopic everyday experience and evolution has not equipped us with the sensory tools to perceive it, its properties are difficult for us to comprehend—they appear enigmatic. Yet, it's the quantum world that shapes our reality, down to the finest detail of our being. Two of their properties lead to a connected group of qubits being able to deliver far more computing power than the same number of "normal" binary bits. One is their ability to superposition, and the other is quantum entanglement. Knowledge of these properties dates back to physicists from the early twentieth century. It is associated with great names like Max Planck, Albert Einstein, Werner Heisenberg, Erwin Schrödinger, and Niels Bohr. But what does this mean concretely?

Qubits, like binary bits, can assume the charge states of zero or one. The difference: they can have both simultaneously. This describes the aforementioned state of superposition. The value of a quantum cannot be determined with certainty, but only with a degree of probability. Only when the state of a qubit is measured does it "collapse" and transition into a definite state of zero or one. Instead of calculating separately with zero and one like a classical computer, a quantum computer calculates with zero and one in a single step due to superposition. With the help of the second property, it gets even better. Quantum bits can be paired with the same charge state, which physicists have referred to as "entanglement" since Erwin Schrödinger. If the value of one entangled qubit is changed, e.g., from zero to one, the value of the other changes absolutely simultaneously and analogously. Thanks to superposition and entanglement, for example, two qubits can be in four states ($2^2$) of zero and one simultaneously. In this way, we have a much larger number of quantum bits available that calculate simultaneously. This works even if the entangled qubits are hundreds of thousands of kilometers apart. Albert Einstein had problems with this, as with other findings of quantum mechanics. One reason is that, according to his experimentally well-proven special theory of relativity, neither information nor matter nor energy can be transmitted faster than light. The question of how this mysterious, truly timeless transmission of states between entangled qubits works remains unresolved to this day.[27]

The performance of qubits can be illustrated with the following small example: With four binary bits, the numbers from one to eight can be represented as follows: 0001, 0010, 0011, 0100, 0101, 0110, 0111, and 1000. A conventional computer processes these bits separately, as mentioned. Four qubits, on the other hand, achieve $2^4 (= 16)$ states and manage to process all eight bits in parallel and at the same time. Bringing more qubits into play increases the processing speed immensely. A quantum computer with 16 qubits can be in $2^{16}$ ($= 65,536$) states simultaneously. With 300 qubits ($2^{300}$), there are more states than estimated atoms in the universe. An even greater technical challenge is to increase the number of usable qubits in a system to several hundred thousand, to manipulate them precisely, and to keep their state stable. This is difficult because they are very susceptible to interference and therefore easily decay. Google's Sycamore calculated with 54 qubits at the end of 2019, and by December 2022, it was already 433. IBM, one of the leading companies in the field of quantum computers, claims it will increase this number to 1121 qubits by the end of 2023.[28]

However, research is not only determined by the race for more and more qubits and the different ways to generate them. Attention is now also being directed towards new hardware architectures that allow processors with fewer qubits to be interconnected. In this way, performance could also be scaled, and quantum computers could find their way into scientific and business practice faster than expected.[29] The whole thing sounds good but involves a number of very complex challenges that research is still working on. Building the hardware, such as for generating, controlling, and stabilizing the qubits, is one of them. Another is equally intricate. Since quantum computers function very differently from our current computers, existing programs are not usable for them. Today's Windows or Excel, a database, SAP's enterprise applications, and our common internet connections would not work with quantum computers from Google, IBM, or D-Wave. For example, the entire complex of development tools, application software, and algorithms must be rethought and rewritten. There is still much to be done, even assuming that quantum computers will never reach the hands of end consumers. The provisional technical end is likely to be a hybrid approach, combining classical supercomputers with quantum computers. This allows the strengths of each system to be utilized depending on the question and the respective weaknesses to be compensated for.

As with the metaverse or Web 3.0, the success of quantum computing will largely depend on its economic utility. Technology for its own sake fails. Therefore, economic use cases, the business cases, are so important. When the benefits of the new computing concept become apparent, the necessary billions from financial investors, large companies, and not least the state will flow. Quantum computing is already a field of cross-sector cooperation between science, industry, and the state. This reflects the success model of the early IT industry in the USA since the 1940s.

In May 2021, the German federal government announced that it would invest two billion euros over four years in both research and practical business applications for quantum computers. After all, the then-chancellor Merkel had been a quantum chemist before entering politics. But it was also about time. Missing the next big wave of IT, as has continuously happened since the postwar period, must no longer happen to Germany and Europe. To ensure practical and economic applicability, an associated innovative ecosystem is to be built, including universities and research laboratories as well as industry.[30]The Fraunhofer Society, representing applied science, is responsible for coordination. For this purpose, it has been operating a quantum computer in southern Germany together with IBM since the summer of 2021.[31] It is expected to offer significant advantages for the economy and science within the current decade, "beyond what would ever be possible with classical computers."[32]

The German Supercomputing Centre in Jülich (JSC) follows the same cooperative philosophy, combining a quantum computer from the Canadian company D-Wave Systems with classical supercomputers and utilizing the best of both worlds depending on the problem at hand.[33] Even though private US companies are technically ahead in quantum computing, the Europeans have taken notice this time. Europe ranks second worldwide in public funding for quantum computing, behind China and ahead of the USA. Within the EU, Germany leads with 40% in state funding, followed by France with 28%, and the EU as an institution accounts for 14% (as of December 2021).[34]

Companies like Microsoft and IBM have focused their efforts from the beginning on gathering and binding as many third-party companies around them as possible. Microsoft is expanding its Azure cloud service into a global AI platform—a leading position in quantum computing for processing gigantic amounts of data is a good prerequisite for this. Such quantum ecosystems consist of developers of hardware components, software solutions, and services. The powerful tech giants prove to be crystallization points of the new technology and are thus a significant advantage for the USA. Microsoft, for example, cleverly leverages its excellent position as a cloud provider by providing its community with access to know-how and hardware and software resources for quantum computing through its Azure cloud.[35] IBM has gathered over 210 Fortune 500 companies, academic institutions, national laboratories, and startups around it.[36]

Investor money logically follows. According to McKinsey, $1.7 billion flowed into this sector in 2021. The sum itself is modest, but the growth of more than 100% compared to the previous year is interesting. Correspondingly, the number of startups has also increased significantly. As a result of this boom, there are now numerous initial practical applications for quantum computers. They are most commonly found in the fields of engineering, chemistry, pharmaceuticals, financial services, transportation, and logistics.[37] Here is an example: We already know quite well how to build batteries for electric vehicles. It is also known how to best use the batteries to achieve a high range. However, what happens on a molecular level in such a battery and what optimization and efficiency potentials lie within it are still largely in the dark. The next generation of batteries thus risks being limited again to process optimization. Daimler AG, in collaboration with IBM, is trying to change exactly that. A similar project supported by IBM Quantum Computing is being pursued by Mitsubishi Chemicals, which involves a different chemical composition of lithium batteries. This is no easy task: to analyze and understand the inner workings of a lithium battery, very complex simulations and modeling must be performed. We are talking about the interaction of billions of atoms of lithium molecules with each other. This results in an enormously large number of variables. Classical computers with classical algorithms are not capable of delivering usable results and getting us out of the lengthy and costly approach of "trial and error." However, quantum computers are capable of this, which can significantly shorten the development of new and more efficient battery types. The resulting competitive advantage for a company can be worth billions.[38]

# Mobility of the Future

The efficiency of batteries is only one aspect of new mobility. Its future in urban environments takes place on the ground and in the air. According to UN estimates, around 70% of humanity will live in cities by 2050, using 2% of the Earth's surface. It is expected that there will then be 43 megacities with more than 10 million inhabitants, which means a very high density of people and vehicles.[39] The challenges associated with mobility in cities are numerous. Air pollution, traffic chaos, accidents, stress, lack of traffic infrastructure, lack of overarching traffic control, and the availability of parking spaces are just a few examples. Urbanization, however, cannot be stopped. Instead of lamenting, we must face its consequences and develop concepts to deal with its negative effects. The key term here is also: information technology. Until now, our understanding of cars has been of isolated vehicles, driven by individuals on a sight-based system, moving through traffic unconnected and without much interaction with their surroundings. What happens at the next corner is largely unknown to them. The resulting lack of coordination with the many other vehicles moving simultaneously with them and in different directions is part of the traffic problem we have in all major cities on all continents. Over 90% of accidents are due to human error or misjudgment.[40]

But a solution is in sight: computers do not play on their phones while driving, they do not get tired, do not drink alcohol, and are not distracted by people in the car or events on the roadside. They can analyze large amounts of relevant environmental data much faster and better than humans, learn independently from it, and react to it in a flash. The US Department of Transportation therefore sees a great opportunity in autonomous driving to significantly improve our traffic safety. Electronic communication with the environment, integration into specially created networks, data-driven and intelligent control of vehicles that coordinate with each other and their surroundings in a predictive manner can provide relief.

Electric cars will predominantly shape road traffic in the foreseeable future. In Germany, the number of new car registrations with purely electric drive increased by 32% in 2022 compared to the previous year, driven also by government subsidies, while hybrid drives recorded an increase of just under 10%. Overall, battery-powered and hybrid vehicles accounted for around 49% of all 2.65 million new car registrations in 2022.[41] The global balance is also positive. China has by far the highest share of electric cars. In 2021, a total of 8.25 million were registered there, which is four times the number in the USA and about half of the global stock.[42] By 2030, 116 million electric cars are expected worldwide—ten times more than in 2020.[43] With their growing share, the importance of IT in vehicles and the IT infrastructure around them is also growing: from the operating system to networking to the various applications in and around the car. Self-driving vehicles represent a qualitative leap in terms of computerization. With their different levels of automation, they will in a not too far future dominate the image of our cities for the transport of people and goods. The market for this is huge. An example of this is Intel's 2017 acquisition of Mobileye. The automotive supplier, founded in 1999 and based in Jerusalem, sees the revenue potential for its assistance systems for semi-autonomous and fully autonomous driving alone at $17 billion by 2030. Mobileye counts BMW, Nissan, and VW among its customers and has become one of the most successful acquisitions in Intel's history.[44]

It is hardly surprising that the platform concept also plays a major role in Intel's mobility strategy. In May 2020, the Mobility-as-a-Service (MaaS) company Moovit was acquired as a complement to Mobileye's offerings. Moovit is a cloud service with over 800 million users in 3,100 cities and 102 countries. It allows comprehensive travel planning, electronic ticketing, and payment services for all public and private transportation.[45] Anyone striving for the introduction of nationwide valid tickets for public local and long-distance transport in Germany may find a good partner in Moovit.

In the future, the platform will include real-time optimized navigation of autonomous vehicles as well as the booking of self-driving robotaxis. A mobile app offers the end user the ability to find, book, and pay for all necessary means of transportation needed on the stages of their journey, from e-scooters to trains to robotaxis. Uber and its likes will face competition. Even car manufacturers must raise their eyebrows in concern given the value chain that Intel can offer from the chip to the autonomous vehicle and new cloud services. We know from the history of the iPhone how quickly telecommunications companies became mere bystanders. To this day, they "only" provide the infrastructure and must survive in a price-driven telecom market, while Apple binds customers to itself with its combination of mobile hardware and cloud services (such as Apple Music) and makes the big money.

To understand the development status of self-driving cars, known as Autonomous Vehicles (AV), it is best to refer to the classification of the Society of Automotive Engineers (SAE), which has become the standard with its 128,000 members worldwide. It divides the degree of automation of cars into levels from zero to five. The first three levels (zero to two) mean that humans still drive themselves and are supported by assistance systems to varying degrees. They must steer, brake, accelerate, and ensure the safety of the vehicle in road traffic. Examples of this form of automation are lane-keeping systems, automatic emergency braking, blind-spot assistants, automatic parking, and adaptive cruise control. Things are different at levels three to five, where the human no longer drives themselves. At level three, however, they must still be able to take over driving at any time upon request by the system, for example, through an acoustic signal. This also means that such vehicles must still have steering wheels and pedals. Since the first half of 2022, Mercedes Benz customers have been able to order the DRIVE PILOT as an optional extra when purchasing an S-Class or an ESQ limousine, which corresponds to level three. However, it may only be activated under narrowly defined conditions. At least, since January 2023, speeds of up to 130 km/h have been allowed in Germany. Previously, the limit was 60 km/h, which was a real killjoy on highways.[46]

At levels four and five, self-driving is no longer required, and the driver is no longer prompted to do so. In Germany, there has been a legal regulation for this since 2021.[47] The difference between the two is that at level four, certain conditions must be met, while level five applies universally and without restrictions. An example of level three would be a traffic jam chauffeur, for level four a car without steering, brake, and gas pedals, but limited to functions such as driverless taxi within a limited radius. Level five represents everything that level four does, but without restrictive conditions.[48]Level four cars are technically almost mature and are currently being tested as prototypes in the field. By 2035, they are expected to have a market penetration of 15% in leading industrial nations. It will take a longer time before level five can be ordered for everyday use on the road. Serious estimates do not expect this before 2035 at the earliest.[49]

In cars of the two highest levels, humans are merely passengers and can spend the travel time according to their own preferences, similar to today in an airplane or on a train. Whether customers who orient themselves by the BMW slogan "Joy of Driving" (Freude am Fahren) from 1972 will find vehicles of levels four and five attractive remains to be seen. Additionally, a whole range of regulatory questions still need to be answered, which will likely influence the degree of "joy." How should the algorithms of a control software be designed, for example, in the event of an accident? Should they prioritize protecting their own occupants or avoiding casualties among other road users? What requirements must a self-driving vehicle meet to protect against hackers? What happens to the movement data? What does autonomous driving mean for car insurance? Who sets the rules in countries like the USA, where traffic laws are determined by the states, or in the EU, where 27 sovereign member states are involved, making the case even more complicated? There cannot be a software version for each individual country, yet cross-border traffic must still be possible without issues. Not only for technical reasons will autonomous vehicles conquer the world only gradually.

"Actually, we are already a software company." With this sentence, Oliver Zipse, CEO of BMW, responded on January 5, 2023, in the ARD Tagesthemen to the moderator's question: "When will BMW, the car manufacturer, become a software company?"[50]The wake-up call from Tesla and the Chinese automotive industry has thus been heard. Zipse was at the interview at the Consumer Electronics Show (CES), an annual IT and electronics trade fair in Las Vegas. This not only signifies the content but also the event itself. The key technology for new mobility is information technology. Three essential tasks for autonomous driving must be solved by the software in conjunction with the hardware:

1. Machine perception of the traffic environment,
2. Understanding the overall situation of the vehicle,
3. Path generation and behavior in this situation.

Anyone who participates in road traffic can imagine the challenges associated with these three tasks.[51] The perception of the environment works through a so-called LIDAR (Light Imaging, Detection and Ranging) and a series of cameras and sensors, with which the vehicle communicates with its external world. Such sensors can, for example, be attached to traffic lights and railway barriers. Behind the LIDAR, a type of radar, is a three-dimensional laser scanner that creates an image of the surroundings. Anyone who has ever seen an autonomous vehicle will remember the small, usually round box on its roof, which contains the LIDAR. The technology is also used for creating digital terrain images. Since the autonomous vehicle must know its exact position in real-time, the radar is supplemented by 3D mapping systems and D-GPS data (Differential Global Positioning System). The latter can correct and refine measurements. Ideally, vehicles are not only networked with their static environment but also with each other. This helps in avoiding accidents, as the driving behavior of other road users can also be taken into account. The Internet of Things (IoT), which has been mentioned elsewhere, comes into play here. The perception of the traffic environment and its evaluation are based on numerous collected data, which are processed in real-time by computers with artificial intelligence. This is thus crucial for traffic safety, as it should be able to capture, interpret, and respond to situations better than humans, but it is not yet sufficiently capable—which brings up the major, still unsatisfactorily solved challenges of autonomous driving once again.

A simple example can illustrate the entire complexity of the topic. If a pedestrian is near the car, for example, on a crosswalk, they will generally not carry a sensor that tells the car: "Here is a pedestrian moving at speed V at coordinates XY in direction Z." The artificial intelligence must recognize them based on the obtained data, even if it is foggy or the street lighting has failed, if it is raining heavily, or if the person is dressed as a horse for carnival and stumbling around drunk. An e-scooter, which moves unusually quickly across the crosswalk with its human cargo, must also be recognized as a "pedestrian." The movement patterns, shape, and other external features are not the same in all these cases, yet a human is behind them. Once all the data is available, a 3D model of the environment is created. This represents the overall situation of the vehicle to the second and is dynamically updated and interpreted. Furthermore, it predicts what will happen next and how the vehicle must behave in relation to all other road users and the static environment (buildings, trees, etc.). In the end, the AI gives instructions for the vehicle's path generation to its individual systems (steering, braking, accelerating, stopping, signaling, etc.). Of course, an unforeseen event, such as a vehicle unexpectedly shooting out of a driveway or a tree falling onto the road during a storm, must also be considered in a split second.

This example shows that it is simply unrealistic to believe that one can comprehensively specify all possible traffic scenarios and the resulting instructions to the vehicle in the software specifications. Classical programming reaches its limits here. Therefore, artificial intelligence and machine learning, which have been explained elsewhere, are used. This also explains the elsewhere quoted sentence from Oliver Zipse about BMW as a software company. It could be further substantiated with many additional examples, such as the connection of vehicles to the internet or their preventive maintenance.

# The Regulation of the Unpredictable

In all regulatory tasks, as exemplified by the issue of autonomous driving, the state is in danger of lagging behind technological development. It really only has a chance to keep up if it works early and closely with research laboratories as well as manufacturers and suppliers of the automotive industry. The same applies to the regulation of other AI-driven technology fields. These include social media, medical technology, and many others. It is not a phenomenon limited to the automotive industry. Autonomous driving is just a good example. Correcting ex post is more difficult than setting the direction and guardrails ex ante within which the end result is allowed to move. Only in this way can the state remain in the proverbial driver's seat. Politics must inform technology early on what desired outcome AI in the car or in other areas is allowed to have and when "good" is also good enough. Even the question of when an autonomous vehicle is allowed to hit the road is not easy to answer. AI systems are not always clearly predictable in their behavior, as they work with very large and changing, growing data sets as well as many parameter values. The data is interpreted by it and thus it makes its decisions. If the result is different from the desired one, one cannot—unlike with classic software—"just" look at the lines of code and check whether the programming rules were correctly applied or the content specifications were correctly implemented by the programmer. AI is not objective and its results are not always predictable. Therefore, a perfect AI system will probably never exist. Some car manufacturers take a more relaxed view and assume that the benefit is large enough to outweigh any potential safety risks, and therefore accept them. Others take a stricter view and want to avoid risks at all costs.[52] The latter not only costs more time and money, but they are also probably not as quick to market as the competition, which can secure its shares in the meantime. The defensive manufacturers then also lack real practical experience, which can lead to product improvements faster than laboratory situations and limited test operations. It is different with more daring states that make more generous legal regulations and are more willing to take risks. They thereby give their companies certain competitive advantages that others do not have.

# Epilogue

## Highway to Hell?

The preface of this book is titled "The Eighth Day of Creation." Looking at the numerous negative assessments of the consequences of the digitization of the economy, politics, and society from the past decades, one might be tempted to change it to "Highway to Hell." Positive portrayals are clearly in the minority; the stereotypically used cliché of the evil algorithms is just one example of this. In 1966, the BBC asked British children what life would be like in the year 2000. The result was captured in a short video that can be seen on LinkedIn.[1] The responses of the children, estimated to be between 13 and 15 years old, were quite pessimistic. Some were afraid of overpopulation or a nuclear war, others feared that computers would take over and destroy many jobs. Two girls believed that their lives would no longer be pleasant but rather quite boring because machines would do everything

J. Müller, *Turning Point*, https://doi.org/10.1007/978-3-658-46079-2

for them. All people and things would be uniform, and diversity would have disappeared. One boy said he would command a horde of robots and attend the funeral of a computer. The tone continued in this manner. In the year 2000, people would only be part of statistics, and they would no longer be perceived as individuals. Animals would only be kept in stalls and no longer in pastures so that they could be fattened more easily. Even the weather would change, "because of all the Sputniks" being shot into the sky—with the result that the ice caps at the poles would melt and only a few mountains of Great Britain would remain, rising as islands from the sea. Human-caused climate change, almost visionary for the year 1966. Optimistic voices were rather rare. Only a few believed that life would be much more "efficient" and there would be fewer diseases.

Of course, the pessimism of the children also reveals the time in which they were surveyed. Despite full employment in Great Britain and rising real wages during the Swinging Sixties, the Cold War with the dangerous Cuban Missile Crisis, the global population explosion, the increasing computerization, and the arms race between the USA and the Soviet Union created a negative background noise. This is reflected in the statements of the children. Contributions such as: "only people with higher IQ" will still have a job, remind us of the modern theme of Social Divide, a social inequality caused by different access to IT.

Pessimism and fear of technology have existed in our recent history since it has been perceived as a defining element of our lives. Sometimes it was the newly invented railway, sometimes the car, sometimes machines and automation, for which Charlie Chaplin's film "Modern Times" from 1936 can serve as an example. Pessimism is part of European cultural history, as we have known at least since Oswald Spengler's book about the "Decline of the West," whose two volumes were published shortly after the First World War. In 1844, there was even a rant against the "modern excessive reading," "for one reads the true and the false indiscriminately."[2] What would the author of this quote say today if he had a Facebook account and watched the vibrant activity on this and other social platforms? His verdict could be transferred to our present time without any modifications. The difference would mainly lie in a technical detail known as hypertext links. Clicking on these links and the resulting rapid consumption of content exacerbates the superficial understanding of "true and false". The information overflow, which describes an unmanageable flood of information, is significantly increased as a result. There is little time left for critical thinking and the reception of what one reads—if that is even intended at all.

Fear, defense, and adaptation as the three typical stages of the progression of technology criticism must today—unlike in the age of railways—happen almost simultaneously. The technological development is too fast, and its widespread dissemination has become too rapid. For this reason, the first two stages are often skipped by many contemporaries. As a result, many suffer from a lack of reflection on the sense and nonsense of our handling of it. It is largely left to the state, which tries to steer the consequences of digitization into the "right" paths through regulation. It need not be emphasized that this happens in strong dependence on the prevailing form of government. Democracies and dictatorships, and all shades in between these two poles, each have their own perspectives. IT has, despite its globally unifying infrastructure, driven the emergence of a multipolar world.

Nevertheless: The internet is the world computer to which everyone is connected. Monopolies of opinion exist only where they are enforced; otherwise, there is a cacophony of very different views. The internet represents one of the opportunities to halt the currently observable, politically motivated disentanglement of our world. Those who see globalization as a danger and its disintegration into old or new economic and power blocs as an advantage will be taught better in the future. A connected world with much communication is better than bloc formation, isolation, demarcation, and speechlessness. Access to information of any kind, anytime and from anywhere, gives people on all continents the opportunity to become more mature. Information monopolies are softened, education is facilitated, problems can be solved cooperatively, and opportunities can be seized. Informed people are less easily manipulated. Politicians and companies must act more transparently, justify their actions more than before, and civil society can organize itself more easily. IT allows us to make work more flexible in terms of time and place, even to a certain extent to individualize it. As a (late) reaction to climate change, we are advancing clean technologies, electrifying and digitizing our cars. In the American Rust Belt, where the facilities of the old steel industry are rotting, battery belts and factories for electric GMs and Fords are emerging. Contrary to the trend, even in cooperation with the Chinese battery giant CATL, as Bill Ford, CEO of the eponymous company, announced in February 2023. Germany's Brandenburg region offers a similar case study with Tesla's presence. We are installing solar panels on our roofs, the old oil or gas heating systems are gradually becoming obsolete and are being replaced, among other things, by heat pumps with intelligent energy management. Photovoltaic systems from companies and private households can be networked into software-controlled virtual power plants, reducing our dependence on large, central energy producers and foreign suppliers.

Our economy has never been as productive as it is today, allowing for distribution margins, facilitating work, and being unimaginable without automation. Knowledge and research results are shared worldwide at the click of a mouse, and mobility is becoming safer. If we now work on our extreme regulatory zeal and the excessive legalization of our lives, then everything will be fine… Nothing works without IT anymore, so understanding its impact is essential. This positive list can be continued indefinitely. Of course, a negative list can also be made. But things do not become bad because they have two sides. They become good or bad by the way we deal with them. Arati Prabhakar, head of the White House Office of Science and Technology Policy, summed up the emerging "AI storm" at the Tech and Creative Conference South by Southwest in mid-March 2023 in Texas. "We are at a turning point. The entire history shows that this kind of powerful new technology can and will be used for both good and bad."[3] Shaping this is our job.

To modern humans, the world increasingly appears not created for them, but by them. This is also why the reference to the eighth day of creation is not exaggerated.—No matter how one ultimately judges this prospect. IT is on the verge of initiating it through generative intelligence and, prospectively, perhaps even through machines capable of consciousness. In this, it is strongly supported by other disciplines, such as life sciences. The convergence between the two is only a matter of time. Connecting the electrical signals of our brain with a computer, through so-called BCIs (Brain-Computer Interfaces), is no longer pure science fiction and can, for example, alleviate or prevent human suffering in medicine. Our future will be determined by technology much faster and more strongly than our past ever was.

It always amazes me in conversations how little big-picture knowledge exists about such a constitutive phenomenon of our modern world as IT. The zeitgeist ignores the zeitenwende (turning point) and is astonishingly resistant in this regard. Romanticizing forgetfulness of life in the past ensures that the good old days are not perceived as what they actually were: significantly worse for the vast majority of the population than today. Those who want to save the world, who want to save our climate, will only achieve this through clean and intelligent technology. Preaching renunciation fails at the latest at national borders. The stages of development of the economies, the political systems, the mentalities, the awareness of problems are too different.

When I tasked my sales team at the beginning of the millennium with analyzing Silicon Valley in terms of our customer potential, it emerged, among other things, that along the 80 km stretch between our office in the north and San José in the south, there were almost 900 companies generating more than a million dollars in revenue. That is one company per 89 meters of road length. Such a vibrant scenario requires much more than "just" venture capital. It is the result of a mindset. IT is the industry of "yes, we can." Nevertheless, it guards itself against human arrogance, sometimes in painful ways. Victory and defeat are closely linked in quick succession, leaving little room for hubris to develop.—Except for some obvious, ego-driven exceptions. I have experienced many quarter-ends at Wall Street-listed employers. "From hero to zero" is a catchphrase that aptly describes this environment in the event of a botched quarterly result. The bursting of the dot-com bubble at the end of March 2000 destroyed 78% of the market value of companies listed on the NASDAQ technology exchange in just seven months and dealt the scandal-ridden "Neuer Markt" on the Frankfurt Stock Exchange a late death blow in 2003. That was also a good pill against arrogance. On vacation in Crete, I read a saying at the entrance of a cave in a former hippie colony: "Live for today, tomorrow will never come." That could have been written on many company buildings in Silicon Valley at the end of the 1990s. I experienced those years there and welcomed the new realism after the crash. The mythological Phoenix rose from the ashes. No longer those who burned the most money against all business sense and sponsored the Super Bowl as a start-up, but those who knew what they were doing were in the game after the bubble burst. Corrective developments of this kind are not only proof of the industry's self-healing power but also a reason for optimism. It stands in contrast to gloomy doomsday scenarios and our infatuation with problems instead of solutions.

Modern technology gives us the opportunity to correct the mistakes of the past and to make the planet better, step by step. Without artificial intelligence and super-fast computing to handle large amounts of data, there is no prosperity and no future for us as a major industrial nation. Without smart IT, there will not even be a voice for Europe that needs to be heard. It is not a problem to make mistakes, just don't make the same ones twice. Only those who try things out and take risks, thereby also being wrong, learn. Otherwise, in a highly competitive world, one quickly ends up on the road to failure, the "Highway to Hell." One does not end up there because one uses technological possibilities, but because one does not. It is good and necessary to approach the current and future achievements of IT constructively and critically, to understand their benefits and impacts, and to minimize their risks. The emphasis must be on constructive. Ideologically motivated objections and a reluctance to embrace the unfamiliar are not legitimate grounds for dismissing new ideas.

Modern computers emerged simultaneously on both sides of the Atlantic. Their future is currently being written on both sides of the Pacific. Information technology is an important part of the tectonic power shift that we are currently experiencing. Europe missed its chance in the 1950s and 1960s, although there were good war-related approaches, especially in England and Germany. War and the post-war period had a catalytic effect on the IT industry in unscathed America, but not in war-torn Europe with its entirely different concerns. However, one can also attribute more foresight to American politics after 1945 in this regard than to those in European countries. Despite the so-called German economic miracle and available financial resources from the late 1950s onward, a network of half-heartedness and digital ignorance stretches over Germany from the first chancellor, Adenauer to present days. If, for example, the EU fills positions like the "Digital Commissioner" or in Germany the "Federal Government Commissioner for Digitization" with people whose expertise does not go beyond reading out the texts of their speechwriters, then one should not be surprised. Some topics are complex and indeed require competence instead of political quota systems and office trading. This applies not only to IT. In the communist German Democratic Republic, the importance of having its own computer industry was recognized early on, forced by the COCOM embargo list of Western countries. Partially successful, sometimes more, sometimes less stringent attempts to build its own state-run IT industry ended with German reunification and the lack of competitiveness of the East German companies. To successfully develop a national or European IT sector, one needs – even with state support—affordable prices and a private sector with a business case that, together with science, takes the lead. The possibility of commercialization is essential. A unified, large domestic market with room to grow and an easily accessible export market for expansion are very helpful.

I sincerely hope that with this book I was able to provide food for thought and convey the "big picture" of IT. Perhaps I even succeeded in passing on some of my optimism regarding the possibilities and opportunities that my industry offers. While writing this book, it was obvious that it actually needs to be updated every six months. All the bots and information sources with their daily updates that I have subscribed to suggest this conclusion. However, for obvious reasons, this does not happen. Hopefully, my IT blog on "Zeitenwende-it.com" provides some relief. Additionally, the allure of my motorcycle and the need to spend more time with my family than before are quite significant. This has both promoted and hindered the writing process. Nevertheless, the mind wants to stay occupied, and the industry does not let me go even after my departure as an "active" member. Knowledge and experiences demand application. As mentioned in the preface, the motto of the hacker collective Anonymous also applies here: "We are Legion. We do not forgive. We do not forget. Expect us." There are already ideas for the next steps.

# Notes

## Notes: Beyond Technology. Our New Life with IT

1. Frick, Walter. Fixing the Internet. In: Harvard Business Review, July–August 2019, https://hbr.org/2019/07/fixing-the-internet [09.03.2023].
2. How much time on average do you spend on your phone on a daily basis? (14.06.2022) https://www.statista.com/statistics/1224510/time-spent-per-day-on-smartphone-us/ [ 11.03.2023].
3. Wie viel Schlaf bekommen Sie durchschnittlich an Wochentagen pro Nacht? (23.11.2021) https://de.statista.com/statistik/daten/studie/1277683/umfrage/schlaf-dauer-der-deutschen [11.03.2023].
4. Aiken, Mary. The Cyber Effect. A Pioneering Cyberpsychologist Explains How Human Behavior Changes Online. London 2016.
5. An informative article can be found on the website of IKK Classic. Cyberchondria: Selbstdiagnose per Doktor

© The Editor(s) (if applicable) and The Author(s), under exclusive license to Springer Fachmedien Wiesbaden GmbH, part of Springer Nature 2024
J. Müller, *Turning Point*,
https://doi.org/10.1007/978-3-658-46079-2

Google.    (n. d.)    https://www.ikk-classic.de/gesund-machen/wissen/cyberchondrie [03/11/2023].

6. Behr, Ines von. Reding, Anaïs. Edwards, Charlie. Gribbon, Luce. Radicalization in the digital era. The use of the internet in 15 cases of terrorism and extremism. Rand Corporation. (2013) https://www.rand.org/pubs/research_reports/RR453.html [03/11/2023]

7. Aiken, Mary. Cyber Effect, p. 137.

8. More on this topic in Chap. 5 of this book. Those who are interested in where internet blockades are currently taking place can follow this in real-time. Mapping internet freedom in realtime. (n. d.) https://netblocks.org/ [11.03.2023].

9. Reported on the website of the US broadcaster NPR National Public Radio. (03/05/2022) https://www.npr.org/2022/03/05/1084739721/airbnb-ukraine-direct-aid?t=1649488606247 [03/09/2023].

10. Internet Statistics And Facts For 2022 https://www.websiterating.com/research/internet-statistics-facts/#summary. Websiterating.com [11.03.2023] advises online marketers and compiles extensive and fairly up-to-date data for this purpose. Another good source for social media statistics is https://datareportal.com with figures on the individual platforms and many other interesting statistics.

11. TikTok says it passes 1 Billion users. (27.09.2021) https://www.theverge.com/2021/9/27/22696281/tiktok-1-billion-users [11.03.2023].

12. How many people use YouTube in 2022. (07.09.2021) https://backlinko.com/youtube-users#monthly-active-users [11.03.2023].

13. Ammann, Thomas. Die Mac#tprobe. Wie Social Media unsere Demokratie verändern. Hamburg 2020, p. 184.

14. As of January 2021 according to their own statements. https://www.redditinc.com/. [11.03.2023].

15. Ranking of the number of Reddit users by country 2020. (20.07.2021) https://www.statista.com/forecasts/1174696/reddit-user-by-country [11.03.2023].

16. The quote is prominently found on the homepage. https://www.minds.com/ [11.03.2023].

17. Ottman, Bill, Harding, Mark, Ottman John, Ottman, Jack. Minds. The crypto-social Network (v.0.4) https://www.minds.com/static/en/assets/documents/Whitepaper-v0.5.pdf [03/11/2023].

18. More on the topic of blockchain in Chap. 4.

19. Further alternatives to Facebook can be found, for example, commented in: Facebook Alternatives 2022. Social Networks that won't sell your Data. (2021) https://makeawebsitehub.com/facebook-alternatives/ [11.03.2023]. Furthermore in: Facebook alternatives 2022—An overview. (2021) https://www.ionos.com/digitalguide/online-marketing/social-media/the-best-facebook-alternatives/ [11.03.2023].

20. As of Q1 2022. TOP 10 insurance companies by the metrics. (02.03.2022) https://www.investopedia.com/articles/active-trading/111314/top-10-insurance-companies-metrics.asp [11.03.2023].

21. How Ping An became a Fin-Tech super app. The Economist. (03.12.2020) https://www.economist.com/finance-and-economics/2020/12/03/how-ping-an-an-insurer-became-a-fintech-super-app [21.01.2023].

22. Al-Khwarizmi. (n. d.) https://de.wikipedia.org/wiki/Al-Chwarizmi [03/11/2023].

23. Anyone who wants to understand this and also learn something about their BMI is recommended this website: BMI berechnen. (n. d.) https://www.barmer.de/gesundheit-verstehen/ernaehrungsgesundheit/body-mass-index/bmi-rechner-231560 [03/11/2023].

24. Such databases can be found, for example, in: Top 10 Face datasets for facial recognition and analysis. (25.07.2022) https://datagen.tech/blog/face-datasets/ [21.01.2023].

25. How it works is very clearly explained on YouTube. In: Künstliche Intelligenz vs. Machine Learning vs. Deep Learning. (2021) https://www.youtube.com/watch?v=I-p1a2JHdt3E [11.03.2023]. Microsoft provides good practical examples for the topic of AI and its manifestations. Was ist Künstliche Intelligenz. Definition und Funktion von KI. https://news.microsoft.com/de-de/einfach-erklaert-was-ist-kuenstliche-intelligenz [11.03.2023].

26. The term inference performance refers to a system's ability to draw conclusions from new data based on a previously learned model. Moore, Samuel. We're Training AI Twice as Fast This Year as Last Year, New MLPerf rankings show training times plunging. IEEE Spectrum. (30.06.2022) https://spectrum.ieee.org/mlperf-rankings-2022 [21.01.2023].

27. An informative article on the use of AI in MRI scans in: Driesser, Ivo. Evaluating brain MRI scans with the help of artificial intelligence, MIT Technology Review, (02.06.2021) https://www.technologyreview.com/2022/06/02/1052942/evaluating-brain-mri-scans-with-the-help-of-artificial-intelligence/.

28. DeepMind uncovers structures of 200 m proteins in scientific leap forward. (28.07.2022) https://www.theguardian.com/technology/2022/jul/28/deepmind-uncovers-structure-of-200m-proteins-in-scientific-leap-forward [11.03.2023].

29. Algorithmen-basierte Diskriminierung im Alltag. Digital Autonomy Hub. Policy Brief #5. February 2022. A fairly broad overview of the advantages and disadvantages of the "algorithmization" of decisions can be found in a paper by the Pew Research Center Code-Dependent: Pros and Cons of the Algorithm Age. (08.02.2017) https://www.pewresearch.org/internet/2017/02/08/code-dependent-pros-and-cons-of-the-algorithm-age/ [11.03.2023].

30. An interesting selection of such—partly serious—cases is shown by O'Neil, Cathy. Weapons of Math Destruction. Bonn 2018. The English original title is aptly Weapons of Math Destruction. New York 2016.

31. Obama, Barack. A Promised Land. New York 2020, pp. 130 f.

32. Lynch, Mike. Barack Obama's Big Data won the Election. (13.11.2012) https://www.computerworld.com/article/2492877/barack-obama-s-big-data-won-the-us-election.html [11.03.2023].

33. Suciu, Peter. Big Data could determine the Outcome of the 2020 Election. (26.10.2020) https://www.forbes.com/sites/petersuciu/2020/10/26/social-media-could-determine-the-outcome-of-the-2020-election/?sh=7bf-632de26f6 [11.03.2023].

34. Russian Interfeence in 2016 US Election. (n. d.) https://www.fbi.gov/wanted/cyber/russian-interference-in-2016-u-s-elections [11.03.2023].

35. This reveals a pattern that can be considered "normal." Arrests are extremely rare, especially in the case of state hackers.

36. Facebook wegen Cambridge-Analytica-Datenskandal verklagt. BBC. (28.10.2020) https://www.bbc.com/news/technology-54722362 [05.03.2023].

37. Ammann, Thomas. Die Mac#tprobe, p. 184 f.

38. Google Virtual Tour. (27.09.2018) https://www.cnbc.com/2018/09/27/google-virtual-tour-of-larry-page-sergey-brins-1998-garage-office.html [11.03.2023]. There you can also find interesting insights into the early phase of the company.

39. Annual revenue of Google from 2002 to 2021. (02.12.2022) https://www.statista.com/statistics/266206/googles-annual-global-revenue/ [11.03.2023].

40. Explore what the world is searching. (n. d.) https://trends.google.com/trends/?geo=DE [03/11/2023].

41. Search Engine Market Share Worldwide. (12.2022)https://gs.statcounter.com/search-engine-market-share [23.01.2023].

42. DuckDuckGo claims to present search results based on relevance rather than commerce, while maintaining high privacy standards. More about this at https://duckduckgo.com/spread [03.03.2023].

43. This is how Google Search works. (23.01.2023) https://www.google.com/search/howsearchworks/how-search-works/ [23.01.2023].

44. 10 Google Search Statistics you need to know. (02.01.2022)    https://www.oberlo.com/blog/google-search-statistics [09.03.2023].

45. Internet Archive. (n. d.) https://archive.org/about [03/03/2023].

46. How many websites are there? (n. d.) https://first-siteguide.com/how-many-websites [03/03/2023]. A real-time insight into the growth of the web and many other interesting statistics in: Internet Livestats. https://www.internetlivestats.com/ [03/03/2023].

47. Vision of pervasive computing drives Novell. (07.05.1995)    https://www.chicagotribune.com/news/ct-xpm-1995-05-07-9505070033-story.html [11.03.2023].

48. Internet World Stats. (07.2022) https://www.internetworldstats.com/emarketing.htm [03/11/2023].

49. Verbreitung und Auswirkungen von mobiler Arbeit und Homeoffice. Forschungsbericht 549 des Bundesministeriums für Arbeit und Soziales, Oktober 2020, p. 27 ff. https://www.bmas.de/DE/Service/Publikationen/Forschungsberichte/fb-549-verbreitung-auswirkungen-mobiles-arbeiten.html [09.03.2023].

50. Homeoffice nach fast zwei Jahren Pandemie. Ein Rück- und Ausblick über die Verbreitung und Struktur der räumlichen und zeitlichen Flexibilisierung von Arbeit in Deutschland, Europa und den USA. January 2022, p. 27. The study offers further numerous and interesting details.

51. Homeoffice nach fast zwei Jahren Pandemie, pp. 26 f.

52. Should in-office workers be paid more? (07.03.2022) https://www.bbc.com/worklife/article/20220307-should-in-office-workers-be-paid-more [11.03.2023].

53. Klinghoffer, Dawn. Hybrid tanked work-life balance. Here's How Microsoft is Trying to Fix It. In: Harvard Business Review. December 08, 2021, https://hbr.org/2021/12/hybrid-tanked-work-life-balance-heres-how-microsoft-is-trying-to-fix-it [03/09/2023]. The article also describes measures that Microsoft has taken to counteract.

54. The ghost colleagues of the remote workplace. (15.03.2022) https://www.bbc.com/worklife/article/20220315-the-ghost-colleagues-of-the-remote-workplace [11.03.2023].

55. ZEW Leibniz Zentrum für Europäische Wirtschaftsforschung. Crowdworking in France and Germany. 2021 There are a number of relevant platforms on the net that act as intermediaries for this. Who are the typical crowd workers? (n. d.) http://www.crowdworker.com/who-are-the-typical-crowdworkers/ [11.03.2023].

56. Amazon Mechanical Turk. https://www.mturk.com/ [11.03.2023]. A German platform example is the App Jobber from Darmstadt, which is active throughout Europe. https://appjobber.com/ [11.03.2023].

57. How technology is redrawing the boundaries of the firm. The Economist. (10.01.2023) https://www.economist.com/business/2023/01/08/how-technology-is-redrawing-the-boundaries-of-the-firm [10.01.2023].

58. McEwan, Ian. Maschibeb wie ich. Zürich 2019.

59. Most Searched Words on Google—Top Keywords. (n. d.) https://www.mondovo.com/keywords/ [03/11/2023].

60. Response from the association to my email inquiry about sales figures from 03/09/2022.

61. AllPornSites Home Page. (11.03.2023) https://allpornsites.net/. The site is continuously updated [11.03.2023].

62. 2021 Year in Review. (14.12.2021) https://www.porn-hub.com/insights/yir-2021 [11.03.2023]. More about the ownership structure and investors in an article by the *New York Post* from 17.12.2020. This shadowy business-man is reportedly behind Pornhub parent MindGeek. (17.12.2020) https://nypost.com/2020/12/17/porn-hub-parent-owned-by-shadowy-businessman-ber-nard-bergemar/ [11.03.2023].

63. The Pornhub Tech Review. (08.04.2021) https://www.pornhub.com/insights/tech-review [03/11/2023].

64. Vilines, Zawn. Porn: is it bad for you? (27.08.2020) https://www.medicalnewstoday.com/articles/is-porn-bad#is-porn-bad [11.03.2023].

65. Detailed results in: Journal of Sex and Marital Therapy, Volume 44, 2018—Issue 4. https://www.tandfonline.com/toc/usmt20/44/4 [19.01.2023].

66. Chinese Gamers are using a steam wallpaper app to get porn past the censors. (21.07.2022) https://www.tech-nologyreview.com/2022/07/21/1056315/chinese-gam-ers-steam-wallpaper-porn [23.01.2023].

67. Court, Andrew. Billie Eilish began watching porn at 11: 'It really destroyed my brain'. (14.12.2021) https://nypost.com/2021/12/14/billie-eilish-says-porn-has-de-stroyed-her-brain/ [03/11/2023].

68. Thompson, Rache. The UK's porn age verification plan is a terrible idea. (09.02.2022) https://mashable.com/article/uk-porn-age-verification [11.03.2023].

69. Das Leben ist kurz. Gönn Dir eine Affäre. (n. d.) https://www.ashleymadison.com/de-de/ [11.03.2023].

70. Ashley Madison Hack. (2021) https://darkwebjournal.com/ashley-madison-hack/ [03/11/2023].

71. Newitz, Annalee. Ashley Madison code shows more women and more bots. (31.08.2015) https://gizmodo.com/ashley-madison-code-shows-more-women-and-more-bots-1727613924 [19.01.2023].

72. Ashley Madison has always denied this, by the way.

73. Aiken, Mary. Cyber Effect, p. 225.

74. AI love you. Japanese man not alone in marriage to virtual character. (17.04.2020) https://mainichi.jp/english/articles/20200417/p2a/00m/0na/027000c [11.03.2023].

75. Top 10 Artificial Intelligence Virtual Girlfriend Apps in 2021. (10.11.2021) https://www.analyticsinsight.net/top-10-artificial-intelligence-virtual-girlfriend-apps-in-2021 [11.03.2023].

76. My virtual girl. (n. d.) https://www.microsoft.com/en-us/p/my-virtual-girl-dream-romance-and-relationships-with-cute-girlfriend/9nwh6bsvfdfh?activetab=pivot:overviewtab [03/11/2023].

77. Raise your child. Live you Life. (n. d.) https://myvirtuallife.com [11.03.2023].

78. Aiken, Mary. Cyber Effect, p. 228.

79. Sex robots of the future. (n. d.) https://www.youtube.com/watch?v=57o380nALxY.

80. Govind, Deepti. The CREEPER Act: The Case For Banning Child Sex Dolls And Robots. (05.08.2021) https://www.biometrica.com/the-creeper-act-the-case-for-banning-child-sex-dolls-and-robots/ [19.01.2023].

81. Can Artificial Intelligence ever be sentient? BBC. (11.03.2023) https://www.bbc.com/reel/video/p0f73vlw/can-artificial-intelligence-ever-be-sentient-? [11.03.2023].

82. More details on the technology in: LaMDA und die Technik dahinter. (24.06.2022) https://www.heise.de/hintergrund/LaMDA-und-die-Technik-dahinter-Wie-viele-Parameter-braucht-s-fuers-Bewusstsein-7146996.html [24.06.2022]. For the publication in the *Washington Post* see The Google engineer who thinks the company's AI has come to life. (11.06.2022) https://www.washingtonpost.com/technology/2022/06/11/google-ai-lamda-blake-lemoine/ [24.06.2022].

83. ChatGPT AI threat pulls Google co-founders back into action. (20.01.2023) https://www.cnet.com/tech/services-and-software/search-engine-you-com-launches-chatgpt-style-chatbot/ [23.01.2023].

84. Smart Doll World. (n. d.) https://www.smartdollworld.com/ [03/11/2023].
85. Responsible Robotics. (n. d.) https://responsiblerobotics.org/ [03/11/2023].
86. Candelon, Francois. AI Regulation is coming. In: Harvard Business Review October 2021, pp. 5 ff.

# Notes: America's Dominance and Europe's Opportunities

1. The periodization of computer generations is not set in stone and is not always uniformly presented in the literature. A good overview is provided by Tanenbaum, A.S. Goodman, J. Computerarchitektur. Strukturen, Konzepte Grundlagen. München 2001, pp. 32–44.
2. Konrad Zuse, John von Neumann & Co. Der Computer hatte viele Väter. BR Wissen. (11.05.2021) https://www.br.de/wissen/konrad-zuse-computer-erfinder-rechner-100.html [24.01.2023].
3. The wit and wisdom of Grace Hopper. (März/April 1987) https://www.cs.yale.edu/homes/tap/Files/hopper-wit.html [24.01.2023].
4. Mark I and its areas of application have often been described. A solid brief presentation can be found in: O'Regan, Cornelius. A Brief History of Computing, p. 54 f.
5. Well-founded and detailed on ENIAC in: Haigh, Thomas. Cerruzzi, Paul. A new history of Modern Computing. Cambridge 2021, pp. 10 ff.
6. ENIAC. (n. d.) https://en.wikipedia.org/wiki/ENIAC [25.01.2023].
7. Traue niemals einem Computer, den Du nicht aus dem Fenster werfen kannst. MacLife. (12/11/2014) https://www.maclife.de/news/steve-wozniak-traue-niemals-einem-computer-nicht-fenster-werfen-kannst-seine-besten-zitate-10060905.html [01/25/2023].

8. Moye, William. ENIAC: The Army-Sponsored Revolution. (01.1996) https://ftp.arl.army.mil/~mike/comphist/96summary/index.html [26.01.2023].

9. Haig, Cerruzzi. A New History, p. 14.

10. ENIAC-on-a-Chip. Moore School of Electrical Engineering, University of Pennsylvania. (09/06/1995) https://www.seas.upenn.edu/~jan/eniacproj.html [02/26/2023].

11. Lavington, Simon. Early British Computers. (05.1980) http://ed-thelen.org/comp-hist/EarlyBritish.html#Ch-02 [05.03.2023].

12. Technology and functionality as well as a brief historical overview of the Enigma are well described in: Oepen, Dominik. Höfer, Sebastian. Die Enigma. (20.04.2007) https://www2.informatik.hu-berlin.de/~oependox/files/Ausarbeitung-Enigma.pdf [26.01.2023].

13. UK-USA Episode One—A Cautious Collaboration. (17.11.2021) https://www.youtube.com/watch?v=ohh-DcFJ1oas [26.01.2023].

14. A well-researched and detailed account of the activities in Bletchley Park and its protagonists can be found in: Copeland, Jack. Breaking the German Tunny code at Bletchley Park. An illustrated history. The Rutherford Journal. (2017) http://www.rutherfordjournal.org/article030109.html [26.01.2023].

15. Thomas Harold "Tommy" Flowers: Designer of the Colossus Codebreaking Machines. IEEE Annals of the History of Computing. Vol. 40. Issue 1. January—March 2018, pp. 72–82.

16. Copeland, Breaking the German Tunny code, p. 6.

17. A good overview of Turing's life and his works in: Andrew Hodges. Alan Turing—a short biography. (1995) https://www.turing.org.uk/publications/dnb.html [26.01.2023].

18. Strick, Hein Klaus. John von Neumann (1903–1957): Vater des Computers. Spektrum der Wissenschaft (26.01.2007) https://www.spektrum.de/wissen/john-von-neumann-1903-1957/861603 [26.01.2023].

19. Tanenbaum,    Goodman.    Computerarchitektur, pp. 37–39. More on this in this book, Chap. 8, section Computing with Quanta and the Reinvention of the Computer.

20. Tom Flowers explained that himself on YouTube in: Tommy Flowers. YouTube. (21.10.2008) https://www. youtube.com/watch?v=yfz8ZYKIO5g [27.01.2023].

21. For the general use of the binary number system in computer technology, see Chap. 8, section Computing with Quanta and the Reinvention of the Computer.

22. Colossus decrypts to be revealed after 75 years. The National Museum of Computing. (05.02.2019) https:// www.tnmoc.org/news-releases/2019/2/5/colossus-decrypts-to-be-revealed-after-75-years [27.01.2023].

23. Thomas Flowers: The hidden story of the Bletchley Park Engineer who designed the code-breaking Colossus. IEEE Annals of the History of Computing. (09.08.2018)    https://publications.computer.org/ annals/2018/08/09/thomas-flowers-code-breaker-wwii-colossus-machines/ [05.03.2023].

24. Copeland, Breaking the German Tunny code, p. 19.

25. Max Newman. (n. d.) https://en.wikipedia.org/wiki/ Max_Newman.

26. Alan Turing. British Mathematician and Logician. Britannica.    (02.12.2022)    https://www.britannica. com/biography/Alan-Turing/Computer-designer [05.03.2023].

27. Wie Konrad Zuse vor 80 Jahren in Berlin den Computer erfand. FAZ.net. (Updated on 12.05.2021)https:// www.faz.net/aktuell/wirtschaft/computer-wie-konrad-zuse-in-berlin-die-erste-rechenmaschine-erfand-17337997.html [05.03.2023].

28. Horst Konrad Zuse zeigt seinen Nachbau des legendären Z3. YouTube. (2011) https://www.youtube.com/ watch?v=_YR5HhWlOgg [05.03.2023].

29. Bauer, Friedrich. Historische Notizen zur Informatik. (2009),    pp. 198 f.    https://link.springer.com/chapter/10.1007/978-3-540-85790-7_34 [05.03.2023].

30. The examination of the topic "Computers from Germany" and the German IT industry as a whole is, in my opinion, still somewhat lacking. There is a need for a scientifically based comprehensive presentation of German IT that appealingly prepares its economic, scientific, and political contexts for a broader audience. A biographical outline of Zuse, his calculating machines, and his significant life stages can be found with further details in a publication of the Deutsches Museum https://kalliope-verbund.info/de/findingaid?fa.id=DE-210A_NL_207&fa.enum=1&lastparam=true [03/05/2023].

31. Univac computer predicts election. CHM Computer History Museum. (n. d.) https://www.computerhistory.org/timeline/1952/ [29.01.2023].

32. Haig, Cerruzzi. A new history, pp. 22 and 25.

33. Ferranti. Wikipedia. (n. d.) https://en.wikipedia.org/wiki/Ferranti and Timeline of Computer History. (n. d.) https://www.computerhistory.org/timeline/1951/ [29.01.2023].

34. Digital Verlustzone. Wie Deutschland den Anschluss verlor. ARD Dokumentation. (26.05.2020) https://www.youtube.com/watch?v=5KbWSr5GBuY.

35. The Graphomat Z64. (23.10.2002) http://www.konrad-zuse.net/zuse-kg/rechner/der-graphomat-z64 [26.01.2023].

36. Manchester Baby. Wikipedia. (n. d.) https://en.wikipedia.org/wiki/Manchester_Baby [29.01.2023].

37. Hashagen, Ulf. Rechner für die Wissenschaft. Scientific Computing und Informatik im deutschen Wissenschaftssystem 1870–1970. In: Hashagen, Ulf. Hellige, Hans Dieter. Rechnende Maschinen im Wandel. (2011), pp. 122 ff. and 177.

38. Hashagen. Rechner für die Wissenschaft, p. 111.

39. Haig, Cerruzzi. A new history, p. 22.

40. A summary of this with further literature references in: History of computing in the Soviet Union. (Updated 04.08.2022) https://wikimili.com/en/History_of_computing_in_the_Soviet_Union [29.01.1023].

41. Hashagen. Rechner für die Wissenschaft, pp. 132/133.

42. 10 Biggest Tech Hardware Companies. (Updated 01.08.2022) https://www.investopedia.com/articles/ investing/012716/worlds-top-10-hardware-companies-aaplibm.asp [29.01.2023].

43. This statistic excludes social media and service giants, such as Amazon. 10 Biggest Software Companies. Investopedia. (10.05.2022) https://www.investopedia. com/articles/personal-finance/121714/worlds-top-10-software-companies.asp [05.03.2023].

44. As early as 1981, Helmut Schmidt, then chancellor of Germany, called for a fiber optic network. T-online Nachrichten für Deutschland. (07.03.2018) https:// www.t-online.de/digital/internet/id_83348004/ewige-breitband-baustelle-schon-helmut-schmidt-forderte-1981-ein-glasfasernetz.html [29.01.2023].

45. The whole thing is recorded on YouTube. Helmut Kohl und die Datenautobahn. YouTube. (03.03.1994) https://www.youtube.com/watch?v=kAfSF-y8Y4U [29.01.2023].

46. Duden. (1967) https://www.duden.de/rechtschreibung/ Computer [03/05/2023].

47. The curious origin of the word Computer. Interesting Literature. (02.2020) https://interestingliterature. com/2020/02/origin-word-computer-etymology/ [05.03.2023].

48. Welt am Sonntag. (03/04/2022), p. 15.

49. Global Cloud Ecosystem Index 2022. MIT Technology Review. (25.04.2022)https://www.technologyreview. com/2022/04/25/1051115/global-cloud-ecosystem-in-dex-2022 [05.03.2023]. Ahead of Germany in the ranking are Singapore, Finland, Sweden, Denmark, and Switzerland.

## Notes: The Rise of IT to World Power

1. Gartner Market Data Book (04.2022) and in brief: Gartner forecasts worldwide IT spending to grow 5.1 % in 2022. (18.01.2022) https://www.gartner.com/en/newsroom/press-releases/2022-01-18-gartner-forecasts-worldwide-it-spending-to-grow-five-point-1-percent-in-2022 [06.03.2023].

2. Gross Domestic Product 2021. (n. d.) https://databankfiles.worldbank.org/public/ddpext_download/GDP.pdf [31.01.2023].

3. 10 größte Unternehmen der Welt 2022. Visual Capitalist. (o. D.) https://www.visualcapitalist.com/wp-content/uploads/2021/06/Biggest-Companies-in-the-World.html [14.04.2022].

4. 10 Biggest Companies in the World 2021. Insider Monkey. (24.03.2021) https://www.insider-monkey.com/blog/10-biggest-industries-in-the-world-in-2021-925224/ [06.03.2023].

5. Samsung takes Semi-Conductor Crown from Intel in 2021. Counterpoint. (28.01.2022) https://www.counterpointresearch.com/semiconductor-revenue-ranking-2021/ [06.03.2023].

6. Cramming more components onto Integrated Circuits. Intel. (n. d.) https://www.intel.com/content/www/us/en/silicon-innovations/moores-law-technology.html [06.03.2023].

7. IBM 7090. (n. d.) https://en.wikipedia.org/wiki/IBM_7090 [03/06/2023].

8. Apples A15 Bionic-Chip powers iPhone 13 with 15 Billion Transistors, new Graphics and AI . (14.09.2021) https://www.cnet.com/tech/mobile/apples-a15-bionic-chip-powers-iphone-13-with-15-billion-transistors-new-graphics-and-ai/ [06.03.2023].

9. More on this in Chap. 8, section Computing with Quanta and the Reinvention of the Computer.

10. YouTube is full of often well-made educational videos on the subject of computer technology and thus also on chips. Particularly recommended are the "Crash Courses Computer Science" by Carrie Ann Philbin, who, with her broad knowledge and charming manner, rightly enjoys a large fan base.

11. Mehr als jedes dritte deutsche Unternehmen nutzt das Internet der Dinge. Pressemitteilung des Statistischen Bundesamtes No. 035 vom 26.Januar 2022 mit Zahlen für einzelne EU-Länder. https://www.destatis.de/DE/Presse/Pressemitteilungen/2022/01/PD22_035_52911.html [31.01.2023].

12. Haig, Thomas. Cerruzzi, Paul. A new history, pp. 87 ff.

13. For Altair see Wikipedia. (n. d.) https://en.wikipedia.org/wiki/Altair_8800 [06.05.2022]. For NEC, see the extensive article NEC. Wikipedia. (n. d.) https://en.wikipedia.org/wiki/NEC [31.01.2023].

14. CPI Inflation Calculator. (n. d.) https://www.in2013dollars.com/us/inflation/1975?amount=1000000 [06.03.2023].

15. The beginnings of the Altair are described in overview by Moore, Anthony. Altair 8800 Computer. Media History and Theory. (01.05. 2015). https://issuu.com/amoore526/docs/altair8800. The information on sales there on p. 6 [31.01.2023].

16. Haig, Thomas. Cerruzzi, Paul. A new history, pp. 144 ff.

17. The representations of the emergence of the PC are, as expected, numerous. For a competent and, contrary to the title chosen there, also easily understandable presentation for non-technicians, I refer to: Crash Course Computer Science. YouTube. Episode 25. (n. d.) https://www.youtube.com/watch?v=M5BZou6C01w [31.01.2023].

18. BASIC stands for "Beginners' All-purpose Symbolic Instruction Code" and the name reflects the concept very well. A brief history of BASIC. Microsoft Community Hub. (12.02.2019) https://techcommunity. microsoft.com/t5/small-basic-blog/a-brief-history-of-basic/ba-p/336312 [06.03.2023].

19. Steve Wozniak: Der Vater des Personal Computers. Mac-History.Net. (10.08.2022) https://www.mac-history.de/2022/08/10/steve-wozniak-apple-co-founder/. A timeline that lists the history of Apple chronologically can be found there in the "Tab Timeline" at https://www.mac-history.de/geschichte-von-apple-seit-1976/ [31.01.2023].

20. These and other interesting facts about Apple's financial development can be found in: Steve Jobs and the Apple story. (Updated 22.12.2022) https://www.investopedia.com/articles/fundamental-analysis/12/steve-jobs-apple-story.asp [06.03.2023]. For Microsoft's market value, see Microsoft hits $1 Trillion market value for the first time. Wallstreet Journal (25.04.2019). https://www.wsj.com/articles/microsoft-hits-1-trillion-market-value-for-first-time-11556201153 [31.01.2023].

21. Gartner says worldwide PC Shipments grew 10.7 percent in fourth quarter of 2020. (11.01.2021) https://www.gartner.com/en/newsroom/press-releases/2021-01-11-gartner-says-worldwide-pc-shipments-grew-10-point-7-percent-in-the-fourth-quarter-of-2020-and-4-point-8-percent-for-the-year [31.01.2023].

22. "This whole vision of a personal computer just popped into my head. That night, I started to sketch out on paper what would later become the Apple I." Quoted from Isaacson, Walter. Steve Jobs. London 2013, p. 55. I have largely taken the events described here from Isaacson's account.

23. Isaacson, Walter. Steve Jobs, p. 40.

24. Nixdorf Computer. Wikipedia. (n. d.) [https://de.wikipedia.org/wiki/Nixdorf_Computer [03/06/2023].

25. Gerstner, Louis. Who says Elephants can't dance? New York 2002, p. 57 ff. Lou had joined IBM as the new CEO in April 1993, with the task of reforming the faltering giant.

26. Fesmina Faizal. The History of Apple. Feedough. (07.09.2021) https://www.feedough.com/the-history-of-apple/ [05.06.2022].

27. The Personal Computer Revolution. YouTube (23.08.2017). Timestamp 6 min and 18 s. https://www.youtube.com/watch?v=M5BZou6C01w.

28. Cortada, James. How the IBM PC Won, Then Lost, the Personal Computer Market. In: IEEE Spectrum. (21.07.2021) https://spectrum.ieee.org/how-the-ibm-pc-won-then-lost-the-personal-computer-market [06.03.2023].

29. A concise and well-founded overview of the Internet and its various developmental phases in: History of the Internet. (n. d.) https://internethistory.org/early-internet/ [06.03.2023].

30. Defense Advanced Research Projects Agency. (n. d.) https://de.wikipedia.org/wiki/Defense_Advanced_Research_Projects_Agency [06.03.2023].

31. A very good, detailed, and easy to understand presentation of the "Post-War Computing" era can be found on YouTube as a nearly ten-hour course by Chuck Severance, a contemporary witness and former employee of the University of Michigan in: Internet History. Technology and Security. YouTube. (n. d.) https://www.youtube.com/watch?v=47NRaBVxgVM [06.03.2023]. The corresponding passages on ARPANET can be found in the section "Early Academic Networking Research".

32. About DE-CIX. (n. d.) https://www.de-cix.net/en/about-de-cix [31.01.2023].

33. The development of the WWW and the collaboration with Robert is depicted by Berners-Lee, Tim. Weaving the Web. New York 1999, pp. 21 ff. Those who do

not wish to buy it can read it for free in the worldwide Internet archive at https://archive.org/details/weaving-weborigin00bern_0/page/21/mode/2up?view=theater. [06.03.2023].

34. Berners-Lee, Tim. Weaving the Web, p. X.
35. A quite informative infographic on the evolution of network speeds can be found in: An Accelerated History of Internet Speed. (n. d.) https://assets.entrepreneur.com/article/an-accelerated-history-internet-speed.jpg [06.03.2023].
36. The underlying data were collected year after year in Silicon Valley. Therefore, they are not necessarily representative of other countries and regions; see: Nielsen, Jacob. Nielson's Law of Internet Bandwidth (27.09.2019) https://www.nngroup.com/articles/law-of-bandwidth/ [06.03.2023]. His information is confirmed by other tracking data since 1990 in: Lee, Xah. Internet Speed Growth Rate (Updated 11.07.2020) http://xahlee.info/comp/bandwidth.html [06.03.2023]. From them, the same formula (+50% annually) was derived. They also originate from the Valley.
37. Haig, Thomas. Cerruzzi, Paul. A new history, p. 330.
38. Windows 95. Wikipedia. (n. d.) https://en.wikipedia.org/wiki/Windows_95 [06.03.2023].
39. A detailed statistic for download in: Statistisches Bundesamt 2021. (n. d.) https://www-genesis.destatis.de/genesis/online?sequenz=tabelleErgebnis&selectionname=48121-0002#abreadcrumb [06.03.2023].

# Notes: The Transformation of the Economy

1. How this looks in detail in different job groups in: Shifting Skills, Moving Targets and Remaking the Workforce. Boston Consulting Group. (05/2022) https://web-assets.bcg.com/c1/c0/649ce92247c48f4efdbf9e38797a/

bcg-shifting-skills-moving-targets-and-remaking-the-workforce-may-2022.pdf [07.03.2023].

2. Examples can be found in large numbers on job forums like Indeed, Stepstone, or Dice.

3. Bard: Google's Antwort auf OpenAIs ChatGPT. Heise online. (02/06/2023) https://www.heise.de/news/Chatbot-Googles-Antwort-auf-ChatGPT-heisst-Bard-7486888.html [03/06/2023]. For Ernie see: Baidu kündigt Konkurrenz zu ChatGPT und Bard an. Handelsblatt (02/10/2023) https://www.handelsblatt.com/technik/it-internet/chatbot-aus-china-baidu-kuendigt-konkurrenz-fuer-chatgpt-und-bard-an/28967090.html [03/07/2023].

4. Microsoft confirms its $10 Billion investment in ChatGPT, Changing how Microsoft competes with Google, Apple and other Tech Giants. Forbes. (27.01.2023) https://www.forbes.com/sites/qai/2023/01/27/microsoft-confirms-its-10-billion-investment-into-chatgpt-changing-how-microsoft-competes-with-google-apple-and-other-tech-giants/ [07.03.2023].

5. ChatGPT is called an iPhone moment in AI. Marketwatch (31.12.2022) https://www.marketwatch.com/story/chatgpt-is-called-an-iphone-moment-in-ai-but-will-it-make-money-like-the-iphone-11672187982 [07.03.2023].

6. ChatGPT passes MBA Exam given by a Wharton Professor. NBC News. (24.01.2023) https://www.nbcnews.com/tech/tech-news/chatgpt-passes-mba-exam-wharton-professor-rcna67036 [07.03.2023]. For the other two exams, see GPT-4 is bigger and better than ChatGPT—but OpenAI won't say why. MIT Technology Review. (14.03.2023) https://www.technologyreview.com/2023/03/14/1069823/gpt-4-is-bigger-and-better-chatgpt-openai/ [14.03.2023].

7. I went into this in more detail in Chap. 1, section Artificial Intelligence and learning machines.

8. NRW allows ChatGPT software in schools. Rheinische Post. (31.01.2023), p. 1.

9. Datenschutz bei Sprachassistenten wie Alexa, Siri & Co.—Orwell's Graus. Datenschutzexperte. (30.06.2022) https://www.datenschutzexperte.de/blog/alexa-daten-schutz-sprachassistenten/ [07.03.2023]. The article lists a series of incidents that reveal much room for improvement in such systems.

10. GPTs are GPTs: An early look at the labor market impact potential of Large Language Models. Cornell University. (23.03.2023) https://arxiv.org/abs/2303.10130 [24.03.2023].

11. Fancy a Bite? UK Restaurant Chain Bella Italia trials Robot Waiters that could help tackle the staff shortage in Hospitality. MailOnline (14.06.2022) https://www.dailymail.co.uk/sciencetech/article-10911461/Restaurant-chain-Bella-Italia-trials-ROBOT-WAITERS-help-address-hospitality-staff-shortage.html [02.02.2023].

12. Wissenswertes zu 5G. Informationszentrum Mobilfunk. (n. d.) https://www.informationszentrum-mobilfunk.de/technik/funktionsweise/5g [02/03/2023].

13. Numerous industry-specific application examples can be found on the Intel website under: 5G Business Opportunities. (n. d.) https://www.intel.com/content/www/us/en/wireless-network/5g-business-opportunities.html [28.06.2022].

14. Further details of the PwC study in: The global economic impact of 5G. PwC Global. (n. d.) https://www.pwc.com/gx/en/industries/technology/publications/economic-impact-5g.html [07.03.2023] as well as in the detailed report that can be downloaded there.

15. VirtualShip® Maritime Simulator. General Dynamics Information Technology. (n. d.) https://www.gdit.com/perspectives/our-stories/maritime-simulation-virtual-ship/ [02/03/2023].

16. There is plenty of literature on this topic. For those who want a concise and precise overview, I recommend: Van Alstyne, Marshall. Parker, Geoffrey. Digital Transformation changes how Companies create Value. Harvard Business Review. (17.12.2021) https://hbr.org/2021/12/digital-transformation-changes-how-companies-create-value [03.02.2023].

17. As of early 2022. According to Statista for the App Store: https://www.statista.com/statistics/268251/number-of-apps-in-the-itunes-app-store-since-2008/. For Google Play: https://www.statista.com/statistics/266210/number-of-available-applications-in-the-google-play-store/ [07.03.2023].

18. Grab Reports Fourth Quarter and Full Year 2021 Results. (03.03.2022) https://investors.grab.com/news-releases/news-release-details/grab-reports-fourth-quarter-and-full-year-2021-results [03.02.2023].

19. Revenue of leading automakers worldwide in 2021. (27.07.2022) https://www.statista.com/statistics/232958/revenue-of-the-leading-car-manufacturers-worldwide/ [03.02.2023].

20. How to operate like a tech company. McKinsey Company. (28.02.2019) https://www.mckinsey.com/business-functions/mckinsey-digital/our-insights/the-platform-play-how-to-operate-like-a-tech-company [07.03.2023].

21. 15 Years Later, Google Remembers Its First Data Center. (06.02.2014)https://www.pcmag.com/news/15-years-later-google-remembers-its-first-data-center [03.02.2023].

22. "We are a tech company that connects the physical and digital worlds to help make movement happen at the tap of a button." About us. (n. d.) https://www.uber.com/gb/en/about/ [21.07.2022].

23. "Risks and uncertainties related to our business and industry include risks and uncertainties associated with … our ability to maintain the trusted status of our

ecosystem, and to maintain or improve the network effects of our ecosystem …" United States Security and Exchange Commission. Form 20-F. Alibaba Group Holding Limited. Part 1, p. 1. Regarding possible regulatory interventions by the Chinese government, see pp. 2 and 3. The Annual Report can be found at: https://docs-src.alibabagroup.com/en/ir/secfilings and can be downloaded there.

24. Annual revenue of Alibaba Group from financial year 2012 to 2022. (27.07.2022) https://www.statista.com/statistics/225614/net-revenue-of-alibaba/ [03.02.2023]. Converted from 853 billion yuan, as of March 2022.

25. "We envision that our customers will meet, work and live at Alibaba". About us. Culture and Values. (n. d.) https://www.alibabagroup.com/en-US/about-alibaba [03.02.2023].

26. Alibaba is well insulated from Evergrande Fallout. Seeking Alpha (18.09.2021) https://seekingalpha.com/article/4455941-alibaba-is-no-evergrande [03.02.2023].

27. Introducing the first end-to-end shopping experience on WhatsApp with JioMart in India. (29.08.2022) https://about.fb.com/news/2022/08/shop-on-whatsapp-with-jiomart-in-india/ [03.02.2023]. In this context, an article by Meta is also interesting: New ways to find and buy from businesses on WhatsApp. (17.11.2022) https://about.fb.com/news/2022/11/find-and-buy-from-businesses-on-whatsapp/.

28. More details in: State of Venture 2021. (12.01.2022) https://www.cbinsights.com/research/report/venture-trends-2021/ [15.07.2022].

29. For Thiel's investment, see The History of Facebook. (28.02.2022) https://www.feedough.com/history-of-facebook/ [04.02.2023]. For Accel Partners' investment, see The Comeback Kid. Forbes. (06.04.2011) https://www.forbes.com/2011/04/06/midas-list-11-jim-breyer-venture-capital-comeback-kid.html?sh=2e9575e62b96 [04.02.2023].

30. Facebook to acquire WhatsApp. Meta. (19.02.2014) https://about.fb.com/news/2014/02/facebook-to-acquire-whatsapp/ [05.02.2023].

31. Solid information about the financiers for tech companies and the amount of capital they have invested in: https://www.crunchbase.com/ [06.07.2022]. There also the information on LinkedIn.

32. Microsoft to buy LinkedIn for $26,2 Billion in its largest deal. Reuters. (13.06.2016)https://www.reuters.com/article/us-linkedin-m-a-microsoft-idUSKCN0YZ1FP [05.02.2023].

33. Motorola Mobility. CBInsights (n. d.) https://www.cbinsights.com/company/motorola-mobility. For Lenovo see Lenovo Completes Acquisition of Motorola Mobility from Google. (30.10.2014)https://news.lenovo.com/pressroom/press-releases/lenovo-completes-full-acquisition-motorola-mobility-from-google/ [02/05/2023].

34. "Data spanning more than a quarter century … make it clear the economy is inverting from one where value was measured by 'touch' to one where value is driven by thought." Intangible Asset Market Value Study. Ocean Tomo. (2022) https://www.oceantomo.com/intangible-asset-market-value-study/ [05.02.2023]. The study is available for download there.

35. Staab, Philipp. Digitaler Kapitalismus. Markt und Herrschaft in der Ökonomie der Unknappheit. Bonn 2019, p. 30.

36. A day in the life of a Chinese robotaxi driver. MIT Technology Review (27.07.2022) https://www.technologyreview.com/2022/07/27/1056472/life-of-chinese-robotaxi-driver/ [05.02.2023].

37. Epic Games Store—Year in Review 2021. (27.01.2022)https://store.epicgames.com/de/news/epic-games-store-2021-year-in-review [06.07.2022].

38. The case naturally had antitrust relevance for the industry and was closely watched. For this reason, the responsible district court of Northern California set up a

website that includes all process-relevant documents and the judgment. Epic Games, Inc. vs. Apple, Inc. United States District Court. Northern District of California. (n. d.)    https://cand.uscourts.gov/cases-e-filing/cases-of-interest/epic-games-inc-v-apple-inc/ [02/05/2023].

39. Ping An Technology. About Us. (n. d.) https://tech.pingan.com/ [02/05/2023].

40. Ping An Company Profile (31.12.2021) pp. 5 and 6. https://group.pingan.com/about_us/who_we_are.html [05.02.2023].

41. "We share leading innovative products and services with others to develop and empower business ecosystems with advanced technologies". Ping An Group. About Us. (n. d.) https://group.pingan.com/about_us/who_we_are. html. [02/05/2023]. Ping An is thus well positioned to become active worldwide under suitable circumstances.

42. How Ping An, an insurer, became a fintech superapp. The Economist (03.12.2020) https://www.economist. com/finance-and-economics/2020/12/03/how-ping-an-an-insurer-became-a-fintech-super-app [05.02.2023].

43. Blockchain explained. What it is and why it matters McKinsey Company. (28.09.2018) https://www. mckinsey.com/business-functions/mckinsey-digital/ our-insights/blockchain-explained-what-it-is-and-isnt-and-why-it-matters [05.02.2023].

44. Blockchain technology market size worldwide from 2017 to 2027. (23.05.2022) https://www.statista.com/statistics/1015362/ worldwide-blockchain-technology-market-size/.

45. Blockchain Market Size. Market Research Report March 2022. (03.2022) https://www.fortunebusinessinsights. com/industry-reports/blockchain-market-100072.    For the figures from Market Research Future see Blockchain Technology Market, February 2020. (02.2022) https://www.marketresearchfuture.com/reports/ block-chain-technology-market-1708. Another variant is offered by IDC with an annual growth of 48%, Global

Spending on Blockchain Solutions. Forecast to be Nearly $19 Billion in 2024. (19.04.2021) https://www.idc.com/getdoc.jsp [23.05.2022].

46. Crypto Winter explained. Tech Target. (26.01.2023) https://www.techtarget.com/whatis/feature/Crypto-winter-explained-Everything-you-need-to-know [05.02.2023]. There also the description of the most striking scandals.

47. Cryptoverse: What crisis? Venture capitalists bet big on crypto. Reuters. (26.07.2022). https://www.reuters.com/business/future-of-money/cryptoverse-what-crisis-venture-capitalists-bet-big-crypto-2022-07-26/ [05.02.2023].

48. An example of this is IBM. Willkommen bei IBM Blockchain. (n. d.) https://www.ibm.com/de-de/blockchain [02/05/2023].

49. Welcome to Ethereum.(o. D.) https://ethereum.org/en/ [05.02.2023].

50. In order to keep the presentation clear, the functional distinction between participants, nodes, and miners of a blockchain is not further elaborated here, among other things. Those interested in further information can easily find literature of any level of detail on the subject. A clear presentation of manageable length is offered by the paper published by the German Federal Network Agency (Bundesnetzagentur): Die Blockchain-Technologie. Grundlagen, Potenziale und Herausforderungen. Bonn. July 2021.

51. Such a platform is represented by IPwe, founded in 2017, which describes itself as "the world's first global patent market." IPwe. (n. d.) https://ipwe.com/ [02/05/2023]. How much this is still in its early stages is shown by Googling terms like IP Trading or Patent Trading. The yield is very thin compared to the number of "normal" search results.

52. More details on this can be found in an article by Handelsblatt. Welche Kryptobörsen sind für den Kauf von Bitcoin & Co geeignet? Handelsblatt. (20.07.2022)

https://www.handelsblatt.com/vergleich/krypto-boers-en-vergleich/ [05.02.2023].

53. How Bitcoin became the leading cryptocurrency. The Daily Californian. (20.12.2021)https://www.dailycal.org/2021/12/20/how-bitcoin-became-the-leading-cryp-tocurrency/ [05.02.2023].

54. Nakamoto, Satoshi. Bitcoin: A Peer-to-Peer Electronic Cash System. (31.10.2008) https://bitcoin.org/bitcoin.pdf, p. 1.

55. How many cryptocurrencies are there in 2022? Exploding Topics. (25.11.2022) https://explodingtopics.com/blog/number-of-cryptocurrencies [05.02.2023].

56. Venezuela dreht Bitcoin Minern den Strom ab. BTC-ECHO Magazine. (12.08.2022) https://www.btc-echo.de/schlagzeilen/ausgeknipst-venezuela-dre-ht-bitcoin-minern-den-strom-ab-123864/ [05.02.2023].

57. Breaking news from the German newscast Tagesschau on 18.06.2022. https://www.tagesschau.de/wirtschaft/finan-zen/bitcoin-wertverlust-101.html [05.02.2023].

58. Kryptowährungen können hohe Zinsen abwerfen. NZZ am Sonntag. Issue of 07.08.2022, p. 33.

59. Collapse of FTX cryptocurrency exchange under scrutiny by federal authorities. The Guardian. (10.11.2022)https://www.theguardian.com/technol-ogy/2022/nov/10/ftx-cryptocurrency-collapse-investiga-tion [05.02.2023].

60. How many cryptocurrencies are there in2022? Exploding Topics. (25.11.2022) https://explodingtopics.com/blog/number-of-cryptocurrencies [05.02.2023].

61. Top 10 cryptocurrencies of 2023. Forbes Advisor. (28.02.2023) https://www.forbes.com/advisor/investing/cryptocurrency/top-10-cryptocurrencies/.

62. Kryptowährungen & Co: Honduras bringt eigenes Bitcoin Valley an den Start. Finanzen.net. (10.08.2022) https://www.finanzen.net/nachricht/devisen/lateinamer-ika-kryptowaehrungen-co-honduras-bringt-eigenes-bit-coin-valley-an-den-start-11608379 [05.02.2023].

63. Iran places first import order using cryptocurrency. Reuters. (09.08.2022) https://www.reuters.com/business/finance/iran-makes-first-import-order-using-cryptocurrency-tasnim-2022-08-09/ [05.02.2023].

64. Ethereum switched to proof of stake. Why can't Bitcoin? MIT Technology Review. (28.02.2023) https://www.technologyreview.com/2023/02/28/1069190/ethereum-moved-to-proof-of-stake-why-cant-bitcoin/ [28.03.2023].

65. The research department of the American Congress scientifically reflects the state of governmental handling of cryptocurrencies as of November 2021. Regulation of Cryptocurrency Around the World: November 2021 Update. The Law Library of Congress https://tile.loc.gov/storage-services/service/ll/llglrd/2021687419/2021687419.pdf. An updated overview of where cryptocurrencies are accepted as a means of payment, where their use is merely "legal," where they are in an unregulated "tolerance zone," and where a ban applies, can be found continuously updated in: Legality of cryptocurrency by country or territory. Wikipedia. (30.01.2023) https://en.wikipedia.org/wiki/Legality_of_cryptocurrency_by_country_or_territory [05.02.2023].

66. More details in: Digital finance: agreement reached on European crypto-assets regulation (MiCA). (30.06.2022) https://www.consilium.europa.eu/en/press/press-releases/2022/06/30/digital-finance-agreement-reached-on-european-crypto-assets-regulation-mica/ [05.02.2023].

67. See above, note 65.

## Notes: IT as Politics by Other Means

1. How Russia killed its Tech Industry. MIT Technology Review. (04.04.2023) https://www.technologyreview.com/2023/04/04/1070352/

ukraine-war-russia-tech-industry-yandex-skolkovo/ [04.04.2023].

2. Iglesias Gerards, Simon. Hüther, Michael. Wirtschaftliche Entwicklung durch Rückschritt.— Zu den Perspektiven der russischen Volkswirtschaft. IW-Report 51/2022. pp. 6 and 34.

3. Clausewitz, Carl von. Vom Kriege. (1832) https:// www.clausewitz.com/readings/VomKriege1832/Book1. htm, Chap. 3. [07.03.3023] The book was first published in Berlin in 1832 and was edited by his widow.

4. A good definition of this term is provided by the German Federal Agency for Civic Education (Bundeszentrale für politische Bildung). "Hybrid warfare stands for a combination of regular and irregular political, economic, media, subversive, intelligence, cyber-technical, and military forms of combat." https://www.bpb.de/themen/kriege-konflikte/dossier-kriege-konflikte/504273/hybride-kriegs-fuehrung/ [11.02.2023].

5. China's Cabinet Stresses Cybersecurity After Data Leak. Bloomberg. (08.07.2022) https://www.bloomberg.com/news/articles/2022-07-07/china-s-cabinet-urges-greater-cybersecurity-after-mass-data-leak [06.02.2023]. The Australian corporate insurance consultancy, Clear Insurance, has compiled a list of the most consequential hacks: 10 Biggest Cyber Attacks in History. (27.09.2021) https://clearinsurance.com.au/10-biggest-cyber-attacks-in-history/ [06.02.2023].

6. Pentagon kept the lid on cyberwar in Kosovo. The Guardian. (09.11.1999) https://www.theguardian.com/world/1999/nov/09/balkans [06.02.2023].

7. A serious scientific presentation of the "IT-Army" and its tasks and structures can be found in a study by the Center for Security Studies at ETH Zurich: Soesanto, Stefano. The IT Army of Ukraine. Structure, Tasking, and Ecosystem. (06.2022) https://css.ethz.ch/content/dam/ethz/special-interest/gess/cis/center-for-securities-studies/pdfs/

Cyber-Reports-2022-06-IT-Army-of-Ukraine.pdf [06.02.2023]. For the number of subscribers, see p. 7 f. There is more than one channel of this name on Telegram. I am referring here to the one that Soesanto calls the "official" one.

8. Soesanto. The IT Army of Ukraine, p. 5.
9. Tracking Social Media Takedowns and Content Moderation During the 2022 Russian Invasion of Ukraine. (Updated 27.05.2022) https://mediamanipulation.org/research/tracking-social-media-takedowns-and-content-moderation-during-2022-russian-invasion [06.02.2023].
10. Facebook also blocked accounts in Ukraine and, according to its own statements, acted at the request of the Ukrainian government. How Silicon Valley's Russia crackdown proves its power—and its threat. The Guardian. (12.03.2022) https://www.theguardian.com/media/2022/mar/11/social-media-facebook-google-russia-ukraine [06.02.2023].
11. How Elon Musks's satellites have saved Ukraine and changed warfare. The Economist. (06.01.2023) https://www.economist.com/briefing/2023/01/05/how-elon-musks-satellites-have-saved-ukraine-and-changed-warfare. [06.02.2023].
12. Elon Musk says around 100 starlinks active in Iran. Reuters. (27.12.2022) https://www.reuters.com/technology/elon-musk-says-around-100-starlinks-now-active-iran-2022-12-26/ [06.02.2023].
13. Ukraine Krieg: Wie Mykhailo Fedorov für Selenskyj und das Digitale kämpft. Heise Online. (13.07.2022) https://www.heise.de/hintergrund/Ukraine-Krieg-Selenskyjs-Kaempfer-fuer-das-Digitale-7178030.html [06.02.2023]. Regarding ClearView AI, their technology, and the support of Ukraine see War in Ukraine. (n. d.) https://www.clearview.ai/ukraine [06.02.2023].
14. Russian Disinformation Technology. MIT Technology Review. (13.04.2017) https://www.technologyreview.

com/2017/04/13/152305/russian-disinformation-technology/ [06.02.2023].

15. Vladimir Putins Chef Troll. Der Spiegel. (18.02.2018) https://www.spiegel.de/politik/ausland/wladimir-putin-und-die-trollfabrik-des-jewgenij-prigoschin-a-1194131.html [06.02.2023].

16. Wie der Kreml Meinung macht. Netzpiloten. (11.06.2022) https://www.netzpiloten.de/russische-trollfabriken-wie-der-kreml-meinung-macht/ [06.02.2023].

17. Office of the Director of National Intelligence, Members of the IC. (n. d.) https://www.dni.gov/index.php/what-we-do/members-of-the-ic [03/07/2023].

18. Intelligence Community Assessment. Foreign Threats to the 2020 US Federal Elections, p. 3. (n. d.) https://s3.documentcloud.org/documents/20515674/intelligence.pdf [07.03.2023] The reference to Ukraine on pp. 7 and 8.

19. Forensic Research Lab, Interference 2020. Foreign Interference Attribution Tracker. (n. d.) https://interference2020.org/ [06.02.2023].

20. Intelligence Community Assessment, pp. 6 and 12.

21. More about them, their methods, and the traces they leave behind, in: Inside Russia's Notorious 'Internet Research Agency' Troll Farm. Spyscape. (2022) https://spyscape.com/article/inside-the-troll-factory-russias-internet-research-agency [07.02.2023].

22. An AI system sees every face as a complex mathematical figure, a series of values that can be translated. The choice of these values—such as for the size and shape of the eyes—changes the entire image. The number of mathematical values used to recognize a human face is significant and varies depending on the system's complexity, the algorithms used and the image resolution. On the page, there are also interesting tips on how to spot clues for a "fake face" by looking closely. Designed to Deceive: Do These People Look Real to

You? The New York Times Interactive. (21.11.2020) https://www.nytimes.com/interactive/2020/11/21/science/artificial-intelligence-fake-people-faces.html [07.02.2023].

23. Russian misinformation seeks to confound, not to convince. Scientific American. (28.03.2022) https://www.scientificamerican.com/article/russian-misinformation-seeks-to-confound-not-convince/ [02.02.2023].

24. Schmutziger Wahlkampf. Wie Desinformation die Bundestagswahl vergiftet. Correctiv. (21.09.2021) https://correctiv.org/faktencheck/hintergrund/2021/09/21/schmutziger-wahlkampf-desinformation-bundestagswahl/ [07.02.2023].

25. Krisen sind Chancen. ARD Tagesthemen. (12.12.2022) https://www.tagesschau.de/inland/innenpolitik/schaeuble-50-jahre-bundestag-mitglied-101.html [07.02.2023].

26. Misdirection, Fake News and Lies. New York Times. (09.06.2022) https://www.nytimes.com/2022/06/09/books/books-disinformation-fake-news.html [07.02.2023]. Translation by the author.

27. Schulze, Matthias. Vom Kalten Krieg zum Informationszeitalter. Bundeszentrale für politische Bildung (02.05.2019) https://www.bpb.de/themen/medien-journalismus/digitale-desinformation/290487/desinformation-vom-kalten-krieg-zum-informationszeitalter/ [07.02.2023].

28. Information about Correctiv can be found here: https://correctiv.org/faktencheck/. The page of Bellingcat: https://www.bellingcat.com/ [07.02.2023].

29. "Unfortunately, the country is incompatible with Internet business at the moment." Reuters. (22.04.2014) https://www.reuters.com/article/russia-vkontakte-ceo-idUSL6N0NE1HS20140422.

30. An Application Programming Interface (API) allows third-party providers to integrate their apps in Telegram in a technically simplified manner. More

on this in the continuously updated guide: Telegram BOT API (n. d.) https://core.telegram.org/bots/api [07.02.2023].

31. 700 Million Users and Telegram Premium. Telegram Blog. (08.2022) https://telegram.org/blog/700-million-and-premium/de [07.02.2023].

32. The Telegram app has a global doxing issue. Wired. (20.09.2022) https://www.wired.co.uk/article/tele-grams-doxing-problem [07.02.2023].

33. For the channel see: Iran International. (n. d.) https://t.me/IranintlTV [03/07/2023]. For Telegram and the protests in Iran see: Iran Proteste: Die Rolle der Telegram App. Deutsche Welle. (01/04/2018) https://www.dw.com/de/iran-proteste-die-rolle-der-telegram-app/a-42032480 [02/07/2023].

34. The website offers a download of the American app version: https://truthsocial.com/ [07.02.2023].

35. As of March 2023, Trump's app was neither available in the German App Store nor on Google Play. Instead, there is a Trump Tracker app on the App Store that disseminates news about his activities.

36. The term is borrowed from the article by Schulze, Matthias. Vom Kalgen Krieg. (see note 27).

37. Digital Dominance: A new global ranking of cyper power throws up some surprises. The Economist. (17.09.2020) https://www.economist.com/science-and-technology/2020/09/17/a-new-global-ranking-of-cyber-power-throws-up-some-surprises [07.03.2023].

38. CIA World Factbook Korea, North, https://www.cia.gov/the-world-factbook/countries/korea-north/#com-munications [02/08/2023].

39. Publicly accessible documentation on this topic is rare. A highlight is the conference paper The All-Purpose Sword: North Korea's Cyber Operations and Strategies. 2019 11th International Conference on Cyber Conflict: Silent Battle. Tallinn 2019. The reference to Kim Jong-un's computer science studies can be found on p. 2. Information about Unit 180 on p.

7. The paper was created by staff from the University of Seoul, South Korea. An easily consumable presentation of its main contents can also be found as a video on YouTube. How North Korea Conducts Cyber Operations. (24.09.2020) https://www.youtube.com/watch?v=KN1oWeGDfQA [08.02.2023].

40. Critical Technology Tracker. Australian Strategic Policy Institute. (02.03.2023) https://techtracker.aspi.org.au/tech/all/?c1=cn&c2=us [02.03.2023]. The evaluation criteria are explained there.

41. Cyberattacken und wie Staaten darauf reagieren. Deutschlandfunk. (29.11.2021) https://www.deutschlandfunk.de/cyberattacken-und-wie-staaten-darauf-reagieren-100.html [08.02.2023].

42. Beijing's costly plans for cybersecurity 'self-sufficiency'. Protocol. (20.07.2021) https://www.protocol.com/china/china-cybersecurity-self-sufficiency [08.02.2023].

43. Cited according to Record Trend. (12.05.2022) https://recordtrend.com/network-security/chinas-network-security-related-expenditure-is-expected-to-reach-us-10-26-billion-in-2021-from-idc/ [08.02.2023]. The site collects the latest research data and makes it publicly available.

44. As Biden stands by, Chinese hackers build dossiers on US citizens. The Hill. (11.08.2021) https://thehill.com/opinion/cybersecurity/567318-as-biden-stands-by-chinese-hackers-build-dossiers-on-us-citizens/ [08.02.2023]. The Hill is the largest independent reporter on the Capitol.

45. China's network security related expenditure is expected to reach US $10.26 billion in 2021. Record Trend, p. 2 [08.02.2023].

46. China's Digitalisierungsstrategie: Gefahr für das deutsche Geschäftsmodell. Institut der Deutschen Wirtschaft. IW Kurzbericht 59/2021, September 3, 2021, p. 1.

47. Beijing's costly plans for cybersecurity 'self-sufficiency'. Protocol. (20.07.2021) https://www.protocol.com/china/china-cybersecurity-self-sufficiency. [08.02.2023].

48. US pushes for TikTok sale to resolve national security concerns. New York Times. (15.03.2023) https://www.nytimes.com/2023/03/15/technology/tiktok-biden-pushes-sale.html [17.03.2023].

49. How Russia killed its Tech industry. MIT Technology Review. (04.04.2023) https://www.technologyreview.com/2023/04/04/1070352/ukraine-war-russia-tech-industry-yandex-skolkovo/.

50. China's Tech Crackdown: A Year-in-Review. LawFare (07.01.2022) https://www.lawfareblog.com/chinas-tech-crackdown-year-review [08.02.2023].

51. Top Chinese companies on NASDAQ. Yahoo Finance. (08.06.2022) https://finance.yahoo.com/news/top-chinese-companies-nasdaq-145128267.html [08.02.2023].

52. China state-owned giants to delist from US stock exchange. Al Jazeera. (12.08.2022) https://www.aljazeera.com/economy/2022/8/12/china-state-owned-giants-to-delist-from-us-stock-exchange [08.02.2023].

53. More on this in the news service China.Table: Home Coming dürfte anhalten. China Table. (29.08.2022) https://table.media/china/professional-briefing [29.08.2022].

54. Five Chinese state-owned companies, under scrutiny in US, will delist from NYSE. Reuters. (12.08.2022) https://www.reuters.com/business/finance/several-chinese-state-owned-companies-delist-nyse-2022-08-12/ [08.02.2023].

55. Landmark US-China audit deal spurs hunt for devils in the details. Financial Times (30.08.2022) https://www.ft.com/content/322e1486-7c11-4582-aa36-39799bf30c51 [08.02.2023].

56. Hung, Tran. Delisting Chinese companies from the New York Stock Exchange: Signs of decoupling. Atlantic Council. (25.08.2022) https://www.atlanticcouncil.org/blogs/econographics/delisting-chinese-companies-from-the-new-york-stock-exchange-signs-of-decoupling/ [08.02.2023].

57. For the "city of the future" Shenzhen with its high-tech industries in the north of Hong Kong, see Sieren, Frank. Shenzhen—Future Made in China. Munich 2021. For a comparison with Silicon Valley, see pp. 15/16.

58. Die neue Weltordnung. Wie umgehen mit China? Richard David Precht im Gespräch mit Frank Sieren. ZDF-Mediathek. (12.02.2023) https://www.zdf.de/gesellschaft/precht/precht-richard-david-precht-im-gespraech-mit-frank-sieren-100.html [13.02.2023].

59. Baisakova, Nurzat. Kleinhans, Jan Peter. The global semiconductor value chain. A technology primer for policy makers. Stiftung Neue Verantwortung. (06.10.2020) https://www.stiftung-nv.de/de/publikation/global-semiconductor-value-chain-technology-primer-policy-makers [08.02.2023].

60. Gartner Says Worldwide Semiconductor Revenue Grew 26 % in 2021. Gartner News Room. (14.04.2022) https://www.gartner.com/en/newsroom/press-releases/2022-04-14-gartner-says-worldwide-semiconductor-revenue-grew-26-percent-in-2021 [08.02.2023].

61. Federal Budget 2022. Investing in the Future and securing Stability. (16.03.2022) https://www.bundesregierung.de/breg-en/news/cabinet-federal-budget-2022-2016888 [07.03.2023].

62. Annual Threat Assessment of the National Intelligence Community. (02.2022) https://www.dni.gov/files/ODNI/documents/assessments/ATA-2022-Unclassified-Report.pdf, p. 6 [08.02.2023].

63. Localization of chip manufacturing rising. Trend Force. (25.04.2022) https://www.trendforce.com/presscenter/news/20220425-11204.html [08.02.2023].

64. Taiwan says Fab4 chip group held first senior officials meeting. Reuters. (25.02.2023) https://www.reuters.com/technology/taiwan-says-fab-4-chip-group-held-first-senior-officials-meeting-2023-02-25/ [25.02.2023].

65. Share of integrated circuit (IC), integrated device (IDM), and fabless company sales in 2021, by HQ location. Statista. (26.01.2023) https://www.statista.com/statistics/1052972/ic-idm-and-fabless-sales-share-by-headquarter-location-of-company/ [08.02.2023].

66. Chip designers made bank in 2021 amid global shortage. The Register. (24.03.2022) https://www.theregister.com/2022/03/24/fabless_chip_designers_made_bank/ [08.02.2023].

67. Share of integrated circuit (IC), integrated device (IDM), and fabless company sales in 2021, by HQ location. see Note 65 https://www.statista.com/statistics/1052972/ic-idm-and-fabless-sales-share-by-headquarter-location-of-company/ [08.02.2023].

68. Baisakova, Nurzat. Kleinhans, Jan-Peter. The global semiconductor value chain, p. 13.

69. U.S. blacklists more than 60 Chinese firms, including SMIC. Bloomberg. (18.12.2020) https://www.bloomberg.com/news/articles/2020-12-18/u-s-to-blacklist-smic-and-dozens-more-china-firms-reuters-says#xj4y7vzkg [08.02.2023].

70. Gartner Says Worldwide Semiconductor Revenue Grew 26 % in 2021, see Note 60.

71. Biden signs $280 billion CHIPS and Science Act. The Verge. (09.08.2022) https://www.theverge.com/2022/8/9/23298147/biden-chips-act-semiconductors-subsidies-ohio-arizona-plant-china [08.02.2023].

72. US bars 'advanced tech' firms from building China factories for 10 years. BBC. (07.09.2022) https://www.bbc.com/news/62803224 [08.02.2023].

73. Intel baut Chipfabrik in Magdeburg. ARD Tagesschau. (15.03.2022) https://www.tagesschau.de/wirtschaft/unternehmen/intel-magdeburg-101.html [08.02.2023].

74. Milliardenpoker um Magdeburg. Die Welt. (11.01.2023) https://www.welt.de/wirtschaft/plus243080269/US-Chipkonzern-Intel-Milliardenpoker-um-Magdeburg.html [08.02.2023].

75. The Inflation Reduction Act 2022. United States Environmental Protection Agency. (Updated 25.01.2023) https://www.epa.gov/green-power-markets/inflation-reduction-act [08.02.2023].

76. Xi Ping wirft USA und Westen Unterdrückung Chinas vor. T-Online. (Updated 07.03.2023) https://www.t-online.de/nachrichten/ausland/id_100139608/china-xi-jinping-wirft-usa-und-westen-unterdrueckung-vor.html [07.03.2023].

77. How are Washington and Beijing Utilizing Industrial Policy to Bolster Domestic Semiconductor Manufacturing? Center for Strategic and International Studies. (29.03.2022) https://www.csis.org/blogs/new-perspectives-asia/how-are-washington-and-beijing-utilizing-industrial-policy-bolster [09.02.2023].

78. Is China's Semiconductor Strategy Working? London School of Economics and Political Sciences. (01.09.2022) https://blogs.lse.ac.uk/cff/2022/09/01/is-chinas-semiconductor-strategy-working/ [09.02.2023].

79. Die ersten 7-nm-Chips aus China: Meilenstein bei SMIC. Heise online. (25.07.2022) https://www.heise.de/news/Neuer-Meilenstein-China-stellt-Chips-mit-7-Nanometer-Technik-her-7189351.html [09.02.2023].

80. European Chip Companies Fare Well in 2021 'Megasuppliers' List. EETimes Europe. (31.12.2021)

https://www.eetimes.eu/european-chip-companies-fare-well-in-2021-megasuppliers-list/ [09.02.2023].

81. Evaluation of investments into chip production on the basis of the 2013 strategy. (07.04.2022) https://www.europarl.europa.eu/doceo/document/E-9-2022-001405_DE.html [09.02.2023].

82. In the global chips arms race, Europe makes its move. The Economist. (12.02.2022) https://www.economist.com/business/in-the-global-chips-arms-race-europe-makes-its-move/21807603 [09.02.2023].

83. Kleinhans, Jan-Peter. Hess, Julia. Denkena, Wiebke. Governments' role in the global semiconductor value chain #1. Stiftung Neue Verantwortung. (07.06.2022) https://www.stiftung-nv.de/de/publication/eca-monitoring [09.02.2023].

84. 2021 State of the Union address. (15.09.2021) https://ec.europa.eu/commission/presscorner/detail/en/speech_21_4701 [09.02.2023].

85. European Chips Act. (02.2022) https://ec.europa.eu/info/strategy/priorities-2019-2024/europe-fit-digital-age/european-chips-act_en#the-need-for-eu-action [09.02.2023].

86. South Korea promotes its chip manufacturers through significant tax reductions, which are effectively equivalent to a subsidy. South Korea plans to invest $450bn to become chip 'powerhouse'. Nikkei Asia. (13.05.2021) https://asia.nikkei.com/Business/Tech/Semiconductors/South-Korea-plans-to-invest-450bn-to-become-chip-powerhouse [09.02.2023].

87. Europas Chipoffensive: 43 Mrd. € für die Aufhol- jagd. Handelsblatt. (08.02.2022) https://www.handelsblatt.com/politik/international/european-chips-act-europas-chipoffensive-43-milliarden-euro-fuer-die-aufholjagd/28048680.html [09.02.2023].

88. ZDF Mediathek. (24.07.2022) https://www.zdf.de/nachrichten/heute-journal/henry-kissinger-ex-aussen-minister-usa-100.html [09.02.2023].

89. Krisen sind Chancen. ARD Tagesthemen. (12.12.2022).
90. Bateman, Jon. U.S.-China Technological "Decoupling": A Strategy and Policy Framework. (22.05.2022) https://carnegieendowment.org/2022/04/25/u.s.-china-technological-decoupling-strategy-and-policy-framework-pub-86897 [09.02.2023]. Jon Bateman is the chairman of the National Security Commission on Artificial Intelligence (NSCAI) of the USA.
91. US chip makers hit by new China export rule. BBC. (02.09.2022) https://www.bbc.com/news/business-62747401 [09.02.2023].
92. The 'internet as we know it' is off in Iran. Here's why this shutdown is different. CNN. (19.11.2019) https://edition.cnn.com/2019/11/19/middleeast/iran-internet-shutdown-intl/index.html [09.02.2023].
93. An overview of the measures taken by Iran can be found in: Isfahani, Sayeh. The Internet has no place in Khamenei's vision for Iran's future. Atlantic Council. (25.07.2022) https://www.atlanticcouncil.org/blogs/iransource/the-internet-has-no-place-in-khameneis-vision-for-irans-future/ [09.02.2023]. For the ban on VPN and other tools see: Islamic Republic of Iran: Computer Crimes Law. (2012) p. 30, https://www.article19.org/data/files/medialibrary/2921/12-01-30-FINAL-iran-WEB%5B4%5D.pdf [09.02.2023].
94. The Internet Society is not the only organization that does this. Constantly updated figures in: Internet Shutdowns. (n. d.) https://pulse.internetsociety.org/shutdowns [02/09/2023].
95. Internet shutdowns: trends, causes, legal implications and impacts on a range of human rights. Report of the Office of the United Nations High Commissioner for Human Rights. (13.05.2022) https://documents-dds-ny.un.org/doc/UNDOC/GEN/G22/341/55/PDF/G2234155.pdf?OpenElement [09.02.2023].

96. The figures from the cited UN report go back to the KeepItOn Coalition, which presents them with interesting interactive graphics. Taxonomy of a Shut Down. (n. d.) https://www.accessnow.org/keepiton/#coalition. The technical tips can be found on Working doc: Digital safety tips for network disruptions. (n. d.) https://docs.google.com/presentation/d/1KVj0Qzs-5jPzrgRvwQ8kzSBZNkGsuypDbwvXKVLMpipE/edit#slide=id.p [09.02.2023].

97. The letter is published and can be found in: Marby to Fedorow. ICANN. (02.03.2022) https://www.icann.org/en/system/files/correspondence/marby-to-fedorov-02mar22-en.pdf [09.02.2023].

98. Cord-cutting, Russian style: Could the Kremlin sever global internet cables? Atlantic Council. Atlantic Council. (31.01.2022) https://www.atlanticcouncil.org/blogs/new-atlanticist/cord-cutting-russian-style-could-the-kremlin-sever-global-internet-cables/ [09.02.2023].

99. In China, the 'Great Firewall' Is Changing a Generation. Human Rights Watch. (01.09.2020) https://www.hrw.org/news/2020/09/01/china-great-firewall-changing-generation [09.02.2023].

100. North Korea Cyber Profile. Comparitech. (27.08.2021) https://www.comparitech.com/blog/vpn-privacy/north-korea-cyber-profile/ [09.02.2023].

101. Google can also determine when certain content was blocked by third parties. Google Government Detailed Removal Requests. (n. d.) https://transparencyreport.google.com/government-removals/overview?hl=en An analysis of the data can be found at: https://transparencyreport.google.com/government-removals/government-requests?hl=en [02/09/2023].

102. GAIA-X. (n. d.) https://www.data-infrastructure.eu/GAIAX/Navigation/EN/Home/home.html [02/09/2023].

103. Merkels Handy steht seit 2002 auf US Abhörliste. Der Spiegel. (26.10.2013) https://www.spiegel.de/politik/deutschland/nsa-ueberwachung-merkel-steht-seit-2002-auf-us-abhoerliste-a-930193.html [09.02.2023].

104. Ausspähen unter Freunden geht überall. Wiener Zeitung. (31.05.2021) https://www.wienerzeitung.at/nachrichten/politik/europa/2106278-Ausspaehen-unter-Freunden-geht-ueberall.html [09.02.2023].

105. Titanpointe. (n. d.) https://sketchfab.com/3d-models/titanpointe-f65fc0abd8ba4c7da6cf0c6ea9e39b07 [02/10/2023].

106. The research department of the US Congress has compiled an interesting document that presents the technology and possible dangers for global internet connections. Undersea Telecommunication Cables: Technology Overview and Issues for Congress. Congressional Research Service. Document R47237. (13.09.2022) https://crsreports.congress.gov/product/details?prodcode=R47237 [10.02.2023].

107. Facebook, Google lead latest undersea cable boom. (12.04.2021) https://www.fiercetelecom.com/telecom/facebook-google-continue-to-lead-latest-undersea-cable-boom [10.02.2023].

108. The Dunant subsea cable, connecting the US and mainland Europe, is ready for service. (03.02.2021) https://cloud.google.com/blog/products/infrastructure/googles-dunant-subsea-cable-is-now-ready-for-service [10.02.2023].

109. Submarine Cable Map. TeleGeography. (n. d.) https://www.submarinecablemap.com/ [02/10/2023].

110. Snowden, Edward. Permanent Record. Frankfurt am Main 2019, p. 209 (German edition of the original from 2013).

111. Titanpointe, The NSA's Spy Hub in New York, Hidden in Plain Sight. The Intercept. (16.11.2016) https://theintercept.com/2016/11/16/the-nsas-spy-hub-in-new-york-hidden-in-plain-sight/ [10.02.2023].

The Intercept is an American non-profit organization funded by billionaire and eBay co-founder Pierre Omidyar. It conducts investigative journalism.

112. Those who are interested in details see Edward Snowden, Permanent Record, pp. 284–287 (Note 110)
113. Buchanan, Ben. The Hacker and the State. Cambridge 2020. pp. 25 and 28 ff.
114. Submarine communications cable. Wikipedia. (n. d.) https://en.wikipedia.org/wiki/Submarine_communications_cable [02/10/2023].
115. Buchanan, Ben. The Hacker and the State. pp. 16–19 and 35.

## Notes: New Hackonomy—The Other Platform Economy

1. Wong, Caroline. How to talk to your kids about Cybersecurity. United States Cyber Security Magazine. (10.10.2022) https://www.uscybersecurity.net/how-to-talk-to-your-kids-about-cybersecurity/ [10.02.2023]. The Hacker News (@thehackernews) can be found on Telegram at https://t.me/thehackernews.
2. Wirtschaftsschutz 2022. Präsentation des Bitkom. (31.08.2022) https://www.bitkom.org/sites/main/files/2022-08/Bitkom-Charts_Wirtschaftsschutz_Cybercrime_31.08.2022.pdf, p. 9 [10.02.2023].
3. Versicherer zu Cyberangriffen: Schäden „im Cyberspace nicht mehr versicherbar". Heise online. (28.12.2022) https://www.heise.de/news/Versicherungswirtschaft-ruft-bei-Cyberangriffen-nach-dem-Staat-7443841.html [10.02.2023].
4. Global cost of cybercrime topped $6 trillion in 2021. TechXplore. (10.05.2022) https://techxplore.com/news/2022-05-global-cybercrime-topped-trillion-defence.html [10.02.2023]. Furthermore: State of Cyber

Security Report 2021. Accenture. (2022) https://www.accenture.com/content/dam/accenture/final/a-com-migration/custom/us-en/invest-cyber-resilience/pdf/Accenture-State-Of-Cybersecurity-2021.pdf, p. 5 ff [10.02.2023].

5. Sicherheitslücke in Teams: Microsoft-Token im Klartext gespeichert. Heise online. (18.09.2022) https://www.heise.de/news/Sicherheitsluecke-in-Teams-Microsoft-Token-im-Klartext-gespeichert-7267922.html [10.02.2023].

6. The different designations for the group can be found in the so-called Malpedia of the Fraunhofer FKIE. Malpedia. (n. d.) https://malpedia.caad.fkie.fraunhofer.de/actor/unc2452 [02/10/2023]. It records known groups with their varying names and is continuously updated.

7. Cyber-attack: US and UK blame North Korea for WannaCry. BBC. (17.12.2017) https://www.bbc.com/news/world-us-canada-42407488 [10.02.2023].

8. A 'Worst Nightmare' Cyberattack: The Untold Story. National Public Radio. (16.04.2021) https://www.npr.org/2021/04/16/985439655/a-worst-nightmare-cyberattack-the-untold-story-of-the-solarwinds-hack [10.02.2023].

9. An example of this: DoppelPaymer Continues to Cause Grief Through Rebranding. Zscaler. (28.07.2021) https://www.zscaler.com/blogs/security-research/doppelpaymer-continues-cause-grief-through-rebranding [10.02.2023].

10. For ARPA, see Chapter 3, section One Network to rule them all.

11. Levy, Steven. Hackers. Heroes of the modern Computer Revolution. New York 1984, pp. 23 as well as pp. 130/131.

12. Krieg im Internet/Darknet. ZDF Dokumentation. (30.08.2018) https://www.youtube.com/watch?v=ifxkayMGoko [10.02.2023].

13. Zerodium homepage. (n. d.) [https://zerodium.com/ [02/10/2023].

14. HackerOne. (n. d.) https://www.hackerone.com/hackers [02/10/2023].

15. Dellago, Matthias. Woods, Daniel W. Simpson, Andrew C. Characterising 0-Day Exploit Brokers. (02.06.2022) https://weis2022.econinfosec.org/wp-content/uploads/sites/10/2022/06/weis22-dellago.pdf, p. 5 [10.02.2023].

16. As of November 2022. Microsoft Bug Bounty Program. (n. d.) https://www.microsoft.com/en-us/msrc/bounty [02/10/2023].

17. Microsoft Digital Defense Report 2022, p. 39. https://query.prod.cms.rt.microsoft.com/cms/api/am/binary/RE5bUvv [02/10/2023].

18. 16Shop Targets Cash App with Latest Phishing Kit. ZeroFox. (01.03.2021) https://www.zerofox.com/blog/16shop-cash-app-phishing-kit/ [10.02.2023]. Those who want to learn about the technically interesting implementation of 16Shops can find a additional information at: 16Shop Phishing Gang Goes After PayPal Users. Threatpost. (21.01.2020) https://threatpost.com/16shop-phishing-gang-paypal-users/152064/ [10.02.2023].

19. Robin Banks might be robbing your bank. IronNet. (26.07.2022) https://www.ironnet.com/blog/robin-banks-a-new-phishing-as-a-service-platform [10.02.2023].

20. Robin Banks phishing service for cybercriminals returns with Russian server. The Hacker News. (07.11.2022) https://thehackernews.com/2022/11/robin-banks-phishing-service-for.html [10.02.2023].

21. Netcraft Homepage. (n. d.) [https://www.netcraft.com/ [02/10/2023].

22. FBI says it ‚hacked the hackers‘ to shut down major ransomware group. National Public Radio. (26.01.2023) https://www.npr.org/2023/01/26/1151696092/fbi-says-it-hacked-the-hackers-to-shut-down-major-ransomware-group [10.02.2023].

23. Such cases rarely become known. An example of this is that of the Russian Denis Mihajlovic Dubnikov, whom the FBI was able to apprehend. Alleged Russian Cryptocurrency Money Launderer Extradited from the Netherlands to the United States. United States Department of Justice. (17.08.2022) https://www. justice.gov/usao-or/pr/alleged-russian-cryptocurrency-money-launderer-extradited-netherlands-united-states [10.02.2023].

24. Top 5 Hacker Forums on the Deep and Dark Web in 2022. Webz.io. (29.06.2022) https://webz.io/dwp/top-5-hacker-forums-on-the-deep-and-dark-web-in-2022/ [10.02.2023]. Translation by the author.

25. Ransomware gangs seek people skills for negotiations. Computer Weekly. (09.07.2021) https://www.computerweekly.com/news/252503773/Ransomware-gangs-seek-people-skills-for-negotiations [10.02.2023].

26. Ransomware-as-a-Service: Enabler of Widespread Attacks. TrendMicro. (10/05/2021) https://www. trendmicro.com/vinfo/us/security/news/cybercrime-and-digital-threats/ransomware-as-a-service-enabler-of-widespread-attacks [02/10/2023].

27. Harding, Emily. Ghoorhoo, Harshana. Hard Choices in a ransomware attack. Center for Strategic and International Studies, p. 3 and p. 13. (28.09.2022) https://www.csis.org/analysis/hard-choices-ransomware-attack [10.02.2023].

28. Cost of a Data Breach 2022 Report. IBM Security, p. 10. (07. 2022) https://www.ibm.com/downloads/cas/3R8N1DZJ [02/10/2023].

29. Deutsche Windtechnik hit by targeted cyberattack. Renewables Now. (14.04.2022) https://renewablesnow. com/news/deutsche-windtechnik-hit-by-targeted-cyberattack-781048/ [10.02.2023].

30. Team Jorge: Wahlmanipulation auf Bestellung? ZDF today (15.02.2023) https://www.zdf.de/nachrichten/politik/team-jorge-israel-desinformation-wahlen-100. html [19.02.2023].

31. Eine kritische Betrachtung der angebotenen Leistungen von Jorge in: Team Jorge und angeblich autonome Bots. Deutschlandfunk Nova. (17.02.2023) https://www.deutschlandfunknova.de/beitrag/wahlmanipulation-auf-bestellung-team-jorge-und-seine-legenden [19.02.2023].

32. Atlas Intelligence Group (A.I.G.)—The Wrath of a Titan. (20.07.2022) https://cyberint.com/blog/research/atlas-intelligence-group/ [10.02.2023].

33. As of July 2022. Sellix describes its business purpose as follows: "Sell subscriptions, tokens, serial keys, digital downloads, video courses, softwares and licenses in a fast, easy and secure way". Sellix Homepage. (08.03.2023) https://sellix.io/ [08.03.2023].

34. A.I.G. post from 10/27/2022 and 10/29/2022 https://t.me/weareaig.

35. "With our connection in some police station we can check and search people's personal information … Service price fixed at 500 € per query." Atlas Intelligence Group (A.I.G.)—The Wrath of a Titan (see Note 32).

36. Hacker Groups take to Telegram, Signal and Darkweb to assist Protestors in Iran. Check Point Blog. (28.09.2022) https://blog.checkpoint.com/2022/09/28/hacker-groups-take-to-telegram-signal-and-darkweb-to-assist-protestors-in-iran/ [10.02.2023].

37. The Atlas Intelligence Group is now hacking Russian sites as some Ukrainian friends asked them to do so. The Tech Outlook. (15.09.2022) https://www.thetechoutlook.com/news/technology/security/the-atlas-intelligence-group-is-now-hacking-russian-sites-as-some-ukrainian-friends-asked-them-to-do-so/ [10.02.2023].

38. Microsoft Digital Defense Report 2022, p. 52.

39. Hackers looted $45 Mio. in global ATM heist. Info Security Magazine. (10.05.2013) https://www.infosecurity-magazine.com/news/hackers-looted-45-million-in-global-atm-heist/ [10.02.2023].

40. Cybercriminals 'drained ATMs' in $45 m world bank heist. BBC. (10.05.2013) https://www.bbc.com/news/world-us-canada-22470299 [02/10/2023].

41. Brazilian Prilex Hackers Resurfaced With Sophisticated Point-of-Sale Malware. The Hacker News. (29.09.2022) https://thehackernews.com/2022/09/brazilian-prilex-hackers-resurfaced.html [11.02.2023].

42. Crypto Bridge Nomad Drained of Nearly $200M in Exploit. CoinDesk Tech. (02.08.2022) https://www.coindesk.com/tech/2022/08/02/nomad-bridge-drained-of-nearly-200-million-in-exploit/ [11.02.2023].

43. Nomad Bridge Funds Recovery Process. Twitter. (03.08.2022) https://twitter.com/nomadxyz_/status/1554679735006859264 [02/11/2023].

44. Regarding the Ronin Bridge: Axie Infinity's Ronin Network Suffers $625M Exploit. CoinDesk Tech. (29.03.2022) https://www.coindesk.com/tech/2022/03/29/axie-infinitys-ronin-network-suffers-625m-exploit/ [11.02.2023]. Regarding the Wormhole Bridge: Jump Trading Backstops Wormhole's $320M Exploit Loss. CoinDesk Business. (03.02.2022) https://www.coindesk.com/business/2022/02/03/jump-trading-backstops-wormholes-320m-exploit-loss-sources/ [11.02.2023].

45. It's Been a Minute. Guess How Much Crypto's Been Stolen Lately? Gizmodo. (09.09.2022) https://gizmodo.com/how-much-crypto-stolen-last-three-months-bitcoin-1849461714 [11.02.2023].

46. As Deepfakes Flourish, Countries Struggle With Response. New York Times. (22.01.2023) https://www.nytimes.com/2023/01/22/business/media/deepfake-regulation-difficulty.html [11.02.2023].

47. BlueBenx Homepage. Explore the crypto economy. (n. d.) https://bluebenx.com/ [23.01.2023].

48. BlueBenx fires employees, halts funds withdrawal citing $32M hack. Cointelegraph. (14.08.2022) https://cointelegraph.com/news/

bluebenx-fires-employees-halts-funds-withdrawal-citing-32m-hack [11.02.2023].

49. Krypto-Diebstahl mit Deepfake eines Hologramms beschert 32 Mio. Dollar. Heise online. (25.08.2022) https://www.heise.de/news/Krypto-Diebstahl-mit-Deepfake-eines-Hologramms-beschert-32-Millionen-Dollar-7242635.html [11.02.2023].

50. Morgan Stanley to pay $60 million to resolve data security lawsuit. Reuters. (02/03/2022) https://www.reuters.com/markets/funds/morgan-stanley-pay-60-mln-resolve-data-security-lawsuit-2022-01-02/ [02/11/2023].

51. Former Uber security chief convicted of covering up 2016 data breach. Washington Post. (05.10.2022) https://www.washingtonpost.com/technology/2022/10/05/uber-obstruction-sullivan-hacking/ [11.02.2023].

52. Former Uber security chief convicted for concealing a felony. BBC. (06.10.2022) https://www.bbc.com/news/technology-63157883 [11.02.2023].

53. Silent Librarian. Malpedia. (n. d.) https://malpedia.caad.fkie.fraunhofer.de/actor/silent_librarian [02/11/2023].

54. Iranian MABNA Hackers. FBI Most Wanted. (23.03.2018) https://www.fbi.gov/wanted/cyber/iranian-mabna-hackers [11.02.2023].

55. Cyberangriffe aus Iran: APT Mabna Institute/Silent Librarian. Verfassungsschutz Baden-Württemberg. (30.04.2021) https://www.verfassungsschutz-bw.de/,Lde/Cyberangriffe+aus+Iran_+APT++_Mabna+Institute_Silent+Librarian_. APT stands for Advanced Persistent Threat [11.02.2023].

56. Iran-Linked Threat Actor The MABNA Institute's Operations in 2020. Recorded Future. Insikt Group. (21.04.2021) https://www.recordedfuture.com/iran-threat-actor-mabna-2020-operations [11.02.2023].

57. Top 5 hacker forums on the deep and dark web in 2022. Dark Web News. (29.06.2022) https://webz.io/dwp/top-5-hacker-forums-on-the-deep-and-dark-web-in-2022/ [11.02.2023].

58. Why do Hackers Attack Dark Web Forums? Dark Web News. (08.06.2022) https://webz.io/dwp/why-do-hackers-attack-dark-web-forums/ [11.02.2023].

59. Buchanan, Ben. The Hacker and the State, pp. 242 ff.

60. A solid presentation of the state of knowledge about Unit 8200 based on publicly accessible sources can be found in a study by ETH Zurich: CSS Cyber Defense Report. The Israeli Unit 8200. An OSINT-based Study (2019) https://css.ethz.ch/content/dam/ethz/special-interest/gess/cis/center-for-securities-studies/pdfs/Cyber-Reports-2019-12-Unit-8200.pdf [11.02.2023].

61. IDF veterans of intelligence unit 8200 behind one of the top 10 VCs in the world. Jerusalem Post. (01.01.2017) https://www.jpost.com/Business-and-Innovation/Tech/IDF-vets-of-intel-unit-8200-behind-one-of-the-top-10-VCs-in-the-world-476945 [11.02.2023].

62. Unit 8200: The only way to succeed in high-tech? Geektime. (07.09.2022) https://www.geektime.com/unit-8200-not-the-only-way-to-high-tech/ [11.02.2023].

63. NASDAQ Stock Screener. (01.11.2022) https://www.nasdaq.com/market-activity/stocks/screener [02/11/2023].

64. Israel mobilizes tech talent through Unit 8200. Bismarck Brief. (14.09.2022) https://brief.bismarckanalysis.com/p/israel-mobilizes-tech-talent-through [11.02.2023].

65. U.S., Israel developed Flame computer virus to slow Iranian nuclear efforts, officials say. Washington Post. (19.06.2012) https://www.washingtonpost.com/world/national-security/us-israel-developed-computer-virus-to-slow-iranian-nuclear-efforts-officials-say/2012/06/19/gJQA6xBPoV_story.html [11.02.2023].

66. SolarWinds hack explained: Everything you need to know. TechTarget. (29.06.2022) https://www.techtarget.com/whatis/feature/SolarWinds-hack-explained-Everything-you-need-to-know [11.02.2023].

67. Cyber Threat Intelligence Report, p. 2. (08.01.2021) https://www.uscybersecurity.net/csfi-cti-report-jan-8-2021.pdf [02/11/2023].

68. Many interesting details about the century hack and its consequences can be found, in addition to the quotes mentioned here, in a contribution by National Public Radio (NPR). A 'Worst Nightmare' Cyberattack: The Untold Story. National Public Radio. (16.04.2021) https://www.npr.org/2021/04/16/985439655/a-worst-nightmare-cyberattack-the-untold-story-of-the-solar-winds-hack [11.02.2023].

69. SolarWinds hackers, Nobelium, once again strike global IT supply chains, Microsoft warns. ZDNet. (25.10.2021) https://www.zdnet.com/article/solarwinds-hacking-group-nobelium-is-now-targeting-the-global-it-supply-chain-microsoft-warns/ [11.02.2023].

70. GRU-Hacker, destruktive Malware und internationale Cyberangriffe. (o. D.) https://www.fbi.gov/wanted/cyber/gru-hackers-destructive-malware-and-international-cyber-attacks [13.02.2023].

71. A whole range of possibilities is described in: How To Bypass Internet Shutdown. MysteriumNetwork. (19.11.2020) https://www.mysterium.network/post/how-to-bypass-internet-shutdown [13.02.2023].

72. Twitter. @YourAnonNews. 24.02.2022.

73. 4chan Homepage. (n. d.) https://www.4chan.org/ [27.01.2023]. Opening the page may take a few seconds as it performs a security check before loading.

74. What is Anonymous? How the infamous 'hacktivist' group went from 4chan trolling to launching cyberattacks on Russia. CNBC make it. (25.03.2022) https://www.cnbc.com/2022/03/25/what-is-anonymous-the-group-went-from-4chan-to-cyberattacks-on-russia.htm [13.02.2023].

75. For example on Telegram: https://web.telegram.org/k/#@ANONM0S]. To the Twitter manifesto @YourAnonNews. 01.05.2019.

76. Anonymous have hacked #Iranian drones and now are in control. Check your monitors we left you a little message. Your flights are useless against our power.

77. Message to Vladimir Putin. (26.02.2022) https://www.youtube.com/watch?v=UpYJ-Mw1trM    [13.02.2023]. The message to Ibrahim Raisi: Anonymous Message To Iranian President. (24.09.2022) https://www.youtube.com/watch?v=qXKNA4XvNUQ [13.02.2023].

78. These are the two most hacked devices in smart homes. Avira Blog. (19.02.2021) https://www.avira.com/en/blog/these-are-the-two-most-hacked-devices-in-smart-homes [13.02.2023].

79. How to protect your baby monitor from being hacked. NordVPN Blog. (17.04.2022) https://nordvpn.com/de/blog/baby-monitor-iot-hacking/ [13.02.2023].

80. Nest camera hacker threatens to kidnap baby, spooks parents. NBC News. (18.12.2018) https://www.nbcnews.com/news/us-news/nest-camera-hacker-threatens-kidnap-baby-spooks-parents-n949251 [13.02.2023].

81. Complete WiFi Hacking Course: Beginner to Advanced. (01.2022) https://www.udemy.com/course/complete-wifi-hacking-course/ [13.02.2023].

82. Die Kamera als Einfallstor. Süddeutsche Zeitung. (06.11.2020) https://www.sueddeutsche.de/digital/ueberwachungskamera-sicherheit-gehackt-1.5103304 [27.01.2023].

## Notes: In the Basement Vault of the Internet

1. NRL History. (n. d.) https://www.nrl.navy.mil/About-Us/History/ [02/13/2023].

2. The corresponding email from Michael Reed is published on the website of Cryptome, a kind of

mini-Wikileaks. TOR Made for USG Open Source Spying Says Maker. (22.03.2011) https://cryptome.org/0003/tor-spy.htm [13.02.2023].

3. The list is continuously updated. TOR Node List. (n. d.) https://www.dan.me.uk/tornodes [13.02.2023].

4. This includes Freenet, I2P, ZeroNet, and MIT's Riffle. The latter claims to be more secure than TOR. The Onion network is still the most used. Those who want to dive into the Dark Web with good or bad intentions usually do so in the Onion network.

5. TOR Project History. (n. d.) https://www.torproject.org/about/history/ [02/13/2023].

6. TOR Made for USG Open Source Spying Says Maker (see above, note 2).

7. According to IRS Code 501(c)(3). Who funds TOR? TOR Project. (n. d.) https://support.torproject.org/misc/.

8. The TOR address is: http://facebookwkhpilnemxj7asaniu7vnjjbiltxjqhye3mhbshg7kx5tfyd.onion. Anyone who wants to reach it effortlessly should search for "Facebook Onion Address" in a browser like Chrome or Firefox and then copy it into the address field of the TOR browser.

9. The CIA is reachable via TOR at: Central Intelligence Agency. (n. d.) http://ciadotgov4sjwlzihbbgxnqg3xiyrg-7so2r2o3lt5wz5ypk4sxyjstad.onion [03/11/2023].

10. CIA's Latest Layer: An Onion Site. CIA Stories. (07.05.2019) https://www.cia.gov/stories/story/cias-latest-layer-an-onion-site/ [13.02.2023].

11. Black Cloud. (n. d.) http://bcloudwenjxgcxjh6uheyt72a5isimzgg4kv5u74jb2s22y3hzpwh6id.onion/; SecureDrop. (n. d.) http://sdolvtfhatvsysc6l34d65ymdwxcujausv7k5jk4cy5ttzhjoi6fzvyd.onion/ [13.02.2023].

12. Deep Web. Reddit. (n. d.) https://www.reddit.com/r/deepweb/ [02/13/2023].

13. Homepage Onion Index. (n. d.) http://oniondxjxs2mzjkbz7ldlflenh6huksestjsisc3usxht3wqgk6a62yd.onion/. [03/11/2023]. The name Torch is a compound of TOR

and SEARCH. Homepage Torch. (n. d.) http://xmh-57jrknzkhv6y3ls3ubitzfqnkrwxhopf5aygthi7d6rplyv-k3noyd.onion/ [02/13/2023].

14. As of November 2022. http://donionsixbjtiohce24abfgs-ffo2l4tk26qx464zylumgejukfq2vead.onion/onions.php [13.02.2023].

15. The page is continuously updated. Dark Web Wiki. Scam Lists. (n. d.) https://darkweb.wiki/scam-list/ [13.02.2023].

16. Alleged Hydra Administrator Dmitry Pavlov Reportedly Arrested in Russia. Bitcoin News. (16.04.2022) https://news.bitcoin.com/alleged-hydra-administrator-dmitry-pavlov-reportedly-arrested-in-russia/ [13.02.2023].

17. Illegaler Darknet-Marktplatz „Hydra Market" abgeschaltet. BKA Pressemitteilungen. (05.04.2022) https://www.bka.de/DE/Presse/Listenseite_Pressemitteilungen/2022/Presse2022/220405_PM_IllegalerDarknetMarktplatz.html [13.02.2023].

18. Justice Department Investigation Leads to Shutdown of Largest Online Darknet Marketplace. United States Department of Justice. (05.04.2022) https://www.justice.gov/opa/pr/justice-department-investigation-leads-shutdown-largest-online-darknet-marketplace [13.02.2023].

19. On its website, Chainalysis explicitly advertises its ability to detect crypto crime. Leverage Chainalysis to detect and investigate crypto crime. (n. d.) https://www.chainalysis.com/solutions/investigations/ [13.02.2023].

20. olizei gelingt Schlag gegen Darknet-Nutzer. Deutsche Welle. (12.01.2021) https://www.dw.com/de/polizei-gelingt-schlag-gegen-darknet-nutzer/a-56201444 [13.02.2023].

21. Australians who view live streaming of child sexual abuse: An analysis of financial transactions. Australian Institute of Criminology. (19.02.2022) https://www.aic.gov.au/publications/tandi/tandi589 [13.02.2023].

22. Child pornography livestreamed from Philippines accessed by hundreds of Australians. 7News.com.

(19.02.2020) https://7news.com.au/news/crime/child-pornography-livestreamed-from-philippines-accessed-by-hundreds-of-australians-c-705273 [13.02.2023].

23. Interview mit Markus Hartmann, Leiter der Zentral- und Ansprechstelle Cybercrime (Central- and Contact-Point Cybercrime) in: NRW. Rheinische Post (27.02.2023), p. A6.

## Notes: Digital Boundary Shift

1. A Short History of the Metaverse. (2022) https://www.youtube.com/watch?v=-DzGaoLh0C0 [24.02.2023].
2. See Chap. 3, The rise of IT to world power, section One network to rule them all.
3. Mark Zuckerberg demonstrates this virtual world in a YouTube video, which is very suitable as a generally understandable, non-technical introduction to the topic. The Metaverse and How We'll Build It Together. (14.04.2021) https://www.youtube.com/watch?v=Uvufun6xer8 [11.03.2023]. Those who want to invest less than a good hour can watch the eight-minute summary on YouTube: https://www.youtube.com/watch?v=b-9vWShsmE20 [24.02.2023].
4. Connect 2021: Our vision for the metaverse. (28.10.2021) https://tech.fb.com/ar-vr/2021/10/connect-2021-our-vision-for-the-metaverse/ [24.02.2023]. About the strategy and goals of the advertising campaign, the Wall Street Journal provides an overview: Meta's New Ad Campaign reminds people that VR is already here. (07.09.2023) https://www.wsj.com/articles/metas-new-ad-campaign-reminds-people-that-vr-is-already-here-c77afc1c [16.10.2023].
5. Colombia court moves to metaverse to host hearing. Reuters. (24.02.2023) https://www.reuters.com/world/

americas/colombia-court-moves-metaverse-host-hearing-2023-02-24/ [26.02.2023].

6. Microsoft to acquire Activision Blizzard in $68.7 billion deal. CNN. (18.01.2022) https://edition.cnn.com/2022/01/18/tech/microsoft-activision-blizzard-acquisition/index.html [24.02.2023]. For the contract conclusion in October 2023, see Microsoft closes $69B Activision deal, overcoming regulators objections. Wall Street Journal. (13.10.2023) https://www.nytimes.com/2023/10/13/technology/microsoft-activision-blizzard-deal-closes.html [13.10.2023].

7. These 8 Tech Giants Have Invested Big in The Metaverse. MUO. (16.02.2022) https://www.makeuseof.com/companies-investing-in-metaverse/ [24.02.2023].

8. Value creation in the metaverse. McKinsey (06.2022), p. 19. https://www.mckinsey.com/capabilities/growth-marketing-and-sales/our-insights/value-creation-in-the-metaverse [24.02.2023].

9. Metaverse. More Evolution than Revolution? Morgan Stanley Research. (23.02.2022) https://www.morgan-stanley.com/ideas/metaverse-investing/ [24.02.2023].

10. Nikeland. (n. d.) https://www.roblox.com/games/7462526249/NIKELAND-CUP-CLASH [24.02.2023].

11. The Amazing Ways Nike is using the Metaverse, Web3 and NFTs. Forbes. (01.06.2022) https://www.forbes.com/sites/bernardmarr/2022/06/01/the-amazing-ways-nike-is-using-the-metaverse-web3-and-nfts. [26.02.2023]. Anyone interested in the concept and details of Nikeland can find more information here: What is Nikeland? A Guide to Nike's Metaverse. Metaroids. (17.08.2022) https://metaroids.com/learn/what-is-nikeland/ [26.02.2023].

12. The products and prices in Ether can be found, among other places, in the shop of OpenSea: Nike Cryptokicks. (07.02.2023) https://opensea.io/collection/rtfkt-nike-cryptokicks [26.02.2023].

13. Nike acquires RTFKT Studios. Nftnow. (12/13/2021) https://nftnow.com/news/nike-acquires-rtfkt-nft-studios/ [02/26/2023].

14. There is an interesting interview with Mark Zuckerberg on YouTube about interoperability and other topics. Web3/Metaverse Chat With Mark Zuckerberg. (2021, 25:49) https://www.youtube.com/watch?v=iwyyxE-JCIuU [26.02.2023].

15. A recommendable, practice-oriented explanation of NFTs and the associated ecosystem can be found at: WTF is RTFKT. (n. d.) https://rtfkt.com/wtf [26.02.2023]. For everyone who does not watch American entertainment films: WTF stands for "what the fuck".

16. Meta enables cross-platform NFT posting on Instagram and Facebook. NFTGATORS. (29.08.2022) https://www.nftgators.com/meta-enables-cross-platform-nft-posting-on-instagram-and-facebook/ [26.02.2023].

17. Microsoft and Enjin bring cross-platform custom NFTs to Minecraft. Coindesk. (11.02.2021) https://www.coindesk.com/markets/2021/02/11/microsoft-and-enjin-bring-cross-platform-custom-nfts-to-minecraft/ [26.02.2023].

18. About Ocavu, formerly Seek: Seek Launches Cross-Platform NFT Solution, Solving Lack of Interoperability in the Metaverse. GlobeNewswire. (16.12.2021) https://www.globenewswire.com/news-release/2021/12/16/2353711/0/en/Seek-Launches-Cross-Platform-NFT-Solution-Solving-Lack-of-Interoperability-in-the-Metaverse.html [26.02.2023].

19. See Chap. 4, The Transformation of the Economy, Section The End of Centralization?—Crypto-Economy and Blockchains.

20. A look at Pavia is worthwhile, as all the characteristics of the spatial Web 3.0 discussed here are realized. This and other early and very interesting Metaverse projects by proponents of the free web can be seen in the

following YouTube video: The best METAVERSE projects that will completely change the internet. (10.2022) https://www.youtube.com/watch?v=Rt9xT_jVhyw [26.02.2023]. Specifically for Pavia, see timestamp 00:28 to 02:24.

21. Google and NASA achieve quantum supremacy. (23.10.2019) https://www.nasa.gov/feature/ames/quantum-supremacy [26.02.2023].

22. A tribute to his achievement can be found in: Remembering Paul Benioff, renowned scientist and quantum computing pioneer. Argonne National Laboratory. (11.05.2022) https://www.anl.gov/article/remembering-paul-benioff-renowned-scientist-and-quantum-computing-pioneer [26.02.2023].

23. China is pulling ahead in global quantum race, new studies suggest. Scientific American. (15.07.2021) https://www.scientificamerican.com/article/china-is-pulling-ahead-in-global-quantum-race-new-studies-suggest/ [26.02.2023].

24. See Chap. 3, The Rise of IT to World Power, section Fresh Chips from Texas.

25. Silicon chips are reaching their limit. Here's the future. Techradar. (28.07.2018) https://www.techradar.com/news/silicon-chips-are-reaching-their-limit-heres-the-future [26.02.2023].

26. After Moore's law. The Economist Technology Quarterly. (12.03.2016) https://www.economist.com/technology-quarterly/2016-03-12/after-moores-law. There is also a graphical overview of the end of Moore's Law expected by experts with the telling title: Faith No Moore. Selected predictions for the End of Moore's Law [26.02.2023].

27. Light propagates at nearly 300,000 km/s. For their research on quantum entanglement, three scientists received the Nobel Prize in 2022. They are the Frenchman Alain Aspect, the American John Clauser, and the Austrian Anton Zeilinger: Nobelpreis für

Physik 2022. Welt der Physik. (04.10.2022) https://www.weltderphysik.de/thema/nobelpreis/nobelpreis-fuer-physik-2022/ [26.02.2023].

28. Ein Quantencomputer mit 1121 Qubits. Digitale Welt. (18.03.2021) https://digitaleweltmagazin.de/interviews/ein-quantencomputer-mit-1121-qubits/ [07.02.2023]. An overview of IBM's quantum development roadmap by fields of work until 2026 can be found in: The IBM Quantum Development Roadmap. IBM. (12.2022) https://www.ibm.com/quantum/roadmap [26.02.2023].

29. IBM's Heron project is a first step in this direction. Hardware statt Qubits: Neue Wege bei Quantencomputern. Heise online. (10.01.2023) https://www.heise.de/hintergrund/Hardware-statt-Qubits-Neue-Wege-bei-Quantencomputern-7450807.html [26.02.2023].

30. Lösungen für komplexe Zusammenhänge. Die Bundesregierung. Presseinformation. (15.01.2021) https://www.bundesregierung.de/breg-de/aktuelles/quantencomputing-1836542 [26.02.2023].

31. Vorhang auf: Fraunhofer und IBM weihen Quantencomputer ein. Fraunhofer press release. (15.06.2021) https://www.fraunhofer.de/de/presse/presseinformationen/2021/juni-2021/fraunhofer-und-ibm-weihen-quantencomputer-ein.html [26.02.2023].

32. A quantum computer with 1121 qubits. Digital World. (18.03.2021) https://digitaleweltmagazin.de/interviews/ein-quantencomputer-mit-1121-qubits/ [26.02.2023].

33. Europas erster Quantencomputer mit mehr als 5000 Qubits in Jülich gestartet. Forschungszentrum Jülich. Pressemitteilung. (17.01.2022) https://www.fz-juelich.de/de/aktuelles/news/pressemitteilungen/2022/2022-01-17-juniq-europas-erster-quantencomputer-mit-5000-qubits [26.02.2023].

34. Quantum computing: An emerging ecosystem and industry use cases. McKinsey. (12.2021) p. 16. https://

www.mckinsey.com/capabilities/mckinsey-digital/our-in-sights/quantum-computing-use-cases-are-getting-real-what-you-need-to-know [26.02.2023].

35. Azure Quantum. (n. d.) https://azure.microsoft.com/en-us/products/quantum/#overviewQuanten-Computer [02/26/2023].

36. Highlights of the IBM Quantum Summit 2022. IBM Quantum. (11/10/2022) https://www.ibm.com/quantum [02/26/2023].

37. Quantum computing: An emerging ecosystem and industry use cases, pp. 13 and 16 [26.02.2023]. See Note 34.

38. Envisioning a new wave in power. IBM Case Studies. (2020) https://www.ibm.com/case-studies/daimler/ [25.01.2023]. For Mitsubishi Chemicals: In quantum pursuit of game-changing power sources. (2020) https://www.ibm.com/case-studies/mitsubishi-chemical/ [26.02.2023].

39. Around 2.5 billion more people will be living in cities by 2050, projects new UN report. UN Department of Economic and Social Affairs. (2018) https://www.un.org/en/desa/around-25-billion-more-people-will-be-living-cities-2050-projects-new-un-report [26.02.2023].

40. Critical Reasons for Crashes Investigated in the National Motor Vehicle Crash Causation Survey. National Highway Traffic Safety Administration. (02.2015), p. 1, Table 1. https://crashstats.nhtsa.dot.gov/Api/Public/ViewPublication/812115 [26.02.2023].

41. Fahrzeugzulassungen im Dezember 2022 – Jahresbilanz. Kraftfahrzeugbundesamt (Federal Motor Transport Authority). (04.02.2023) https://www.kba.de/DE/Presse/Pressemitteilungen/Fahrzeugzulassungen/2023/pm01_2023_n_12_22_pm_komplett.html [26.02.2023].

42. Anzahl von Elektroautos weltweit von 2012 bis 2021. Statista. (09.06.2022) https://de.statista.com/statistik/daten/studie/168350/umfrage/

bestandsentwicklung-von-elektrofahrzeugen/ [26.02.2023].

43. Größe der Elektrofahrzeugflotte weltweit 2020 bis 2030. Statista (06.2020) https://de.statista.com/statistik/daten/ studie/1261909/umfrage/anzahl-der-weltweiten-elektro-fahrzeuge/ [26.02.2023].

44. Intel's Mobileye sees $17 bln in assisted-driving product revenues by 2030. Reuters. (05.01.2023) https://www. reuters.com/technology/intels-mobileye-sees-17-bln-as-sisted-driving-product-revenues-by-2030-2023-01-05/ [26.02.2023].

45. Intel acquires Moovit to accelerate Mobileye's Mobility-as-a-Service offering. Intel News Release. (04.05.2020) https://newsroom.intel.com/news-releases/ intel-may-2020-acquisition/ [26.02.2023].

46. Level 3-autonomes Fahren: Definition, Autos, Gesetze. Bußgeldkatalog. (23.12.2022) https://www.bussgeldkat-alog.org/level-3-autonomes-fahren/. For the speed limit of 130 km/h see: Autonomes Fahren in Deutschland mit 130 km/h erlaubt. Golem. (03.01.2023) https:// www.golem.de/news/mehr-geschwindigkeit-auto-nomes-fahren-in-deutschland-mit-130-km-h-er-laubt-2301-170873.html [26.02.2023].

47. Bundestag nimmt Gesetz zum autonomen Fahren an. Deutscher Bundestag Dokumente. (20.05.2021) https:// www.bundestag.de/dokumente/textarchiv/2021/kw20-de-autonomes-fahren-840196 [07.02.2023].

48. More details on this in SAE Levels of Driving Automation™ Refined for Clarity and International Audience. Society of Automotive Engineers. (03.05.2021) https://www.sae.org/blog/sae-j3016-up-date [26.02.2023].

49. Digital Auto Report 2021. PricewaterhouseCoopers and strategy&. Vol. 1, p. 3. https://www.strategyand. pwc.com/de/en/industries/automotive/digital-auto-re-port-2021/strategyand-digital-auto-report-2021-vol1. pdf [26.02.2023].

50. Future of BMW. CEO Oliver Zipse in the german NewscastTagesthemen. (01/05/2023) https://bit.ly/3V-VD0lF [02/07/2023].

51. In the following, I refer to a presentation by the Fraunhofer Institute for Cognitive Systems IKS. Autonomous Driving (n. d.), https://www.iks.fraunhofer.de/de/themen/autonomes-fahren.html, as well as a podcast by Prof. Simon Burton about Artificial Intelligence in vehicles: KI in Autos – komplexe Herausforderung, aber machbar. Autonomes Fahren. (13.05.2022) https://www.fraunhofer.de/de/mediathek/podcasts/podcasts-2022/podcast-ki-in-autos.html [26.02.2023].

52. KI in Autos – komplexe Herausforderung, aber machbar. [26.02.2023]. See note 51

# Notes: Epilogue

1. CBInsights. (14.02.2023) https://www.linkedin.com/posts/cb-insights_kids-in-1966-predictions-for-the-year-2000-activity-7031077117446475776-i8gZ/ [14.02.2023].

2. See Rödder, Andreas. 21.0. Eine kurze Geschichte der Gegenwart. München 2016, p. 36. He describes fear, resistance, and adaptation as typical patterns of technological criticism. The quote is taken from his book (p. 37).

3. Chat GPT4: is the world prepared for the coming AI storm? BBC. (16.03.2023) https://www.bbc.co.uk/news/world-us-canada-64967627 [16.03.2023].